# WE
# FIRST

## HOW BRANDS AND CONSUMERS USE
## SOCIAL MEDIA TO BUILD A BETTER WORLD

### SIMON MAINWARING

palgrave
macmillan

*Dedicated to*

*Talia, Aisha, Monna, and Fruzsina,*

*who lit the way.*

WE FIRST
Copyright © Simon Mainwaring, 2011
All rights reserved.

First published in 2011 by PALGRAVE MACMILLAN® in the United States—a division of St. Martin's Press LLC, 175 Fifth Avenue, New York, NY 10010.

Where this book is distributed in the United Kingdom, Europe, and the rest of the world, this is by Palgrave Macmillan, a division of Macmillan Publishers Limited, registered in England, company number 785998, of Houndmills, Basingstoke, Hampshire RG21 6XS.

Palgrave Macmillan is the global academic imprint of the above companies and has companies and representatives throughout the world.

Palgrave® and Macmillan® are registered trademarks in the United States, the United Kingdom, Europe, and other countries.

ISBN: 978-0-230-11026-7

Library of Congress Cataloging-in-Publication Data
Mainwaring, Simon.
  We first : how brands and consumers use social media to build a better world / Simon Mainwaring.
     p.   cm.
  Includes bibliographical references and index.
  ISBN 978–0–230–11026–7
  1. Social responsibility of business.  2. Capitalism.  3. Social media— Economic aspects.  4. Branding (Marketing)  5. Internet marketing.  I. Title.
HD60.M327   2011
658.8—dc22

                                                          2010048454

A catalogue record of the book is available from the British Library.

Design by Letra Libre

First edition: June 2011

10  9  8  7  6  5  4  3  2

Printed in the United States of America.

# CONTENTS

# ACKNOWLEDGMENTS

Writing a book is a great way to get a lot of time alone. Ironically, you spend much of that time reflecting on the people who have helped you along the way. These are people who care about the same things as you do, or who simply care about you. Some shared their advice and others listened, but all offered encouragement when writing these final acknowledgments seemed a long way off.

First, the book would not have been written but for the inspiration provided by leaders who have proven that powerful transformation is possible. They include business pioneers Jay Coen Gilbert, Scott Harrison, and Blake Mycoskie, marketing legend Dan Wieden, powerful storyteller and filmmaker Jesse Dylan, and global leaders President Clinton and Bill and Melinda Gates.

*We First* was made possible through the support of my agents at William Morris Endeavor Entertainment, including Mark Akner and Erin Malone, who took a risk on some new guy with a funny accent. Enormous appreciation also goes to Rick Benzel, whose editorial assistance and friendship have been invaluable in shaping the book. Emily Carleton at Palgrave Macmillan kept this first-time author on course and on time, and provided a vital contribution to the final manuscript. My gratitude also goes to Sarah Hanson for her copyediting work. Huge thanks as well to Mark Fortier, Kevin Small, and Mat Miller for their great support in PR, marketing, and promotions. Finally, thank you to those in my social community on Facebook and Twitter whose support, retweets, and comments on my weekly posts reassured me that what I was doing was meaningful and worthwhile.

This book is the result of love and support from Bo Eason, Patsy Rodenburg, Larry Moss, John Gerzema, Robert Tercek, Joe and Sophie Uliano, Dr. Jeremy Brooks, Theresa Drew, Bill Corcoran, Steve Robertson, Carol Case,

Todd Brown, Leyla Bader, Kate Larkin Laverge, Alexander Ouvaroff, Ania Badja, Mark Caroline, Aaron Strout, Derrick Ashong, Kathy Hepinstal, Lingotek, Ryan Hessel, Nelly Ma, Bill Chiaravalle, Phillip Squier, Sara Goldblatt, Lawrence Azzerad, Tod Rathbone, Josh Beane, Damon Webster, Deborah Morrison, Russell Grin, Sara Lavery, Larry Biehl, David Levy, Phil Sieb, Katherine Jennings, Jennifer McCabe, Paull Young, Paloma Vazquez, Kevin Ohannessian, Piers Fawkes, Sean Rad, Sally Hogshead, Valerie Maltoni, Brian Reich, Jason Falls, Charlene Li, Brian Solis, Mel Exon, Ben Malbon, Maria Popova, Priscilla Cohen, Cole Winans, Cameron Smith, Luke Stettner, Sam Saddigh, Craig Davis, Gotham Chopra, Max Lugavere, Jason Silva, Sean Carasso, Terry Savage, Philip Thomas, Patrick O'Neill, Rob Schwartz, Randi Fiat, Stephen and Patty Dewey, Chris Hughes, Rishad Tobaccowala, Liz Heller, Scott Case, Beth Harper, Ken Rutkowski, Peter Guber, Ryan Scott, Brian Sirgutz, Corrie Frasier, Alec Ross, Farah Pandith, and Queenie of Harbor Island.

Closer to home, special appreciation goes to Chris Leahy, without whom I would not have found my peace, purpose, or a sense of fulfillment.

Enormous gratitude and love also goes to my brother, Paul, for his tireless support throughout the writing process, and to my sister, Justine, for her encouragement over the last two years. This book is also dedicated, in loving memory, to my father Nigel.

My mother, Fruzsina, has served as an example of what intelligence, discipline, and heart can achieve throughout my life. Thank you for a lifetime of love and inspiration whether I was in your arms or at the end of a phone.

To my daughters Aisha and Talia, I say a thousand thank-yous. Thank you for saying it was OK for Daddy to work when it wasn't. Thank you for sounding interested when you didn't understand what I was talking about. Thank you for wanting the book to do well when all you really wanted was me.

Thank you to my wife, Monna. Every home has a hearth and ours is her heart. We've climbed many mountains together, first with bags on our backs as we traveled around the world for my advertising career and then with kids in tow as I started my own business. In recent years I have learned that the greatest achievement a man can enjoy is the success of his family. Thank you, Monna, for your love, patience, and understanding throughout this most recent climb.

Finally, thank you to all those who read this book and take its message to heart knowing that the future is ours to create. With open hearts and minds united by a common purpose there's nothing we can't achieve.

# PROLOGUE

Is this the world you want?

I hope it's not. I hope you want to live in a better world, with greater prosperity for more people and less poverty wasting so many lives; where people have meaningful jobs that advance the happiness and productivity of our societies; where there are no infants and children with underdeveloped minds and malnourished bodies due to a lack of resources, disease, unclean water, or war. A world that educates and inspires its youth, teaching them that the human race has the capacity to find solutions to all of our problems if we put our collective minds and hands to work.

Today's world falls far short of the one I want, for both myself and my children. I do not believe it is naïve or utopian to imagine a better world or to share that dream with others in the hope of inspiring change. I believe—as I will demonstrate in these pages—that we have entered an amazing and exciting era in human history. We are fast acquiring the knowledge and technology to meet the challenges of poverty, malnutrition, child mortality, and the myriad social ills that blight our planet. Enabled by the Internet and social media, we are connecting with each other across geographic, cultural, and language barriers, reawakening our innate capacity for empathy and allowing ourselves to derive great satisfaction from social contributions as well as our self-interested endeavors.

If this is not the world you want, I ask that you read on with an open mind, as we will be examining how to change capitalism. This book provides the rationale for a new way of thinking about how we can transform the role of the private sector, including both corporations and consumers, to build a better world. I have coined the title and term "We First" as a desperately needed counterpoint to the "Me First" mentality that informs much of the capitalist self-interested behavior that led us to where we are today.

I was inspired to explore this line of thinking after reading a speech that Bill Gates gave to the World Economic Forum in January 2008. At the time, Gates was both the world's richest man and its greatest philanthropist, an irony that intrigued me in light of his message. He described a new logic for why companies should accept responsibility for developing solutions that address the many crises that plague our planet, especially in the Third World, where poverty often precludes sufficient profit to merit corporate participation. He praised the groundbreaking (PRODUCT)RED campaign founded by U2 lead singer Bono and Bobby Shriver as an example of how civic-minded companies could help change the world, but he also stressed that current philanthropic efforts still fall far short of what is needed to transform the lives of millions of less fortunate people on the planet. He ended by laying down a challenge to the delegates, business leaders, and heads of state at the conference.

> I'd like to ask everyone here—whether you're in business, government, or the nonprofit world—to take on a project of creative capitalism in the coming year. It doesn't have to be a new project; you could take an existing project, and see where you might stretch the reach of market forces to help push things forward. When you award foreign aid, when you make charitable gifts, when you try to change the world—can you also find ways to put the power of market forces behind the effort to help the poor?[1]

His words "creative capitalism" and "change the world" lodged in my mind, prompting several questions: How could capitalism harness market forces to work for a better world? How might corporations reimagine their role in a way that balances their interest in profit with the imperative to massively increase the efforts and resources dedicated to global social transformation? And how could such a vision not only undo the damage done in the past, but also remake the capitalist business world into a sustainable engine of progress?

As a branding and advertising professional, I had spent years working on creative ideas for the advertising campaigns of multinational brands, including Nike, Toyota, and Motorola. My job was to take business problems and recast them as creative opportunities, helping companies own what is known in the ad business as the "emotional high ground" within their category in order to motivate changes in consumer thinking or behavior. This ensures that corporate messaging meets consumer needs in order to achieve a desired business result.

Gates's challenge struck me as a messaging opportunity of the highest order. A mass migration of consumer eyeballs away from traditional media like network television, magazines, and newspapers to the Internet, social media, and smartphones was already under way. I wondered if these transformations in corporate and consumer engagement could unlock a solution for social change that was never possible before.

The result of my thinking on this was a concept I called "contributory consumption," a comprehensive system of mindful consumerism in which *every single transaction* for products and services would include a contribution toward building a better world. Implicit within this solution was an end to the false opposition we make between profit and purpose, between living and giving that animates so much of free market capitalism. Contributory consumption would provide a systemic solution to spread prosperity throughout the world.

Furthermore, contributory consumption would be the natural outgrowth of the new dynamics emerging between consumers and brands due to social media. Consumers all around the world are connecting as never before, gaining access to communication platforms such as email, blogs, Facebook, and Twitter that allow them to expose bad corporate behavior by raising their voices in protest or to reward conscionable and well-intentioned brands with purchases, referrals, and recommendations. The combination of consumer power to both reward and punish would drive contributory consumption.

I saw this new dynamic as the key to answering Gates's challenge to develop a more "creative capitalism," as he called it. I imagined that, given the enormity of our consumer society, contributory consumption could generate huge financial resources that could be used to fund philanthropy and perhaps help achieve the eight United Nations Millennium Development Goals (MDGs) that seek to eradicate poverty, starvation and malnutrition, illiteracy, lack of healthcare and sanitary conditions, and other persistent problems of today's world. My goal with contributory consumption became *to transform every mall, store, and warehouse from a monument of consumer self-interest into a motor of social change for the benefit of all.*

## A GLOBAL WAKE-UP CALL

Then something occurred that completely changed the scale and scope of my thinking. As I fleshed out the business architecture for contributory consumption, I watched the U.S. financial system collapse during the fall of 2008. Like every concerned citizen, I read about the millions of Americans and people around the world who were losing their jobs, their life savings, and, in many cases, their homes. I saw how many corporations were downsizing their workforces and altering their business strategies for a long recessionary haul.

Why had capitalism gone so awry that it left many of the world's economies in shambles, throwing hundreds of millions of people, as well as thousands of companies, in the United States, Europe, and even Asia, into the worst financial conditions since the 1930s? How, in light of this, could contributory consumption be implemented if fewer and fewer people had jobs and household incomes declined, causing consumer spending to contract? The number of poor and destitute people in the developing world was already heartbreaking. Now more and more people in the most prosperous developed countries were joining their ranks.

I began to see contributory consumption as just one piece of a bigger and more critical solution. With each passing day, it became more obvious to me—and to many thought leaders around the world—that the entire system of free market capitalism, as it is practiced in the United States and in many Western nations, is leading us further and further down the wrong path, toward a world dominated by narrow self-interest, greed, corporatism, and insensitivity to the greater good of humanity and to the planet itself. Short-term thinking and the single-minded pursuit of profit are increasingly subverting an economic system that otherwise has the capacity to benefit everyone. Although I conceived my idea of contributory consumption primarily as a way to help the poor of the developing world, it had now morphed into a much larger belief that all of us—consumers, corporations, governments, and nonprofits—must begin working together in new ways to redirect the daily practice of capitalism away from a self-destructive future.

## FROM ME FIRST TO WE FIRST

I realized that my idea for implementing contributory consumption was not enough. We now need to infuse a new desire to build a better world deep into the core of free market capitalism. Consumers and corporations need to become partners in reengineering the foundational principles of capitalism to honor not only profits but also purpose, mutual self-interest, sustainability, human values, collaboration, and collective prosperity.

Many corporations already have "corporate social responsibility" (CSR) programs that fund important environmental and social causes. But these efforts alone are insufficient. Building a better world has to become *what corporations do every day* as a function of how they make their profits, not something done *after* profits are made. Consumers, too, need to commit themselves to supporting this movement, by rewarding those brands that take on this task, punishing those that refuse to, and modifying their own consumption habits so that they become partners in creating a new practice of sustainable capitalism.

My goal in writing this book has grown. I now seek to persuade all readers—whether you are an executive, an entrepreneur, a marketing professional, or a consumer—that we need to break out of this destructive Me First economy we have enabled into a self-sustaining We First economy.

*We First* presents a wide-ranging and comprehensive argument about why we must alter or "temper" the excesses of free market capitalism. It proposes specific ideas for how we can transform the entire private sector—corporations and consumers alike—into a force for global renewal. Once we agree to redefine prosperity as the well-being of many, not the wealth of a privileged few, the path to transforming capitalism becomes logical and clear. A We First mindset helps us cut through the quagmire of philosophic debates and economic disagreements so that we can focus on pragmatic, realistic, and actionable solutions to improve the world.

You may wonder why I believe we can now accomplish this change. The answer is the advent of social media. The Internet and social networking websites such as Facebook and Twitter have created an entirely new relationship between brands and consumers that is transforming almost every industry. Social media empowers consumers to become a strong voice in how corporations conduct themselves, but it also gives brands more opportunities to connect with their customers and respond to their needs. Leveraged in the right way, social media offers a win-win situation for both brands and consumers to transform capitalism into the engine we need to build a better world.

## A NEW VISION

I am certainly not the first to suggest that capitalism has lost its way and needs a serious overhaul. Like other authors and thought leaders who have already contributed to this discussion, I hope to inspire everyone reading this book to begin participating in a national and global conversation about how we can begin making real progress toward building a better world.

I am not an economist. What I offer are insights into brand marketing, consumer behavior, and the substantial impact of social media, all of which are already reshaping capitalism. Consumers are now seamlessly connected as they float between the off- and online media and shopping worlds, with new power to influence business strategies and corporate social responsibility. At the same time, corporations and their brands are increasingly aware of the need to be relevant, meaningful, and sharable within the online world in order to build communities that earn them goodwill, loyalty, and profit.

As this book goes to press, the world is witnessing the ability of social media to connect people and spread the ideas, values, and courage needed for significant political and social transformation in several countries. I am referring specifically to the events of early 2011 in Tunisia, Egypt, and beyond in the Arab world, where citizens used Facebook and Twitter to support their movements to overthrow each nation's entrenched ruler. In Egypt especially, social media played three key roles in what became a broad-based people's revolution. First, it helped citizens organize the first protest march on January 25 that sparked the wider movement among Egyptians to peacefully demonstrate for regime change. Second, despite the Egyptian government's temporary shutdown of the Internet and cell phones, the tools of social media allowed citizens to control and shape the narrative rather than allowing the government-run media to portray them as radicals. And third, social media was vital in informing the outside world of what actually happened in and around Tahrir Square and in arousing global empathy for the Egyptian people's cause.

This is not a book about the power of social media to support political revolutions. My principal focus is on how brands and consumers can use social media to create a new version of capitalism that establishes them as partners in building a better world. Nevertheless, these political events confirm that we can no longer doubt the role that social media increasingly plays to inspire and connect people, spread ideas, and help orchestrate popular movements in the name of positive social transformation.

It is my hope that this book will facilitate the intellectual and behavioral shifts that must occur for the entire private sector to come together as a third pillar of social change, working with governments and philanthropic organizations to advance the well-being of all. To this end, the first half of this book, chapters 1–5, examines why we need to change the thinking behind our current practice of capitalism, while the second half of the book, chapters 6–10, explains how we go about doing it.

My wish is that future generations will take for granted that corporations and consumers both have an enduring responsibility to make the world a better place.

*Never doubt that a small group of thoughtful committed citizens can change the world; indeed, it's the only thing that ever has.*

—Margaret Mead

# 1

# TRANSFORMING THE ENGINE OF CAPITALISM

OCTOBER 24, 1929

On this day, Black Thursday, the Dow Jones Industrial Average dropped nearly 13 percent, leading to a week of investor frenzy. Orders to sell overwhelmed the market. By the following week, on October 29, Black Tuesday, another precipitous drop extended the decline to nearly 23 percent, and by mid-November, the Dow had lost nearly 40 percent of its September value. These market losses led to nearly ten years of unmitigated economic hardship for hundreds of millions of people not only in the United States, but also around the world, who lost their life savings, their jobs, and their homes. . . .

OCTOBER 6, 2008

During what has become known as Black Week, the Dow Jones Industrial Average closed lower every day, wreaking market havoc. By the end of the week, the Dow had lost 18 percent, and the S & P 500 index more than 20 percent. By early November, the S & P was down 45 percent from its 2007 high. These market losses led to what some economists predict will be years of unmitigated economic hardship for hundreds of millions of people in the U.S. and around the world, many of whom will lose their life savings, their jobs, their homes and sometimes their families. . . .

The parallels between the Great Depression of the 1930s and the Great Recession of the late 2000s are uncanny. It almost seems as if history is repeating itself.

It is.

How the two events started and spread throughout the world are so aligned it leaves little doubt that we have failed to learn the lessons of economic history. One of the most perceptive economists of the late twentieth century, John Kenneth Galbraith, called this human tendency to neglect economic history "the pathological weakness of the financial memory."[1]

The Great Recession represents a major failure of capitalism, and we are still experiencing it. We are all familiar with the statistics and the stories about the millions of the people (including you, perhaps) who have found themselves unemployed, lost their homes, fallen into poverty, or who are worried about when and how the world's economy will reset itself. We know that this period is not an ordinary blip in history. It has rained economic ruin and social disruption on hundreds of millions of people, not only in the United States, but also around the globe. Almost no developed nation has been spared the calamities of the financial meltdown, and the loss of their prosperity has dramatically impacted the developing world through the resulting loss of funding from government and philanthropic sources.

In the book *This Time Is Different*, economists Carmen Reinhart and Kenneth Rogoff characterize the Great Recession as a profound game changer. Mincing no words, they write,

> The global financial crisis of the late 2000s, whether measured by the depth, breadth, and (potential) duration of the accompanying recession or by its profound effect on asset markets, stands as the most serious global financial crisis since the Great Depression. The crisis has been a transformative moment in global economic history whose ultimate resolution will likely reshape politics and economics for at least a generation.[2]

*At least a generation?* This prediction is ominous. It goes against the grain of what we have been taught to believe—that free market capitalism is the best economic system the world has ever known, one that steadily delivers widespread and enduring prosperity and wealth. This incongruity should inspire us all to ask a fundamental question: Can we afford to continue living with a system that creates so much economic chaos rather than fulfilling the promises we expect of it?

## DOES CAPITALISM NEED REPAIR?

*We First* is about a new way of looking at capitalism. It seeks to initiate a greater degree of honesty and frankness into our thinking about free market capitalism as the engine that propels our society. Without becoming defensive or accusatory, this book proposes that we need to take a serious look at the results that the past practice of capitalism has brought us—and more important, where it is leading us in the future.

This book is not about doing away with capitalism. It is about recognizing the advantages of capitalism as a generator of progress and prosperity, but at the same time acknowledging the mounting criticisms—if left unchecked, a capitalist system will run off its own rails. Many noted economists, thought leaders, and social visionaries around the world are all recognizing that capitalism has become dysfunctional. It has lost its way as an effective, self-regulating, and sustainable economic system. It has devolved into the single-minded pursuit of profit and wealth for a small elite at the expense of the overall society.

What the Great Depression, the Great Recession, and all the decades in between should have taught us is that free market capitalism is in need of repair. It embeds a wide range of systemic problems that are slowly choking our societies and preventing our economic institutions from achieving what the human race ultimately needs—a steady march of upward prosperity and progress for everyone on the planet.

The noted economist Milton Friedman led a movement during the second half of the twentieth century that proclaimed that corporations have no social responsibility to society. As the leading voice on President Ronald Reagan's Economic Advisory Board, he championed supply-side economics and the view that the only role of corporations was to make profits for their shareholders, regardless of any consequences their actions might cause to society or the environment, so long as they complied with existing regulations. Friedman's philosophy has now guided three decades of government policy, leading to a massive deregulation of industries and the growth of powerful corporations.

Reasonable people disagree on whether this approach has succeeded in producing the economic benefits it claims. But more important, and not up for debate, is that deregulation has led directly to the increasing impoverishment of the American middle class and the erosion of the belief that the American Dream is still possible. Barring government intervention and voluntary restraint, free market capitalism has become effectively uncontrollable.

Admittedly, the freedom of unregulated capitalism can be at times its greatest strength. The potential rewards of capitalism inspire people to start companies, innovate, and create new businesses that both enrich themselves and advance the world. The United States in particular prides itself on being the leading-edge nation that attracts the best and brightest minds to reap capitalism's benefits—a strong investment community, an educated workforce, and a vast market of consumers. But at the same time, the unregulated market and the growth of corporations have altered the character of our society and transformed capitalism for the worse.

What are the systemic flaws of capitalism that prevent it from fulfilling its greater promises?

- Capitalism allows a small class of people to amass most of the wealth and use it to dominate the investment markets, corporations, and the overall business environment.
- It is prone to inflationary periods and bubbles that eventually collapse, wiping out investments.
- It is prone to allowing, in the name of profit, the worst of human nature, namely greed and selfishness, to run rampant and manipulate the system, especially when government regulations are absent.
- It is subject to unstable behavior on the part of investors, whose impulsive actions can seriously impact global markets.
- Its single-minded pursuit of profit above all other factors takes a huge toll on average workers and their families, who are cast aside when wealthy investors and corporations are willing to sacrifice social progress for purely personal gains.
- It encourages corporations and businesses to think only about short-term profits at the expense of the environment.

These systemic flaws are increasingly negating the advantages of capitalism, preventing us from steadily expanding prosperity and building a better and more stable world. If we are to be honest and responsible citizens who accept the stewardship of our nations and this planet, how can we not recognize that this engine is in need of a serious overhaul?

## REPEATING THE SAME MISTAKES

It is critical that we begin to take stock of our situation and make changes immediately, as the financial crash of 2008 and its ongoing aftermath have cast capitalism's flaws into stark relief. The power brokers on Wall Street and within many corporations are already reverting to their pre-recession thinking and behaviors. Many of the systems and architects that wrought the financial meltdown are reemerging—as if nothing happened.

Enormous CEO salaries and bonuses are back on track, and corporate success is still tied to short-term market gains. Wall Street analysts, powerful hedge funds, and wealthy investors are again dictating that profits are the only results that matter. The old guard of Wall Street investors have returned to their old tricks, but this time they have become "high-frequency traders" who buy and sell securities up to one thousand times per second using smartly programmed computers. As a result, Wall Street's biggest banks, including Goldman Sachs Group Inc., JPMorgan Chase & Co., Bank of America Corp., Citigroup Inc., and Morgan Stanley enjoyed their most profitable two years in investment banking and trading between 2009 and 2010.[3]

Meanwhile, corporations are hitting all-time record profits in 2010, according to the U.S. Department of Commerce.[4] One reason for this is that companies are refusing to hire back workers to jump-start the sluggish economy. In the middle of 2010, Moody's Investor Services reported that U.S. corporations were sitting on $1 trillion in cash, due partly to their lower expenses and partly to increased profits from the nascent recovery.[5] But even with that cash, few of them were starting to hire. Numerous reports indicated that many of these companies were instead using the savings from their lower payrolls to invest in laborsaving technologies to further reduce their workforce, while other companies began buying back their stock to increase its value for shareholders. Some economists euphemistically called this strategy a "jobless recovery," while Robert Reich, former Secretary of Labor under President Bill Clinton, referred to the trend as an outright "decoupling of profits from jobs."[6]

The result of the recession and the continuing effects of unemployment are creating a dire situation in the United States—the virtual disappearance of the middle class. In her insightful book *Third World America: How Our Politicians Are Abandoning the Middle Class and Betraying the American Dream*, Arianna Huffington argues that capitalism has decimated the buying power of the average American family to such a degree that it has destroyed our once sacred notion of the "American Dream," turning the United States into the equivalent of a Third World nation. In the book, she presents a dire perspective of the middle-class situation.

> The warning lights on our national dashboard are flashing red: Our industrial base is vanishing, taking with it the kind of jobs that have formed the backbone of our economy for more than a century; our education system is in shambles, making it harder for tomorrow's workforce to acquire the information and training it needs to land good twenty-first century jobs; our infrastructure—our roads, our bridges, our sewage and water and transportation

and electrical systems—is crumbling. And America's middle class, the driver of so much of our creative and economic success—the foundation of our democracy—is rapidly disappearing, taking with it a key component of the American Dream: the promise that, with hard work and discipline, our children will have the chance to do better than we did, just as we had the chance to do better than the generation before us. . . . So long as our middle class is thriving, it would be impossible for America to become a Third World nation. But the facts show a different trajectory. It's no longer an exaggeration to say that middle-class Americans are an endangered species. [7]

These are some of the facts that confirm the crisis of the middle class.

## DISPARITY OF INCOME

The gap between the rich and the middle class is widening sharply. Between 1979 and the present, the top 1 percent of income earners has seen their incomes nearly triple, up by 281 percent, while the bottom quintile has seen their incomes rise only 16 percent. The middle 20 percent is up just 25 percent. [8]

## DISPARITY OF WEALTH OWNERSHIP

A small class of wealthy people owns nearly all the resources in the United States. Between 1983 and 2004, of all the new financial wealth created by the American economy, the top 20 percent of the population captured 94 percent of it, while the bottom 80 percent received only 6 percent. Furthermore, the top 10 percent of Americans owns 80 to 90 percent of all stocks, bonds, trust funds, and business equity, and more than 75 percent of non-home (commercial) real estate. The concentration is even greater further up the wealth scale: the top 1 percent of wealthy individuals owns 38.3 percent of all privately held stock, 60.6 percent of financial securities, and 62.4 percent of business equity. [9]

## RISING POVERTY

The rise in poverty in the United States has hit record levels. In 2010, more than 44 million Americans lived below the official government-set poverty line—that's one in seven people—the highest rate since 1994. As of May 2010, 40.2 million Americans were living on food stamps, and this figure rose to 43.6 million by January 2011, representing more than 14 percent of the U.S. population. Among them, 6 million report they have no other income, so roughly one in every fifty Americans lives in a household surviving entirely on a food-stamp card. [10]

## DESCENT INTO DEBT

Debt is rising. In a 2009 survey, 61 percent of Americans say they "always or usually" live paycheck to paycheck, up from 43 percent in 2007. Over 1.4 million Americans filed for personal bankruptcy in 2009, a 32 percent increase over the previous year. In 2010, banks estimated they would foreclose on 1 million homes.

THESE ARE NOT ENCOURAGING STATISTICS, and the plight of the middle class is fast becoming grim. They portend an economic environment that is not conducive to the type of healthy economy that can support long-term corporate growth and success. It is not logical that corporations would want to support a version of capitalism that weakens people rather than turning them into strong, prosperous, and loyal customers. It is difficult to rationalize this behavior unless we concede that capitalism is taking us down the wrong path.

> *The biggest problem with runaway inequality . . . is that it undermines the unity of purpose necessary for any firm, or any nation, to thrive. People don't work hard, take risks and make sacrifices if they think the rewards will all flow to others.*
>
> —Steve Pearlstein, *Washington Post*

## CAPITALISM'S MISSED OPPORTUNITIES

Meanwhile, not only has capitalism failed the richest nations on Earth, but it is failing vast stretches of the developing world as well. The United States has a long history of being among the most generous countries on the planet in regard to sharing its national wealth to help other nations in need—in 2009, for example, the United States was providing assistance to 150 countries with an Official Development Assistance budget of about $30 billion. The size of our foreign aid is testimony to the fact that, since the end of World War II, the foundations of capitalism have failed to integrate what we formerly called the Third World nations (and which we now call the "developing nations") into a prosperous global economy.

Certainly, we cannot blame capitalism for all the problems of the less-developed world. History shows that in many of these nations, it is their own internal conflicts and political corruption that has stymied their progress. But it is simply incorrect to think that capitalist enterprises have done all they could in the second half of the twentieth century, given that so much of the developing world has failed to achieve steady progress toward prosperity.

As a result of decades of missed opportunities to integrate prosperity in the developing nations, the world is now faced with humanitarian problems on an unfathomable scale in the twenty-first century. Consider some of the challenges the underdeveloped nations of the world must endeavor to solve.

- 1.4 billion people on the planet live on less than $1.25 per day, while another 2.56 billion people live on less than $2.00/day.[11]
- 1 billion children live in poverty worldwide, roughly 1 out of every 2 children.[12]
- 8.1 million children died in 2009 before they reached the age of 5, half of them in Africa, most succumbing to illnesses that could have been easily prevented by access to inexpensive drugs and care.[13]
- 925 million people are undernourished in the world as of 2010.[14]
- Nearly 800 million people in the world are illiterate.[15]

*In a system of pure capitalism, as people's wealth rises, the financial incentive to serve them rises. As their wealth falls, the financial incentive to serve them falls—until it becomes zero. We have to find a way to make the aspects of capitalism that serve wealthier people serve poorer people as well.*

—Bill Gates

### IT'S YOUR CHOICE

Can we change capitalism to repair these problems and avoid the possibility of another recession or depression? The answer starts with a personal decision. Each of us must decide whether we want to continue endorsing and accepting the current policies of capitalism as practiced by Wall Street and the majority of corporations in the world. We need to ask ourselves where we stand on questions like these:

- If you are a corporate executive, do you want to continue endorsing an economic system that compromises the quality of life

## THE UNITED NATIONS MILLENNIUM DEVELOPMENT GOALS

In an attempt to gain traction on the dire circumstances of the developing world, the United Nations formulated the Millennium Declaration in 2000, which was signed by 189 nations. The declaration proposed eight Millennium Development Goals (MDGs) that it sought to achieve by 2015.

Goal 1: Eradicate extreme poverty and hunger.

Goal 2: Achieve universal primary education.

Goal 3: Promote gender equality and empower women.

Goal 4: Reduce child mortality.

Goal 5: Improve maternal health.

Goal 6: Combat HIV/AIDS, malaria, and other diseases.

Goal 7: Ensure environmental sustainability.

Goal 8: Develop a Global Partnership for Development.

To finance these goals, the U.N. asked 22 of the world's wealthiest countries to donate 0.7 percent of their Gross National Income (GNI), an amount calculated to be enough to fund the estimated $195 billion per year needed to meet the goals. British Prime Minister Tony Blair, U.S. President George Bush, French President Jacques Chirac, and 19 other world leaders signed the agreement. As of the end of 2010, however, only 5 of these 22 nations have met their agreed-upon donation. A few others have created a schedule by which they intend to reach it. But the United States, Australia, Canada, Japan, New Zealand, and Switzerland have yet to do either.

for your employees and surrounding community? Is it really in your company's best interest to support an economic system that prevents so much of the population from enjoying prosperity?

- If you are a member of a board of directors, should you continue to allow Wall Street to hold your company hostage to short-term results that satisfy the profit demands of your small group of investors and shareholders, or would you prefer to provide the leadership needed to build a more stable and sustainable society for all?

- If you are a trader, banker, or broker on Wall Street, do you want to continue pursuing as your life's mission the accumulation of wealth that lacks a constructive purpose in building a better world?

- If you are an investor, do you want to continue investing your money in a market whose vagaries and manipulations could cause your wealth to vanish overnight? Even if it has not yet happened to you, what is to prevent the day from coming when your own investments will disappear?
- If you are a consumer, should you continue to support corporations that fail to implement conscionable business practices and are damaging to society?

---

### THE GROWING CONSUMER ANGER WITH CORPORATE BEHAVIOR

Evidence from several different surveys shows that consumers are angry with corporate behavior, leading them to distrust companies and agree that the government must step in to regulate them further.

#### LOSS OF TRUST
In 2009, only 38 percent of U.S. consumers trusted corporations to do the right thing, according to the Edelman Trust Barometer, one of the most respected surveys of public sentiment about corporations. This was the lowest level of trust in ten years. The figure rose to 51 percent in 2010, but it is still barely one-half of the population who trust companies—not an impressive fact. Meanwhile, only 26 percent of U.S. consumers say they trust CEOs to communicate with credibility. Consumers are also no longer respectful of the corporate profit motive. In 2010, they ranked "transparent and honest practices" and "a company I can trust" as the two most important factors in a company's reputation, far above "financial returns," which came in last place.

#### SUPPORT FOR MORE GOVERNMENT REGULATION
According to a 2010 McKinsey report, consumers around the world favor more government regulation over businesses. The report cites that 65 percent of consumers surveyed across 20 countries agree that governments should impose stricter regulations and greater control over business in all industry sectors in the future.[16]

Years ago, consumers had few outlets to channel their feelings about economic issues, but today they do. The Internet and social media now give them a voice, and they will increasingly use it as leverage to argue for changes in corporate behaviors and for more regulation over Wall Street.

- As a human being, should you allow the pursuit of profit to hijack the engine of capitalism without regard for the consequences for the rest of the world?

We could go on asking many more such questions, but what it comes down to is that change begins within each individual. Each of us must decide whether we want to support a practice of capitalism that has only a modest and unstable record of economic and social achievement—or whether we want to help collaboratively reengineer its future.

*No society can surely be flourishing and happy, of which the far greater part of the members are poor and miserable.*

—Anonymous

## CAPITALISM IS NOT IMMUTABLE

The esteemed British Prime Minister Winston Churchill was once asked whether he thought democracy was the best form of government in history. He sardonically replied, "Democracy is the worst form of government, except for all those other forms that have been tried from time to time."[17] Defenders of free market capitalism often use a similar tactic when they are asked about our economic system, insisting that it may have its flaws but is nevertheless the best economic system among all others. Yet this answer skirts the fact that a broken system still needs to be fixed.

Capitalism is not immutable. We need to moderate its excesses, regulate its potential for abuse, and temper its rough edges to transform it into a more powerful engine of prosperity. In the past decade many thought leaders, economists, and policy experts have proposed changes to the system of capitalism. Their ranks include leaders of the World Economic Forum and G20 nations, five Nobel Prize–winning economists, numerous past and current political and business leaders, writers, academics, and even some of the wealthiest people in the world, including Bill Gates, Warren Buffett, and George Soros. From their insights have arisen many interesting ideas for changing how we practice capitalism, including such plans as ethical capitalism, co-op capitalism, conscious capitalism, creative capitalism, constructive capitalism, and philanthrocapitalism. These proposals are each nuanced in different ways, but they all fundamentally share one characteristic: a strong opposition to accepting that the

United States and other leading industrialized nations can continue down the path that free market capitalism is now on.

## INTRODUCING WE FIRST CAPITALISM

Alongside the other creators of new versions of capitalism, I propose another pragmatic and actionable one—*We First capitalism*. The core premise of We First capitalism is that all corporations, businesses, consumers, and citizens need to begin using capitalism *as a driver of prosperity for the greater good*. We First stands in opposition to Me First, the traditional driving force of free market capitalism. But at the same time, We First is inclusive of Me First: Serving everyone's interests also serves our own.

We First is neither anti-capitalist nor anti-wealth. It is pro-prosperity. The We First approach acknowledges that companies have a right and an obligation to make money for their shareholders. Entrepreneurs, inventors, and innovators deserve to gain from the fruits of their ideas and their labor. But We First insists that corporations can no longer remain in the isolation of their executive meeting rooms. They must begin to see that we live in an increasingly complex, interconnected world, where self-interest can no longer be viewed in narrow terms and where profits can no longer be defined strictly in terms of dollars made for shareholders. Today's corporate self-interest is tomorrow's oil spill, groundwater contamination, food shortage, shuttered factory, unemployment line, or even international conflict. Today's profits are tomorrow's corporate collapse, market bubble, or global recession.

We First asserts that capitalism needs to turn its productive capacity to purposeful activities that contribute to building a better world for everyone. Rather than short-term profits, corporations must seek to create *enduring* value and prosperity. Consumers, too, must accept a higher level of responsibility for creating the world they want by caring about the products they buy and reducing how much they consume.

Above all, We First capitalism seeks to put corporations, consumers, and government together as partners and collaborators working toward a realistic goal of improving life for as many individuals on the planet as possible. This can be done through a market-based economy, but one guided by mutual self-interest, purposeful profit, sustainability, and ethical values.

We First won't solve all our problems. Even if We First principles are adopted broadly by developed nations, they will still end up clashing with despotic regimes whose attitudes are antithetical to political and social freedom and open markets. We First will also need to overcome the old vanguard of CEOs and investors who continue to follow Friedman economics or who believe that corporations should serve solely as their personal wealth generators. We will still need to persuade traditionalist economic thinkers who believe in the "invisible hand of the free market" and supply-side economics. But unless we begin transforming—or perhaps *tempering* is the better word—capitalism, we cannot start down a new path toward finally implementing rational solutions to the many debilitating, unconscionable problems of this world.

Many people will find it difficult to reorient their perception of capitalism to this We First proposal. Some will reject the concepts of this book as simply revisionist or as progressive thinking. But given the vast range of problems we face around the globe, it is no longer possible to deny that we need a paradigm shift before it is too late. We have reached a moment in history in which the survivability of the planet and the economic and social well-being of billions of its inhabitants are in jeopardy. We cannot keep making the same myopic mistakes in managing the world's economies—the consequences are too dire. If wide swaths of the world's population remain impoverished, the middle class in the developed world disappears, and the planet doesn't survive, it won't matter that capitalism is arguably history's best economic system.

*The best way to predict the future is to create it.*

—Peter Drucker, noted business thought leader

## CHANGE MORE POSSIBLE THAN EVER BEFORE

Why is changing capitalism more possible today that at any other prior time? What makes this time more realistic or actionable? And why should corporations and consumers care?

The answer is *social media.* Just as the Industrial Revolution transformed manufacturing and the digital revolution transformed communications, the social-media revolution is transforming the way business is conducted. It is doing this by giving citizens and consumers new platforms to influence the purpose of capitalism through their conversations and the strength of their purchasing power. Just as the Internet democratized information, social media is democratizing the market, providing people with new leverage to push back against corporations that misuse their resources, expertise, and mission only to create profits for themselves without regard for the world.

The impact of social media is an example of what Austrian economist Joseph Schumpeter famously called "creative destruction"—the idea that some innovations advance the world while simultaneously destroying the archaic industries they replace. We have all witnessed the creative destruction that occurred recently in the music, movie, media, and publishing industries, each of which tried yet failed to stall the march of change. In the same way, the new dynamics instigated by social networking, smartphone apps, location-based services, augmented reality, social gaming, virtual goods, and the emerging g-commerce (gaming commerce) are equally upending traditional business models, destroying old monopolies, and, as a consequence, transforming the business world. Social media is effectively the next incarnation of creative destruction in the technology and communications fields, remaking the very capitalism that birthed it and enabling the transition from Me First to We First. The two transitions are complementary.

Many people fail to understand the power that social media has to change the world, still believing that blogging, Facebook, Twitter, and YouTube are merely forms of entertainment, distraction, and narcissism. While it is true that social media can serve those purposes, it is a neutral technology that can be used for meaningful or trivial purposes. There is no doubt that as social media matures, consumers will grow in their awareness of how it can be put to good use by connecting people everywhere and accomplishing meaningful work in the name of building a better world. We have already seen, for example, how Twitter was used as a critical method of communications after the earthquake in Haiti and during various political conflicts such as in Iran and most recently in both Tunisia and Egypt during their 2011 popular revolutions.

Indeed, never before have the world's citizens been able to so easily link up with one another to share their concerns, inform themselves through deeper analysis, and strategize how to use their power to persuade corporations to become responsible global citizens. Never before have consumers had access to free, web-based platforms from which to express their feelings directly to companies that disregard the environment, treat workers poorly while paying CEOs exorbitant salaries, and fail to contribute to creating healthy societies.

Social media is the technological differentiator that makes change possible as never before. It enables consumers to punish and reward, to contribute their ideas and creativity, and to engage with brands in real-time dialogues about their concerns as customers and citizens. It gives them ways to bypass the usual power brokers of business to become a force for social transformation in their own right.

Social media has reawakened us to the fact that we are humans with feelings—empathic creatures who crave connection and an opportunity to express ourselves and create purpose and meaning in our lives. It channels our natural impulses to care about others and to impose a social spirit into all that we do. It enables consumers to translate their deep desire for a sustainable and socially responsible world into a movement that has the potential to transform capitalism into conscionable business.

To understand and implement We First capitalism, we must first address four shifts in mindset that need to occur within both companies and consumers before it becomes clear how and why social media can be mutually beneficial. These mindsets involve examining our notions of self-interest, purpose, sustainability, and values—the topics of the next four chapters. After we examine these, the final five chapters will address how both brands and consumers can use social media as complementary elements in the new dynamic of We First capitalism.

### CHAPTER TAKEAWAYS

- The Great Recession and the Great Depression can both trace their roots to the same systemic problems in capitalism.
- We can change free market capitalism if we want to; as an economic system, it is not immutable. Many thought leaders have already offered recommendations for other types of capitalism.
- We First is a pragmatic solution to reengineer capitalism so that it serves the needs of all stakeholders and delivers prosperity to all.
- The rise of social media gives consumers new leverage to persuade corporations to accept greater social responsibility for their behaviors, while at the same time offering corporations opportunities to strengthen ties to their customers.

# 2 REDEFINING SELF-INTEREST FROM ME FIRST TO WE FIRST

Meet Bob Wilson, *a cheerful 52-year-old sales rep living in the heartland of the United States. His successful 30-year career afforded his family a very comfortable lifestyle. They have a large, 3,000-square-foot home in an exclusive development, with a pool, a barbecue area, and a lawn that Bob enjoys mowing with his tractor mower, although his neighbor hates the noise. For years, business was booming, and he profited handsomely. Bob also seemed to have a knack for picking high-performing stocks—oil and tobacco companies, a few computer hardware and chip companies, and so on. His neighbor tried to convince him to invest in a "social venture fund" that focused on socially responsible companies, but Bob didn't trust that he would make money on it.*

*Bob doesn't worry much about the costs of his lifestyle. His wife shops at the big box stores to get the lowest prices on all their groceries and household goods. Gas for the car and the mower are relatively cheap, and the coal-fired power plant in his county keeps his electric and heating bills manageable. He loves grilling steaks, watching his 50-inch Korean-made TV, taking his sons to stock car races, and occasionally scuba diving in the Caribbean. With his stock market earnings, he purchased a 15-foot pleasure boat made in Australia and an SUV to tow it to the nearby lakes. When the two boys graduated college, he rewarded each of them with new cars, though he did save some money by buying Japanese-made ones rather than American.*

*One of Bob's sons, Nick, is engaged to a woman who was working for one of the major banks, but she lost her job in the financial meltdown of 2008. A week ago, she began teasing Bob about how much his lifestyle contributes to global warming. She pointed to the two 60-gallon trash containers overflowing* each week with food cartons and plastic packaging, to all the gas their cars and boat consume, and to thousands of kilowatt-hours of electricity they use while the coal plant nearby refuses to upgrade its equipment to reduce emissions. She even joked about Bob's love of beef, telling him about some scientists she read about who are attempting to modify cow belches so they are more like those of kangaroos. Both animals have a foregut digesting process, but cows produce large amounts of methane gas that is about 21 times more potent than $CO_2$ and makes up about 10 percent of the total amount of greenhouse gases emitted into the air, whereas kangaroo belches have zero methane.[1] Bob laughed and promised to read up more about global warming.

About 9,000 miles away, it's an impeccable 85-degree July day in Malé, capital of the Maldives and home to about 100,000 people. A nation made up of about 1,200 islets off of Sri Lanka, the Maldives is well known for its spectacular coral reefs and lagoons that attract a billion-dollar tourist industry.

But Malé and the other islands of the Maldives are facing a serious challenge: none of them is more than two meters above sea level. That's about the level some estimates predict the oceans will rise to by 2100 due to global climate change. The former Maldivian president, Maumoon Abdul Gayoom, considered the potential disaster so seriously that he began taking steps to protect Malé. He was the first signer of the 1997 Kyoto Protocol to halt global warming. He got the Japanese government to pay $60 million to build a concrete seawall entirely around Malé.

Gayoom also initiated the construction of an artificial island across Malé's lagoon. The two-square-kilometer island, Hulhumalé, is several meters higher than the rest of the Maldives' islands and will help relieve congestion in Malé and serve as a safe haven for at least 50,000 Maldivians by 2020. Inaugurated in 2004, it is currently home to about 5,000 people. To pay for all this, Gayoom exhorted other countries of the world to contribute, on the rationale that it was they who caused global warming, so why should Maldivians have to pay for it?

In 2008, the first democratically elected president of the Maldives, Mohamed Nasheed, took over from Gayoom. He began yet another initiative to save the country. Using money from the profitable tourism trade, he established a global-warming relocation fund to literally buy a new homeland for the entire country, should the high waters come. He and his ministers have so far evaluated real estate in Sri Lanka, India, and Australia, but no choice has been made.

*Back in the United States, Bob and his wife have received an excited phone call from Nick and his fiancée. They picked a wedding date. They also decided that, for their honeymoon, they would go scuba diving in an exotic country some friends had told them about. It's called the Maldives. Bob promises to read up on it.*

## CAPITALISM AND THE CONFLICTS OF SELF-INTEREST

Bob and millions of consumers like him want to exercise their natural self-interest—to live the good life, have a great job, make money in the markets, and consume to their hearts' content. Corporations that sell products to consumers like Bob want to exercise their self-interest—to maximize their profits, expand their business around the world, and utilize whatever resources are necessary to their production. Investors in companies that sell to the Bobs of the world likewise have their own self-interest—to get the best return on their investments and move their money wherever returns are the greatest. Citizens like Bob have further self-interest—in freedom, peace, and stability; in living in decent communities with good schools and low crime; and in having hope for the future. And with the Maldives, we see that even the smallest of nations have self-interest to preserve themselves from the rising seas created by all the Bobs, corporations, investors, and citizens of other nations.

*The dilemma we face in today's world is that all competing self-interests are increasingly selfish, turning the practice of capitalism into a clash of Me First agendas, each seeking to fulfill only his, her, or its own needs.*

The problem with operating capitalism under this Me First attitude is that our world has changed faster than our minds have been able to adapt. We struggle today because our narrow self-interested behaviors are no longer functional in an interconnected, globalized world. Our old concept of self-interest is now anachronistic, ineffective, and even counterproductive. To make capitalism work again, we need to update our understanding of self-interest to fit the world we now live in.

*We're in a giant car heading toward a brick wall and everyone's arguing over where they're going to sit.*

—David Suzuki, scientist and environmental activist

## IS IT HEALTHY SELF-INTEREST OR SELFISHNESS?

In principle, we have always conceived of self-interest as the natural driver of our thoughts and behaviors. It ensures our survival, getting us what we need to continue living—food, water, money, sex, friendships, attachment, and community. Fulfilling our self-interest helps us receive pleasure and avoid pain. Even helping other people can disguise an act of self-interest. For example, many people contribute to charities solely to enhance their own reputation in the community or to inscribe their family name on something for posterity. Self-interest is not a bad human motivation. It is our automatic impulse to seek out what benefits us in order to survive and thrive.

Capitalism is often said to be the perfect match for humans to gratify their self-interest. Free market capitalism sanctions self-interest by giving us the right to own personal property and to work hard to generate our own rewards. The free market enables motivated individuals to buy and sell, to experiment, to innovate, and to create. This is all healthy and good self-interest, and we know it works. The potential rewards of self-interest have spurred thousands of entrepreneurial thinkers to devote their lives to inventing the new machines of the industrial and digital revolutions: railroads, cars, planes, thousands of branded products, television, computers, and high technology in myriad forms.

But there is a dark side to the perfect match between capitalism and self-interest. It is the unhealthy drive in humans to pursue self-interest so vigorously that it becomes selfishness. *Every act of healthy self-interest taken too far becomes destructive selfishness.* In the context of capitalism, good self-interest benefits society because it fulfills the needs of individuals while respecting those of others, but selfishness detracts from society because it fulfills only one individual's needs at the cost of others' well-being.

We can see selfishness manifested in numerous forms of economic behavior. It is evident when people decide the free market allows them to buy and sell anything imaginable—body parts, women and children, fraudulent business schemes, toxic or nonexistent property, illegal weapons, medical waste, rare birds, fake artworks, and all the schemes that eventually cost taxpayers millions of dollars in criminal court cases and prison expenses. It is truly astonishing how far people will stretch the limits of self-interest to profit at the expense of others.

Selfishness also appears when companies and individuals conduct business without regard for the consequences of their actions. Indifference to and disregard for the harm one's actions might bring to fellow citizens or to the environment is a persistent problem in the world. We routinely see a constant stream of self-centered acts of commerce that are clearly systemic fraud: contractors whose buildings collapse after they've cut corners on construction, trash companies that dump their hauls wherever no one is looking, factories that leak their chemical waste into the soil or waterways, and more.

The pursuit of self-interest is capitalism's dilemma. The inability of reasonable people to agree on what makes for productive self-interest that contributes both to individual happiness and to society versus what constitutes selfishness that fulfills only one individual's needs makes it difficult, if not impossible, to control the flaws and abuses of capitalism. There is no grand vision of capitalism that we can agree on and use to establish a standard of operation in our daily affairs—much less to teach our children. Over time, the standards regarding permissible selfishness have degraded further and further. Selfishness is now routinely confused with self-interest.

*The genius of capitalism lies in its ability to make self-interest serve the wider interest. The potential of a big financial return for innovation unleashes a broad set of talented people in pursuit of many different discoveries. This system driven by self-interest is responsible for the great innovations that have improved the lives of billions.*

—Gordon Brown, former prime minister of the United Kingdom

## ME FIRST CONSUMERISM

Consumers are equally guilty of enabling a selfish Me First mentality. One does not need to look far to find proof of how Me First consumerism has driven millions of consumers to overspend relative to their income. Lured by decades of advances in technology that made life easier and created millions of new products, consumers leveraged their incomes to pursue a better life for themselves and their families. Between 1982 and 2007, household debt in the United States skyrocketed from about 60 percent of income to more than 130 percent. Consumers kept spending until personal savings fell below zero percent for the first time since the Great Depression—meaning that people borrowed more than they saved. In March 2010, the average American household carried $16,007 in credit card debt. On average, today's consumer has a total of 13 credit obligations, including credit cards, store charge cards, gas cards, and bank cards, as well as installment loans on cars, mortgage loans, and student loans.[2]

> *As we have discovered to our cost, the problem of unbridled free markets in an unsupervised marketplace is that they can reduce all relationships to transactions, all motivations to self-interest, all sense of value to consumer choice and all sense of worth to a price tag.*
>
> —Gordon Brown, former prime minister of the United Kingdom

---

### UNEARTHLY LEVELS OF CONSUMPTION

For a true understanding of the impact of Me First consumerism on the world, consider that the 1 billion citizens of North America, Western Europe, Japan, and Australia consume resources (such as oil and metals) and produce waste (like plastics and greenhouse gases) at a level 32 times higher than the populations of the developing world. Should the 1.3 billion people of China decide that they, too, aspire to the same Western standard of living, it would triple the world's consumption of resources and production of wastes. And if the entire world consumed at that pace, it would be the equivalent of having 72 billion people living on Earth—not 7 billion, the current total. The burgeoning middle class in China has already started to experience some of the same effects of mass consumerism that we see in the United States, such as wild shoppers stampeding a store running a sale, killing workers and other shoppers; and the now infamous 60-mile traffic jam in the summer of 2010 that took ten days to unravel.

---

### COMING TO TERMS WITH SELF-INTEREST

The unresolved tension between self-interest and selfishness is not a philosophical debate. It is at the root of corporate and individual economic behavior, shaping how brands and consumers participate in capitalism on a daily basis. It affects the choices we make about our use of natural resources, our habits of consumption, our views of investment and profit, our attitudes toward both poverty and ethical business conduct, and the political debates that ultimately determine what type of society we want to live in.

If we are to repair the capitalist engine of prosperity, corporations and consumers need to come to terms with a fundamental distinction between self-interest and selfishness. We can voluntarily reengineer capitalism to become a productive and powerful force for progress and prosperity everywhere—or we can do nothing and let the engine run itself into the ground through selfishness.

The first challenge to changing capitalism is to regain control of Me First selfishness that seeks to fulfill only individual needs. To do this, it comes down to a single question: *How can we convince reasonable people that some types of self-interest are, in fact, forms of selfishness that are destroying the larger benefits that capitalism could deliver to the entire world?* Can we construct a logical argument with enough intellectual and emotional power to persuade the entire private sector that its current view of self-interest—the version that allows destructive selfishness to occur—no longer makes any sense? Can we get corporate boards, executives, and consumers alike to ask themselves the following questions?

- How much is enough pay for a CEO, compared to the lowest employee in the firm?
- Is it self-interested or plain selfish for companies to pay large dividends to investors when employees do not make real living wages?
- Is it fair for corporations to receive staggering financial benefits through offshore tax havens while the states in which they operate struggle to provide even such basic services as a good education for the next generation of citizens?
- Is it conscionable for companies to profit handsomely by investing taxpayer money provided by the federal government's Troubled Asset Relief Program (TARP) while those same taxpayers lose their jobs, homes, and security?
- Is it justifiable for the developed nations to seek ever-higher standards of living at the cost of the livelihoods and lives of the impoverished billions in the rest of the world?

*We have always known that heedless self-interest was bad morals; we know now that it is bad economics.*

—Franklin Delano Roosevelt

## SEVEN REASONS TO REDEFINE SELF-INTEREST

I believe that we are finally able, with good reason, to redefine our concept of self-interest. This rationale is based on a single premise: *We now live in a mutually dependent and connected world so transformed that it requires us to apply a fresh context for how we exercise our self-interest in the practice of capitalism.*

This new world is observable, palpable, and undeniable. It contrasts sharply with the world we used to know, even as little as a few years ago. Here is how I would describe this new world:

> We now live in an unpredictable, rapidly changing, highly connected, globalized world of nearly 7 billion (and growing), in which new technologies are empowering consumers and citizens (especially the emerging generation, the Millennials) to collaborate in new social venues to communicate about what's meaningful to them, to seek personal freedom, to rebalance prosperity, to reduce conflict, and to protect the planet from environmental destruction through a growing consciousness and focus on smart, sustainable thought and action.

Embedded in this description of our new reality are seven dynamics that literally force us to consider a new context in which our self-interest must operate.

1. The globalization of business and geopolitics
2. The virtual and real interconnectedness of citizens
3. The complexity of problems
4. The population explosion and its impact on consumption
5. The power shift to consumers and citizens
6. The reality of environmental threats
7. The demographics of change

Let's review each of these.

### 1. THE GLOBALIZATION OF BUSINESS AND GEOPOLITICS

From a geopolitical point of view, globalization has minimized the value of maintaining purely local or nationalistic self-interests. The degree of integration and interdependence among countries, governments, institutions, businesses, and people in the modern world is tightening and unstoppable. The world's leading industrialized nations have already recognized the need to create international agencies and quasi-governmental structures to help regulate their increasingly intertwined affairs. The European Union is one such body, representing the need for Europe's formerly antagonistic rivals to accept the benefits of coordinating their economies and collaborating on their collective future. Numerous regional and continental associations have similarly emerged, such as the Union of South American Nations and the African Union, to combine the interests of smaller, less powerful nations against the industrialized heavyweights of the world.

Economically, globalization has altered the landscape for capitalism. It increasingly allows companies to compete, and sometimes collaborate, across a larger map. Just 60 years ago, it was unusual for companies to operate on multiple continents. But by 1990 there were 3,000 multinational companies in the world, and by 2009 that number had skyrocketed to 63,000.[3]

Through today's digital technologies, companies can manage large value chains of suppliers, workers, and customers around the world. Thousands of companies outsource their manufacturing and customer services to workers in emerging market countries, especially in high-tech industries. The employment they generate has raised the standard of living for millions of people in these countries. India, for example, has been growing at an average of 8.3 percent per year since 2004,[4] and in 2009, produced 25 new billionaires on top of the 24 it already had.[5]

In such a globalized world, companies are discovering that self-interest is more complicated and more difficult to practice when viewed only from a narrow perspective. There is a growing awareness that formerly single-nation problems like inflation, unemployment, energy shortages, trash, drug trafficking, pollution, and control of epidemics are now so globalized they must be tackled at the regional or international level.

Figuring out how to create global financial stability is an especially difficult challenge. The tight linkages among global financial systems today, the multinational reach of corporations, the internationalization of brands, and the unavoidable transparency of actions provided by the Internet all lead to one conclusion: *Almost any decision taken in narrow-minded self-interest is selfish if the people involved fail to consider—and heed—the larger global and political consequences of their actions.*

*The perception that businesses must choose between turning a profit and improving the communities where they operate is outdated and irrelevant in our interdependent world.*

—Bill Clinton

## 2. THE VIRTUAL AND REAL INTERCONNECTEDNESS OF CITIZENS

The Internet and mobile telephony are key factors in the need to create a new context for self-interest in capitalism. Billions of citizens are now connected to others inside and outside their own borders. Centuries-old boundaries of nationality, culture, and language are weakening or disappearing. We can see the whole world in nearly real time, allowing us to hear about events anywhere, whether they are natural disasters, political rallies, corporate malfeasance, or new innovations.

Through the Internet, a remarkable thing is happening. *Technology is reawakening our innate human sense that we are all connected.* The most obvious proof of this is the enormous growth of social networks. According to Alexa's Global Traffic Rank, by December 2010 Facebook had over 550 million registered users (as distinct from unique and active users); MySpace, 91 million; Twitter, 90 million; LinkedIn, 50 million; and Ning, 42 million.[6] Such numbers are in addition to the enormous networks built through email and the many other messaging services, including Skype, with 590 million users; Windows Live Hotmail, with 360 million; Yahoo Mail, with 284 million; and Gmail, with 173 million. In early 2010, 7 of the 15 most trafficked websites in the world were social networking sites, according to George F. Colony of Forrester Research, a technology and market research company.[7]

Such people-driven networks, operating and evolving independently from traditional media monopolies, are developing their own cultures and rules of engagement. These dynamics are growing more important as the entire web becomes increasingly social. This process is already under way, evidenced by the launch of Facebook's Open Graph platform in April 2010, which connects Facebook users with any of the tens of thousands of participating third-party websites using its "Like," "Unlike," and "Recommend" buttons. These developments have the potential to change the fundamental relationship between corporations and consumers connected by the Internet and social media.

The expansion of mobile technology also portends vast changes in capitalism's context. Currently there are 4.6 billion cell phones in use, with 10 billion expected by 2015. The facility of both voice and data communication among people worldwide will create new businesses, new markets, and new forms of commerce. Mobile technology is already opening up formerly remote and chronically impoverished areas in many of the least developed countries, where there is little infrastructure for land telephone lines or connections to the Internet.

Because of this new global interconnectivity, corporate self-interest must be moderated by dialogue, transparency, authenticity, accountability, interactivity, community, and collaboration—precisely the operating dynamics within social networks.

*We are living in the middle of a remarkable increase in our ability to share, to cooperate with one another, and to take collective action, all outside the framework of traditional institutions and organizations.*

—Clay Shirky, NYU professor, leading authority in Internet technologies, and author of *Here Comes Everybody*

---

### TECHNOLOGY IS TEACHING US TO BE HUMAN AGAIN

Numerous surveys show that social networking has become the dominant activity for time spent on the Internet. An August 2010 report from The Nielsen Company indicated that Americans devote 36 percent of their time online to communicating and networking across social networks, blogs, personal email, and instant messaging.[8] In January 2010, the average American was already spending 7 hours per month on Facebook, up from 4.5 hours in June 2009.[9] But why is this so?

Frankly, it does not take much analysis to understand that social networks fulfill a deep-seated human need to care about others that modern society has increasingly eroded in many Western nations. As the digital world has ushered in simple and real-time tools to connect people, a powerful reaction has occurred: technology has literally resuscitated our innate need to share our emotions with each other. Such technology reawakens our empathy for other people and allows us to congregate around shared values. People around the globe are reconnecting on an emotional level around what unites rather than divides us, especially over our common concerns about the condition of the planet and the future we will leave for our children. Some events especially touch people emotionally, such as the highly publicized shooting death of the young girl, Neda Agha-Soltan, during the 2009 presidential election protests in Iran—reinforcing a growing recognition among people that we must figure out how to take better care of each other.

In an insightful presentation at the 2010 TED (Technology, Entertainment, and Design) conference, Nicholas Christakis, author of *Connected*, discussed his 30 years of research into social networks. He found that networks of people have memory, a flow within them, and resilience over time. They also have an internal intelligence, in that they can operate like a collective in the same way as a beehive, or as a flock of birds pooling their navigational wisdom to find a speck of an island in the ocean on which to rest during migration. His research supports many of the concepts embedded in the theory of the "wisdom of the crowds," as outlined by James Surowiecki in his book of the same name, suggesting that a diverse group of people can find solutions to problems far better than a narrow group of experts.

Christakis summed up his presentation: "We form social networks because the benefits outweigh the costs. The spread of good and valuable things is required to sustain and nourish social networks. Similarly, social networks are required for the spread of good and valuable things like love, kindness, happiness, altruism, and ideas. If we realized how valuable social networks are, we'd spend a lot more time nourishing and sustaining them. Social networks are fundamentally related to goodness. And what the world needs now is more connections."[10]

## 3. THE COMPLEXITY OF PROBLEMS

One of the most salient differences about this new world we inhabit is that our problems are far more complex today than ever before. Compared with the simple villages and rituals of family life in which the majority of humans lived for centuries, life is now faster, more challenging, and more complicated for more of the world's population. While 4 billion people continue to live a simple, rural subsistence lifestyle, more than 2 billion people now work in what is called "the money economy" of commerce and business. Of these, 800 million constitute the affluent rich, who consume 75 percent of the world's energy and resources.[11]

But with progress have arrived two problems on a scale never before imagined. One of these is energy. The economic hubs of the world consume energy at an annual rate that will nearly double between 1980 and 2015, from 283 quadrillion BTUs to 583 quadrillion BTUs.[12] The need for energy is one of the leading factors in the complexity of global problems, because it creates numerous repercussions the world must learn how to deal with: politics between petro-rich and petro-poor nations; competition and economic instability due to unpredictable energy prices; global warming, pollution, and acid rain from burning fossil fuels; and the further destruction of the environment from oil drilling, coal mining, and deforestation.

A second major challenge is how to deal with massive urbanization as millions of formerly rural citizens flock to cities for jobs. Worldwide, 51 percent of humanity now lives in a city, with the prediction that this will become two out of three people by 2025. Projections estimate that, by that date, the world will have more than 30 megacities whose populations exceed 8 million each, and more than 500 cities with populations greater than 1 million.[13] This will result in enormous costs to build the necessary infrastructure—housing, roads, communications, educational and medical facilities—to accommodate such huge urban populations.

It is not surprising that we continue to struggle to wrap our minds around this new level of complexity in the world and its effect on our ability to exercise our self-interest. Historically, the great civilizations of the world have protected their self-interests by amassing armies to wage war. Today, however, the rise of prosperous capitalist businesses and multinational corporations requires more peaceful solutions to settle competing national self-interests. This suggests that capitalism, to be successful, must enable humanity to improve its techniques and methodologies for solving problems in more peaceful and mutually self-interested ways.

> *With more countries, more customer segmentation, more media, and more distribution channels, companies and their CMO's are waging a battle with complexity.*
>
> —*The McKinsey Quarterly*

## 4. THE POPULATION EXPLOSION AND ITS IMPACT ON CONSUMPTION

In 5000 BC, the world's population is estimated to have been about 15 million people. In AD 1000, it had grown to 310 million. Jump to 1950, when humans numbered 2.5 billion. Now, 60 years later, we are roughly 6.8 billion souls. It is estimated that by 2050, the Earth will contain 9 billion people.

The rising number of people is not itself a problem for capitalism. The challenge will be how this growing number of people can become the same type of consumers who now populate the developed world. If every one of those 9 billion people wanted to satisfy their self-interests in the same way the most prosperous countries now do, the world's resources could not support it.

Jared Diamond, a University of California–Los Angeles professor of geology and physiology and the author of *Collapse: How Societies Choose to Fail or Succeed,* suggests that the developed world—and by extension, all of capitalism—will need to make substantial sacrifices in production and consumption if we are to avoid a catastrophic disaster of resource scarcity. This includes lowering our consumption of oil and food stocks, and mastering sustainability in such areas as fishing and forestry. Should this fail to happen, Diamond offers a chilling prognosis.

> People in the third world are aware of this difference in per capita consumption, although most of them couldn't specify that it's by a factor of 32. When they believe their chances of catching up to be hopeless, they sometimes get frustrated and angry, and some become terrorists, or tolerate or support terrorists. Since Sept. 11, 2001, it has become clear that the oceans that once protected the United States no longer do so. There will be more terrorist attacks against us and Europe, and perhaps against Japan and Australia.[14]

Diamond is not the only thinker to remark on these potential consequences. In *Hot, Flat, and Crowded,* Thomas Friedman also argues that we are already well on our way to incurring serious problems of an Earth populated with more people eager to have prosperity. He predicts that we will face a growing demand for scarcer energy supplies and natural resources; a massive transfer of wealth to oil-rich countries and their petro-dictators; disruptive climate change; and rapidly accelerating biodiversity loss, as plants and animals become extinct at record rates.[15]

The world's population explosion necessitates collaboration and cooperation in adjudicating conflicting self-interests. In the same way that we have created laws to prevent self-interested monopolies from taking over entire industries in the private sector, we will need to find solutions to ensure that any assertion of capitalistic self-interest does not preclude a more equitable division of the Earth's resources—if not to create prosperity for all, at least to avoid increased conflict.

## 5. THE POWER SHIFT TO CONSUMERS AND CITIZENS

In early January 2009, a college student named Arlen Parsa wrote a blog entry to expose how a business (Belkin, maker of routers) was hiring people to write fake reviews of its products on Amazon.com. In June 2009, citizens in Iran, which has state-controlled media, tapped into Twitter as their only means to inform the world about the anti-government protests. In ten days in January 2010, more than $30 million to help Haitian earthquake relief was raised from Americans using their cell phones to text in their $10 pledges.

Stories like these have become commonplace today, as consumers and citizens are capitalizing on the new world of communications to equalize what has been called an "information asymmetry" that formerly prevented them from having complete knowledge and insight into events and situations. But now the various tools of social media are empowering citizens to form large collective groups for social activism. Thanks to email, SMS, blogging, social networks, YouTube, Flickr, and smartphones, any person has the tools to expose individuals, companies, or governments for acts of duplicity, lying, manipulation, or greed. The ability for any company or government to bury mistakes and transgressions is fast approaching zero, while the capability of people to root out corruption and unite in digital protest is skyrocketing.

Living in this newly transparent and highly networked digital world completely alters the balance of self-interest in the former hierarchy of authority. For decades, companies, advertising agencies, and the media held sway over what information consumers saw, heard, and shared, with few tools available for citizens to ferret out the truth or to connect directly and readily with each other. Today governments, companies, and individuals are finding it nearly impossible to manipulate the truth or to make decisions that others perceive as selfishly motivated—at least not without engendering pushback from informed and angry citizens. The rapidity and force of public reprimand will increasingly impact governments and companies that fail to consider the interests of their citizens or customers. Larry Weber makes this point succinctly with the title of his recent book: *Sticks and Stones: How Digital Business Reputations Are Created Over Time and Lost in a Click.*[16]

Henry Jenkins, a noted professor at the University of Southern California and an authority on media and communications, calls the power shift to citizens a fundamental reversal in who controls the "storytelling." In the past the institutions in power (whether a government or a company) wrote the narratives of history. Now the power dynamic is reversed, as the members of the public have access to the tools of the new media, which allows them to rewrite the story as *they* see and live it.

This shift in power to consumers and citizens is not temporary or the product of faddish technology. It is clearly one of the most fundamental and enduring characteristics of the modern digital world, and it will influence how capitalism moves forward. Kevin Kelly of *Wired* magazine goes so far as to call it "digital socialism" that will apply pressure to all centralized forms of authority and lead us into a new world of mutual self-interest and collaboration. He writes, "We're not talking about your grandfather's socialism. In fact, there is a long list of past movements this new socialism is not. It is not class warfare. It is not anti-American; indeed, digital socialism may be the newest American innovation. While old-school socialism was an arm of the state, digital socialism is socialism without the state. This new brand of socialism currently operates in the realm of culture and economics, rather than government."[17]

Some forward-thinking companies have accepted this change and are making adjustments in how they assert their capitalist self-interest. For example, they are actively tapping into "crowdsourcing," using the social networks to seek out collective mind power, ideas, and feedback that not only accelerate their innovation process but also help build a large community of customers who are emotionally invested in the company. This power shift to consumers will become an increasingly important dynamic in changing capitalism in the future, as technology enables consumers to organize themselves around shared values—and to defend those values when companies breach them, such as through boycotts and online protests.

## 6. THE REALITY OF ENVIRONMENTAL THREATS

Respect for our planet is not a modern concept. Centuries ago, indigenous cultures in many parts of the world lived by the rule that each generation is a guardian of the Earth for future generations. But in the last century, human activity in the name of progress and profit has forgotten that ancient rule, mindlessly destroying the environment and consuming resources as if there is no end to them.

Four decades of scientific research have now yielded nearly universal acceptance of three critical environmental concepts: one, that human activity impacts the Earth; two, that the health of the planet is jeopardized by our continued use of carbon-based fuels, which are causing global climate change; and three, that the Earth has finite resources, which once consumed cannot be replaced. Chief among these are the rainforests, which once covered 14 percent of the world and are now down to 6 percent, with projections that they could completely disappear within 40 years.[18]

The overwhelming opinion on this issue, issued by the Intergovernmental Panel on Climate Change (IPCC), a panel established in 1988 by the World

Meteorological Organization (WMO) and the United Nations Environment Programme (UNEP), is that the increase in greenhouse gases caused by humans burning hydrocarbons and the release of methane is responsible for creating a measurable global atmospheric warming trend over the past 50 years. The warming is not part of a natural planetary cycle. The IPCC's conclusions have been endorsed by more than 40 scientific societies and academies of science, including all of the national academies of science in the major industrialized countries.

Until the most recent decade, environmentalism was the complete antithesis of capitalist self-interest. For most of the twentieth century, the majority of capitalist enterprises viewed environmental issues with disdain; sustainability was not in their vocabulary. The pursuit of short-term, profit-oriented Me First capitalism neglected the long-term consequences of overfishing, overfarming, deforestation, and overproduction.

But the consequences of such myopic thinking can no longer be denied in light of increasingly worrisome statistics. By 2005, the United Nations Food and Agriculture Organization (FAO) already reported that 52 percent of all fish stocks were fully exploited (caught at their maximum biological capacity to reproduce), while 16 percent of wild fish were overexploited, and 7 percent were depleted.[19] In 2008, the FAO released reports that global deforestation was happening at the rate of about 13 million hectares annually.[20] The FAO also reported in 2008 that land degradation, defined as a long-term decline in ecosystem function and productivity, was

> increasing in severity and extent in many parts of the world, with more than 20 percent of all cultivated areas, 30 percent of forests and 10 percent of grasslands undergoing degradation. An estimated 1.5 billion people, or a quarter of the world's population, depend directly on land that is being degraded. The consequences of land degradation include reduced productivity, migration, food insecurity, damage to basic resources and ecosystems, and loss of biodiversity through changes to habitats at both species and genetic levels. [21]

Many environmental issues are complex, with conflicting priorities on both sides of an argument—e.g., agribusiness vs. food shortages; industries providing jobs vs. clean air and water; the need for easy transportation vs. pollution; saving forests vs. wood fuel for the indigenous poor. Some solutions to environmental problems lead to other environmental problems, such as the use of computers and the Internet, which on one hand help people work virtually from their homes, while on the other hand create huge heat farms and mountains of unrecyclable components in landfills.

Environmental issues are some of the most divisive for free market capitalism and profit-making corporations. The industrial economies of the world want to expand their access to the Earth's resources, while the emerging economies demand equal rights and underdeveloped nations sit powerless on the sidelines. The conflicts of negotiating which countries must yield their self-interest in the effort to slow global warming is evident in the hollow success, if not failure, of almost every single international climate change attempt since the Kyoto Protocol in 1997, including the 2009 Copenhagen and the 2010 Cancún Climate Change Summits.

Nevertheless, the reality of serious environmental damage to the Earth is now a factor that requires rethinking corporate and consumer self-interest.

## 7. THE DEMOGRAPHICS OF CHANGE

The final argument that we live in a new world relates to the fact that the vanguard of the Millennial generation is moving toward taking over major government and industry leadership roles throughout the developed world. Baby Boomers still control many top positions of power, but the past decade marked the beginning of a generational change that will shortly affect Me First capitalism by 2020. The Millennials are the first generation to have come of age with computers and mobile phones constantly at their disposal. It is their comfort level with the digital world and their expansive, global, and connected worldview that will dictate how capitalism and self-interest play out in the future.

There is no doubt as to the disruptive impact that Millennials will have on the false distinction corporations make between profit and purpose. We already know from noted researchers William Strauss and Neil Howe, among others, that Millennials prefer collaboration to competitiveness, sharing to hoarding, connection to isolation, bottom-up decentralization to top-down centralized authority, diversity to homogeneity, free expression to control, and "free" to having to pay for something.

Millennials arrived with the digital revolution and so are naturally using these tools to express their political and social views. They have eagerly plunged into the new world of social technologies such as Napster, MySpace, Facebook, Twitter, YouTube, Foursquare, Second Life, and Zynga. Their desire to be connected at all times is reflected in the mission statements of many digital companies—Twitter aims to be the "Pulse of the Planet" while Zynga's marketing platform is "Connecting the World through Games." Moreover, the same Millennials that drove the success of these companies are now pushing brands into dialoguing with them about such issues as corporate social responsibility, sustainability, ethics, and the fair treatment of employees, all of which were formerly a company's sole province.

Given the pace at which Millennials are already coercing traditional media to remake itself in their image (e.g., simple to use, easy to understand, transparent, authentic, always on, and free), they will bring the same perspective to altering how business and governments function throughout the globe. They will eventually take over the reins of leadership, eager to fulfill the words of noted entrepreneur and author Paul Hawken, who told a graduating class of Millennials at the University of Portland in 2009: "The Earth needs a new operating system. You are the programmers, and we need it within a few decades."[22]

## A NEW VIEW OF SELF-INTEREST

The new world circumscribed by these seven dynamics plays havoc with our old conceptions of individual and corporate self-interest and our propensity to let Me First selfishness dominate our economic behaviors. The current free market business models are simply no longer valid in a globalized world with nearly 7 billion inhabitants, with more than 120 countries vying for limited resources, interconnected economies, and new technologies that are altering the balance of political and media power. Continuing our Me First practices is shortsighted and self-destructive—and it will only lead to disastrous social, economic, and political consequences. Me First is a mismatch for this new world.

In its place, we need capitalism to begin operating under a new order that recognizes two changes. First, our perspective must look beyond our immediate needs and acknowledge that sometimes our self-interest is best served through compromise or solutions that promise gains over the longer term, rather than immediately. Second, we need to begin respecting the possibility of mutual self-interest, or We First, in which every party comes away with something to gain.

The application of We First means that corporations must recognize that they are part of society and have a responsibility to create something more than profit. As for consumers, they, too, need to understand that they play a role in preserving the Earth and helping a better form of capitalism take root by requiring the businesses they support to become responsible corporate citizens. In short, the only way capitalism will survive and thrive in this new world is to build a society based on the fulfillment of mutual self-interest. Fortunately, there are many ways that can be accomplished.

## CHAPTER TAKEAWAYS

- The dilemma we face in today's world is that everyone has self-interests, and they are becoming increasingly selfish.
- We now have a clear rationale to redefine self-interest—which is that we living in a complex and unpredictable, interconnected, globalized world in which new technologies are empowering citizens and consumers to alter the nature of capitalism.
- We need to move away from Me First self-interest to We First mutual interest.

# 3

# THE FUTURE OF
# PROFIT IS PURPOSE

Anyone who works in branding and marketing knows that humans are complex creatures whose purchasing habits can be very difficult to predict. Corporations and brands spend millions of dollars each year to learn what makes consumers tick. They conduct focus groups, taste tests, and surveys to delve into the consumer mindset. They invite influential bloggers to spend time at their offices, telling them what they and their audiences think. But despite millions spent in these research efforts, consumer behavior remains elusive for many brand managers to pin down with precision.

In 2005, a professor of social sciences at Harvard, Michael J. Hiscox, and his student, Nicholas F. B. Smyth, conducted an experiment to see if consumers are motivated by factors other than low prices in retail sales. Hiscox and Smyth were looking to find out if people might pay more for products they know to have been produced by workers toiling under good conditions rather than in sweatshops. The conventional wisdom of profit-maximizing corporations is that people want to pay less for goods, which justifies their using offshore labor paid as cheaply as possible, even if it means inhumane working conditions.

The research duo performed their test in an upscale retail store, ABC Carpet and Home, in New York City. The store had two brands of towels for sale. Both were made from organic cotton, and both had been made under certified Fair Trade conditions where factories had been monitored by inspectors and the workers were reasonably paid. For the first phase of the experiment, Hiscox and Smyth monitored sales of both sets of towels to get a baseline measure of their sales ratios.

In the next phase of the experiment, they designed a label based on ABC's logo for their "Fair and Square" merchandise—items produced under certified

Fair Trade conditions. Their label included the statement: "These towels have been made under fair labor conditions, in a safe and healthy working environment which is free of discrimination, and where management has committed to respecting the rights and dignity of workers." They placed the label on signs above and near just one set of towels, but not the other, implying that only the one set was Fair Trade and not the other. In the next month, unit sales of the labeled towels went up 11 percent, with a dollar sales increase of almost 5 percent, while sales of the other brand dropped.

Next, Hiscox and Smyth raised the price on the labeled towels by 10 percent. Unit sales increased another 20 percent over the other towels, generating a 62 percent gain in net dollars because of the higher price. This phase lasted another month. Then they raised the price of the labeled brand again by 20 percent, and unit sales rose another 4 percent, with an additional increase of 17 percent in net dollars. Finally, they reversed which towels had the label displayed over them and found the sales of the formerly labeled brand dropped back to near baseline levels, while the newly labeled brand saw its sales climb.[1]

Numerous other research experiments have yielded similar results, proving that consumers are not interested only in price. In 2008, the respected cause-marketing consulting company Cone tested consumer behavior in conjunction with Duke University's noted Fuqua School of Business. In this experiment, they tracked purchasing habits on four products. The test subjects were first shown magazine advertisements. Some ads had copy stating that sales of the products supported a certain cause, while the other ads showed no cause affiliation. The results showed a 28 percent increase in those consumers' purchases of toothpaste affiliated with a cause in the advertisements versus toothpaste that had only a standard advertisement. A shampoo had a 74 percent increase in sales based on the advertising linking it to a cause, compared with a regularly advertised shampoo.

There is a clear moral to experiments like these: people are not always motivated by low price when they recognize another benefit gained through their purchase—that of having helped build a better world. Whether it is towels, toothpaste, or tomatoes, consumers appear to understand that their way of life cannot be a race to the lowest possible price if the process compromises the lives of those who produced the products or harms the Earth. It is results like these that suggest consumers are wiser than brands may think. *Perhaps what consumers want is not "retail" but "Wetail."*

## THE PRICE OF PROFIT WITH AND WITHOUT PURPOSE

One of the fundamental inherent flaws of free market capitalism is that it condones a mindset that profit for *profit's sake* is all that matters. Profit itself is not an evil force. We know that profits are a necessary component of capitalism. Corporations, small companies, and entrepreneurs count on making profits beyond their cost of goods and labor so as to generate funds for growth, research, and innovation, and to pay themselves for their hard work and reward investors for the risk of their investments.

Yet profit mania is the source of the malaise we are now experiencing, because it seeks to enrich people without adding a meaningful purpose to society. Profit for profit's sake is a mindset that drives too many investors, businesses, and corporations to neglect three critical issues that We First capitalism seeks to change: one, the methods of producing profits; two, the consequences of profits, and three, the social implications of profits. Let me explain each of these.

Regarding methods, companies need to change the tactics and techniques they use to generate profits. Thinking only about profits for profit's sake blinds them to unsafe, unsound, and unsustainable production methods. It causes them to do things like cut corners on design or manufacturing, overlook safety precautions, abuse the use of chemicals in their production processes, dump toxic refuse, cheat on compliance regulations, and take other illicit actions intended to reduce costs and maximize gains.

In this approach, customers become mere purchasing entities whose larger social needs, concerns, and desires are irrelevant to the company. Disinterest in customer well-being is why so many corporations have struggled for years with customer service—and why even today, most companies still fail to understand how to connect with consumers using social media.

In terms of consequences, a profit-for-profit's-sake mentality encourages executives to make decisions based purely on maximizing financial gains. They are not asked to account for any social, political, or environmental impacts of their business. This includes both the visible and the invisible negative externalities that companies create in the world, from pollution and depleted resources to displaced populations and unemployed workers to cities blighted by urban decay.

The third issue neglected in the profit-for-profit's-sake equation is actually one of the most important mind shifts we need to make—the consideration of the social implications of profits. Decisions made in the name of profit have long-term effects on the cultural and social fabric of our communities. Being a society focused on profit has increasingly defined us as a culture that elevates get-rich-quick schemes, infomercials, a convenience mentality, easy solutions, instant celebrity, and a substantial loss of basic human values.

To be fair, the opportunity to earn big profits is why so many talented people join corporations where they can take advantage of opportunities for education, innovation, entrepreneurship, and earnings from their hard work. But if we acknowledge this advantage of capitalism, we must also acknowledge the destructive downside of its social implications on our culture. We cannot praise capitalism for its virtues if we are not willing to accept criticism for its vices.

Let me summarize these three problems in a single phrase: *Profit for profit's sake is selfish, insensitive, and asocial.*

The opposite of profit for profit's sake is *profit with purpose.* By "purpose" I am referring to a model in which businesses, while making a profit, also have a positive impact on the world. A business that commits to purpose seeks to infuse greater meaning into the lives of all the stakeholders it touches— employees, customers, suppliers, distributors, community members, and all other parties affected by the business's presence.

To summarize this version of capitalism in a single phrase: *Profit with purpose is mindful, contributory, and socially oriented.*

> *Long-term profits are maximized by not making them the primary goal.*
> —John Mackey, founder and CEO, Whole Foods

## THE NEW DYNAMICS BETWEEN PROFIT AND PURPOSE

As a society that includes corporations, businesses, investors, boards of directors, consumers, and citizens, we must engage in a new conversation about profits and purpose to foster a more constructive spirit in capitalism. Happily, such a dynamic is already emerging, and it will increasingly drive how corporations and consumers negotiate the balance between gains and costs. This dynamic is created by two complementary market forces that are reshaping the relationship between corporations and customers.

1. Consumers want a better world, not just better widgets.
2. The future of profit is purpose.

## TWO EXAMPLES OF MARRYING PROFIT AND PURPOSE

Scores of smaller and midsized companies committed to merging profit and purpose have emerged in the past decade. Here are two examples that demonstrate the range of purposeful goals that companies can establish at the strategic core of their businesses.

### DANCING DEER BAKING COMPANY

Dancing Deer, founded in 1994 in Boston, originated as a bakery selling primarily to restaurants and cafés. It quickly expanded with a line of packaged baked goods. Word of Dancing Deer's tasty pastries spread rapidly, and the company was profiled on national television. Since then they have grown into a nationally known brand, with sales over $10 million in 2007. From the beginning, the company has poured its profits back into the larger purpose of helping homeless families out of shelters and into homes: its Sweet Home Project donates 35 percent of the retail price of all specially labeled Sweet Home Gifts to fund scholarships for homeless mothers.

### GUAYAKI YERBA MATE

Founded in 1996, this company has established a clear purpose beyond profits: it seeks to create 1,000 jobs and restore 200,000 acres of rainforest by the year 2020. Given that the company's sales are roughly $12 million annually, it must grow by 25 percent per year to reach those goals. But rather than rapidly expanding just a few of their fields, the company has chosen to build a network of certified Fair Trade growers to help create jobs for indigenous peoples of Brazil, Paraguay, and Argentina. To start, the company has partnered with the Marrecas community in Brazil to restore 40,000 acres of Atlantic rainforest while harvesting the mate plant. This alone will provide jobs for 250 families. The company is also teaming up with several American and South American universities to create sustainability-education programs.

These are but two examples of the plethora of new business models merging purpose and profit that are capturing the attention of consumers today.

These two forces are intertwined and mutually fulfilling. As more consumers insist that capitalism works in the service of a better world, companies will become increasingly purposeful, and thus more profitable. Replacing the old capitalist paradigm of supply and demand, this dynamic between profit and purpose will become the new economic principle that drives the marketplace. Consumers who want a better world will drive the profits of corporations that provide greater purpose through their activities. Meanwhile, corporations that provide too little purpose for consumers will fail.

## CONSUMERS DESIRE A BETTER WORLD

The first inklings that consumers truly desire a better world arose in the early years of the environmental movement. Beginning in the 1960s and 1970s, environmentalism was the launching point for a new consumer consciousness that business practices were negligently destroying the Earth by poisoning and polluting the air, water, and soil for profit's sake. In the United States, this consciousness then morphed in the 1990s into a wider movement that became known as corporate social responsibility (CSR), by which consumers sought to hold companies responsible for a broad range of sound business practices.

It's worth noting that in Europe, environmentalism and CSR had already been part of the tacit contract between corporations and society, and many of those governments regulated corporate activities more highly to begin with. But the strength of the CSR movement in America and the increasing globalization of companies have made the consumer push for socially responsible companies into a global cause.

Consumers desiring a better world have already achieved some successes in this regard, helping to transform several industries from the ground up. In the car business, for example, consumers clamoring for a more environmentally responsible car got Toyota's attention—and the Prius and its Hybrid Synergy Drive engine were born. Consumers also helped reshape the grocery industry through their desire for organic and healthier foods, opening the door for companies like Whole Foods and Wild Oats, whose successes in turn forced traditional grocery chains to begin adding organic foods as well. Consumers acting in conjunction with advocacy organizations like Greenpeace have also leaned on companies like Nestlé and Cadbury to encourage them to source their supplies such as palm oil from vendors that don't deforest the land or threaten the species that live there.

While consumer power for a better world is still nascent, it's poised to skyrocket. Consumer pressure will greatly expand the breadth and depth of CSR, forcing companies to willfully change their practices. This consumer drive will become unstoppable for three reasons. First, following the Great Recession, many consumers are simply frustrated and angry at corporations. Millions of them have been personally affected by the relentless corporate drive for profit above all else, having lost their jobs. These are people who are now distrustful of corporations and intolerant of selfish behaviors that negatively affect their lives and their planet.

Second, many consumers, especially those of the Millennial generation, are no longer willing to tolerate corporations and brands that neglect purpose or prevaricate about their efforts to be responsible citizens. They will especially vilify companies caught "greenwashing" (exaggerating or lying about the eco-friendliness of their products), "cause-washing" (advertising their support for a cause, only to be revealed later as having donated little or no money), or "local-washing" (claiming their products are made from local produce or materials when, in fact, they are not).

Third, and perhaps most important, consumers are simply becoming more aware of the need for capitalism to evolve. They want to see companies adopt a more constructive rationale in the practice of their businesses, and they will have less tolerance for those that fail to place purpose at the core of their missions and strategies. Such consumers will increasingly seek to conduct their business transactions only with corporations and brands that practice purposeful capitalism with transparency, authenticity, and accountability throughout their entire supply and sales chains.

Today's consumers are eager to become loyal fans of companies that respect purposeful capitalism. They are not opposed to companies making a profit; indeed, they may even be investors in these companies—but at the core, they want more empathic, enlightened corporations that seek a balance between profit and purpose. The 2009 Edelman "Goodpurpose" survey of 6,000 consumers aged 18–64 across ten countries overwhelmingly confirmed this consumer sentiment. Here are some of the statistics that show the extent to which consumers want a better world and are willing to support those corporations that make an effort to deliver it:

- 83 percent of consumers are willing to change their consumption habits if it can help make tomorrow's world a better place to live.
- 82 percent agree that supporting a good cause makes them feel better about themselves.
- 61 percent have bought a brand that supports a good cause even if it was not the cheapest brand.
- 64 percent would recommend a brand that supports a good cause, up from 52 percent last year.

- 59 percent would help a brand promote its products if there was a good cause behind it.
- 56 percent believe the interests of society and the interests of businesses should have equal weight in business decisions.
- 66 percent of people globally believe it is no longer enough for corporations to simply give money to a good cause; they need to integrate good causes into their day-to-day business.
- 59 percent of people globally (61 percent in the United States) have a better opinion of corporations that integrate good causes into their business, regardless of the reasons why they do so.
- 65 percent of people have more trust in a brand that is ethically and socially responsible.
- 64 percent of consumers say they expect brands today to do something to support a good cause.
- 63 percent of consumers want brands to make it easier for them to make a positive difference in the world.
- 67 percent would switch brands if a different brand of similar quality supported a good cause.[2]

Results from another survey, the 2010 Cone Cause Evolution Study, also confirm these findings from consumers, especially in regard to the beliefs about corporate responsibility held among the two important demographic groups for brands of "Moms" and "Millennials." This survey found the following statistics:

- The Millennial generation has an even stronger preference to do business with responsible companies than the average consumer. In 2010, 85 percent said they would switch their brand if it was involved in a good cause and the price was the same, versus 80 percent of all adults.
- 53 percent of Millennials reported having purchased a cause-related product in the past year, versus 41 percent of all adults; and 85 percent of them would buy a product where a portion of the cost supports a cause, versus 81 percent of all adults.
- Self-identified "Moms" show the highest preference for doing business with socially responsible corporations, even beyond

Millennials: 93 percent said they would switch their brand if it were involved in a good cause and the price were the same, versus 80 percent of all adults.

- Among Moms, 61 percent have purchased a cause-related product in the last year, versus 41 percent of all adults.
- 92 percent of Moms would buy a product where a portion of the cost supports a cause, versus 81 percent of all adults.[3]

Moreover, these statistics do not exist in a vacuum, as consumers are increasingly enabled to vote for responsible brands with their wallets. Dozens of websites showing product and company reviews, and smartphones loaded with mobile shopping applications are quickly making "socially mindful consumerism" a reality. For example, consumers can now scan a product's bar code using any of several smartphone apps and learn if its manufacturer is environmentally responsible, treats its employees well, and conducts sustainable practices. Technologies such as location-based services and augmented-reality apps (smartphone applications that add layers of information to what the user sees through the screen) will soon allow consumers to gain even more information at the point of purchase about the companies whose products and services they buy.

Over the long term, the potent mix of consumer frustration with irresponsible companies, the greater capacity for consumers to communicate, the newfound ease of informing oneself, and the strong concerns of important consumer groups like Moms and Millennials will transform consumer sentiment into a viable force on behalf of change in corporate behavior. Simply put, those corporations that resist merging purpose with profit will fail to win customers' loyalty, goodwill—and sales.

*From Day 1, we wanted a balance between profitability and social conscience.*

—Howard Schultz, CEO, Starbucks

*If business remains on its present path and continues to insist that market-driven incremental change is all that's needed, soon there won't be much of a world to do business in.*

—Jeffrey Hollender, founder and former CEO, Seventh Generation

## SEVENTH GENERATION: THE COMPANY AND THE CONCEPT

Seventh Generation is one of the first major companies committed to producing Earth-friendly, nontoxic, and recycled household and paper products. Seeking to end the environmental damage caused by poisonous and carcinogenic chemicals that bio-accumulate in the food chain and water systems, Jeffrey Hollender founded the company in 1988 when he set out to produce household cleaning products made from natural plant compounds, as well as toilet paper and diapers made from recycled paper. To acknowledge his grand purpose, he named the company after the Great Law of the Native American Iroquois tribe: "In our every deliberation, we must consider the impact of our decisions on the next seven generations."

Over the decades, Seventh Generation has become a noted leader in corporate social responsibility, placing its corporate purpose as high as its revenues ($140 million in 2009). The company's efforts have contributed to raising "eco awareness" in society and transforming public opinion about environmentalism. Seventh Generation and companies like it have most certainly played a role in the fact that, according to a 2009 Experian Simmons consumer survey, 75 percent of U.S. adults now feel they have a personal obligation to be environmentally responsible, and 65 percent believe companies should play a role in facilitating this, an enormous reversal from the 1980s, when environmental products were uncommon.[4] Although Seventh Generation was not profitable for its first 13 years, its recent successes caught the leading traditional corporations off guard. Clorox, S. C. Johnson, and Kimberly-Clark have all now launched new eco-friendly brands to compete.

Seventh Generation is committed to redefining traditional capitalism in numerous ways. Its "Return on Purpose" donates 10 percent of its profits to community, environmental, and health nonprofits working for change. It is an active proponent of fair trade with its suppliers. It promotes "conscious consumption" among consumers, educating them through its website, marketing materials, and information on its packaging how to buy less and avoid waste. Hollender refused, on principle, to sell his products to Walmart until 2010, when the mega-retailer began demonstrating to the company that it was committed to sustainable business practices.

In 2009, Hollender stepped down from his role as CEO of Seventh Generation (he remains executive chairman), admitting that, given the scale of crises we face, he had barely made a dent in changing the world. His goals are now to defeat the vast army of lobbyists working against global climate change legislation, and to consult with United Nations officials about the climate crisis and social inequities. He also speaks to business students, educating them about a new type of corporate legal structure, the B Corporation, which forces boards to consider social and environmental impact along with profit models.[5]

Despite Hollender's departure, Seventh Generation remains a model of the type of thinking needed in not one but thousands of companies in order to evolve a new corporate social consciousness about capitalism.

## THE FUTURE OF PROFIT IS PURPOSE

The corollary of consumer desire for a better world is a new attitude that corporations will have to develop about the nature of profits. Companies need to recognize that the best way to increase their profit potential is to respond authentically to the growing consumer desire for purpose.

Some companies have been heading in this direction, but the validity of this premise remains only superficially accepted. A brief look at the history of corporate social responsibility confirms why this is so.

Beginning in the 1970s, in response to the environmental movement, a small number of corporations began adhering to higher standards of production and manufacturing to cut down on their polluting effects. Companies like Anita Roddick's Body Shop and Ben & Jerry's ice cream company launched Earth-friendly, socially responsible products. But these were anomalies at the time, and few corporations followed their lead.

It took decades, but eventually other companies started seeing the positive benefits of socially responsible behavior, and CSR efforts began flourishing. By the late 1980s and early 1990s, more and more firms were improving their environmental business practices by cutting energy usage, reducing waste in packaging, streamlining inefficient processes, and initiating more focused charitable contributions. Corporate executives participated in CSR workshops, read the slew of books that began appearing in the 1990s and early 2000s about CSR, and started benchmarking CSR best practices. The top graduate schools started offering management degrees with a CSR focus, and working it into their core curriculum. In recent years, many corporations have even put a chief responsibility officer (CRO) in charge of corporate ethical behavior and corporate giving. Some companies even hired a chief giving officer (CGO) to manage their charitable budgets and dole out funds to a variety of local, national, or global causes selected to match their customers' interests. Today, almost every major Fortune 500 company boasts an environmental and CSR initiative.

Meanwhile, in the 1980s and '90s, many of the largest and wealthiest corporations also tried something new: they spun off independent nonprofit philanthropic foundations to fund good-works programs specifically chosen to match the company's mission. The Foundation Center, a national nonprofit service organization of philanthropies, reports that the number of corporate foundations has mushroomed in just a few decades, with about 2,500 corporate foundations now in the United States alone.[6]

The 1980s and 1990s were also decades in which corporations began testing out a new technique called cause-related marketing, or CRM, as yet another way to respond to consumer concerns about the state of the world. American Express is credited with the first CRM campaign in 1983, when it advertised it would donate to the Statue of Liberty restoration fund one cent for every transaction its cardholders made, plus $1 for every new card application. The effort proved an enormous success, raising more than $1.7 million to restore the venerable American icon of freedom.[7] Since then, hundreds of companies have launched CRM campaigns, partnering with nonprofits to raise cash for their causes.

One of the most well-known ongoing CRM campaigns, for example, is Yoplait's "Lids to Save Lives" campaign, started in 1998. During specific months each year, for each pink Yoplait lid consumers mail in the company donates ten cents to the Susan G. Komen for the Cure fund supporting breast cancer research. The campaign generates such strong interest that teams of people eagerly compete against each other to raise the most money. Another notable CRM example comes from Procter & Gamble. In 2008, the company linked up with UNICEF and offered to pay for one tetanus shot for an expectant mother in one of 12 African nations for every pack of specially marked Pampers diapers sold.

Cause-related marketing is perhaps the first solid demonstration of the complementary nature between corporate profit and consumer desire to effect global change through their purchasing power. In challenging consumers to prove how much they care about a chosen cause, CRM efforts effectively turn consumers and brands into partners in building a better world. Today, scores of companies conduct CRM campaigns, such as Chase Bank's "Community Giving," Target's "Bulls-eye Gives," Kraft's "Huddle to Fight Hunger," Ford's "Invisible People," and Pepsi's "Refresh Project." Cause-related marketing has become the primary method corporations use to show their social responsibility. Tracking studies from Chicago-based consulting firm International Events Group show that corporate donations from CRM have risen exponentially, from zero in 1983 to $125 million in 1990. That figure quadrupled, to $545 million, in 1998, and skyrocketed to $1.52 billion in 2008.[8]

When you put all this together, there has been a steadily rising tide of funding in the name of a better world. In 2009, corporations gave $14.1 billion in charitable donations, including an estimated $4.42 billion in grants from corporate-based foundations.[9] Yet many consumers and watchdog groups remain suspicious of how sincere corporations are in their commitments to social transformation. On average, most corporations donate only about 1 percent of their total pretax profits to charitable causes, and the figure rarely exceeds 1.5 percent. By comparison, corporations generate trillions of dollars for their shareholders, while top corporate executives individually receive salaries and bonuses in the tens of millions.

Corporations have a long way to go to show consumers that they understand why the future of profit is purpose. Given the multiple and massive global crises we face, $14 billion is simply not enough. Corporate social responsibility, cause-related marketing, and corporate foundations may be the start of purposeful engagement in many companies, but real purpose must go deeper into the core of their strategic plans and into the heart and soul of the companies.

There are several leading companies and brands—including Starbucks, Ford, Pepsi, Nike, Walmart, Procter & Gamble, and Unilever—that are leading the way to making the future of their profit truly about purpose. These companies wisely recognize the business and social efficiencies of marrying purpose and profit. They are models for others to follow, beacons pointing to the future of We First thinking and capitalism.

> *The whole corporate social responsibility idea is trying to graft something onto the old profit maximization model. What we need is a transformation [in] the way we think about business, what it's based on. People want businesses to do good in the world. It's that simple. . . . We need a deeper, fundamental reform in the essence of business.*
>
> —John Mackey, CEO, Whole Foods

## FILLING THE VOID FOR PURPOSE

Consumer desire for purposeful business is mounting, and many are becoming impatient as they wait for the corporate world to change. As a result, the free market is already responding with an entirely new industry of companies, online communities, and entrepreneurial individuals committed to transforming capitalism themselves.

For example, there are a number of associations that have formed to advocate for socially mindful capitalism and to serve as networks for responsible businesses. The most noted of these is the Social Venture Network (SVN), which since 1987 has sought, as its website states, "to provide forums, information, and initiatives that enable leaders to work together to transform the way the world does business."

Another response is represented by B Labs, a nonprofit formed to create an alternative to the traditional C-corporation legal structure for businesses that want to commit themselves to corporate social responsibility. Any business that wants to abide by a commitment to socially mindful business practices can become a B Corporation by going through a rigorous certification process so that consumers will know they are dealing with a socially responsible company.

New types of media, entertainment, and technology companies have also been created to serve the needs of leading-edge brands, executives, and consumers who want to support causes through their business practices. Here are a few:

- Causecast is a company that offers cause marketing, CSR, employee engagement, and opportunities for public cause participation to both for-profit and nonprofit companies.
- Freeform is a purpose-driven media and production company creating content for brands, nonprofits, and academic institutions committed to social change.
- Participant Media creates entertainment that seeks to inspire change, such as Davis Guggenheim's 2010 documentary on the state of education in America, *Waiting for Superman*.
- Conscious Capitalism Alliance is a professional organization for entrepreneurial corporate executives who are deeply committed to personal growth and transformation to a conscious business model.
- SocialVibe is a marketing and advertising company that helps brands engage consumers using social media. Through its online community it allows consumers to identify charities and find brands that support them. SocialVibe members who want to support those charities can then purchase from the sponsoring brand.

We are also seeing new socially oriented business being implemented in many industries as nonprofit or low-profit companies are starting to compete with regular corporations. In banking, for example, numerous microfinance companies have appeared to offer easy-term loans to entrepreneurs and farmers living in developing countries or with low incomes who would not normally qualify for business loans. The most famous of these is the Grameen Bank, founded by Muhammad Yunus, who was awarded the Nobel Peace Prize in 2006 for his microfinance work in helping new small businesses in Bangladesh.

And finally, there is a wide assortment of social entrepreneurship training and funding organizations whose missions are to help create socially minded businesses that can compete with the traditional corporations of the world. For example, Ashoka, founded in 1981, provides support for 2,000 social entrepreneurs in 60 countries using a venture-capital approach that teaches people how to compete with for-profit businesses. The Skoll Foundation is another example, investing in social entrepreneurs "whose work has the potential for large-scale impact in critical social areas: economic and social equity, environmental sustainability, health, institutional responsibility, peace and security, and tolerance and human rights."[11]

## TOMS SHOES AND THE ONE-FOR-ONE CONCEPT

In the past, several companies have hosted cause-marketing efforts where they invited consumers to bring in a gently used item, such as a pair of glasses or sneakers, and the company would donate it to a cause. But few companies have gone so far as TOMS Shoes. Founded in 2006 by Blake Mycoskie on a single premise—"With every pair you purchase, TOMS will give a pair of new shoes to a child in need. One for One"—consumers' awareness of the company has skyrocketed in just a few years. The company's canvas shoes are based on a simple design worn by farmers that Mycoskie saw while traveling in Argentina. He was motivated to create a shoe company after noticing how many children in rural Argentinean communities were shoeless, and how merely providing them with shoes would help secure their future health and education, as shoeless children are not allowed to go to school and are vulnerable to a fungus that destroys the lymphatic system.

As of November 2010, TOMS had donated more than 1 million pairs of shoes to children in Argentina, Ethiopia, Guatemala, Haiti, Rwanda, South Africa, and the United States. The company is also adapting its one-for-one concept to other endeavors, enticing such partners as Polo Ralph Lauren and Element Skateboards, which sell co-branded products whose sales also donate footwear. Furthermore, as the company's website says, "It is TOMS' hope that as our One for One movement continues to grow, more and more companies will look to incorporate giving into what they do."

In essence, all these new types of companies, organizations, networks, training, and funding groups reflect the decades of consumer frustration and impatience waiting for the traditional capitalist corporations of the world to transform themselves into purposeful social businesses. They are a testament to the number of socially minded individuals who are working at closing the gap between living and giving that profit-making corporations have long ignored.

> *It is in the interest of the enterprise to take care of the economic and social environment; to create value for shareholders but also to create value and wealth for customers, employees, and regions where the companies operate, because our company is an economic and social project.*
>
> —Franck Riboud, CEO, Groupe Danone

## PURPOSE ON A MASSIVE SCALE

If this new dynamic between brands and consumers is already under way, why not just allow it to continue along its path? Why not trust that the free market will reach a natural balance point between profit and purpose on its own? Maybe corporations will begin giving more, or perhaps they will create better social responsibility and cause-related marketing programs. After all, they are already doing their best in these tough economic circumstances to give back to the world. Thousands of corporations already honor consumer concerns through their extensive CSR and CRM programs that contribute upwards of $14 billion to causes.

The problem is, such contributions are simply not enough and we cannot wait any longer for capitalism to change. Too much damage has already been done, and the more we wait, the more damage will be created. We need corporations to immediately scale up their responses to problems in three ways: vertically within each corporation, horizontally across industries, and collaboratively between businesses and consumers.

First, companies need to extend their commitment to socially responsible behaviors far beyond the attention they currently give CSR. Although most of the world's major corporations have adopted some form of CSR, truly purposeful business practices remain largely on the sidelines. Purpose must be reconceived as a driver of profit in corporate decision making, not as an afterthought. It must infuse the entire organization from top to bottom with consistent, vertical alignment. By extension, boards of directors, executives, and investors need to rethink the greater potential value they can get from long-term contributions toward making a better world against their limited, short-term profits.

The second dimension of scaling is instituting reforms horizontally. Any meaningful altering of capitalism requires a larger universe of companies to adopt a commitment to integrate purpose with profit. Without a massive expansion of purpose across tens of thousands of companies and businesses, the paltry size of current contributions—financial, human, and operational—will simply not meet the scale of crises we face in the world today.

The third dimension of scaling is that we need to leverage the connections between the hundreds of millions of consumers in the world and all their brands so they become partners working together in the name of social transformation. As the Edelman Goodpurpose study puts it, we need to replace the rather narrow idea of corporate social responsibility with *mutual* social responsibility. To achieve this, we need to speed up the mutually reinforcing dynamic between consumers who want a better world and corporations committed to purposeful profits.

If corporate behavior over recent decades is any indication, it seems clear that consumers will need to take the lead in persuading corporations to become willing participants in the transformation of their business practices. This is especially true as new digital and social technologies for communication and shopping are being passed on directly to consumers—often for free—leaving companies and brands to catch up with their customers as well as their competitors. But if consumers put their desire for a better world to work using these technologies, brands will increasingly follow suit, and we could be well on our way to achieving the level of purposeful social engagement and contributions that are urgently needed to mend our world.

## CHAPTER TAKEAWAYS

- The future of profit is purpose: Consumers want a better world, not just better widgets.
- Substantial proof shows that consumers, especially Moms and Millennials, want to do business with responsible companies and are willing to change their purchasing habits to support them.

- The Internet, smartphones, and mobile applications are quickly making it easy for consumers to perform "socially mindful" shopping.
- Despite corporate charitable contributions, consumers remain suspicious of how sincere companies are in their commitment to social responsibility.
- A new category of socially mindful companies and entrepreneurs is emerging to circumvent the traditional corporate models of CSR that are taking too long to effect change.
- To remain competitive with these new social entrepreneurs and their businesses, traditional corporations will have to adapt.
- We need to scale up the corporate responses to social transformation—and consumers must take the lead.

# 4 CREATING SUSTAINABLE CAPITALISM IN FIVE WAYS

More than 2,000 miles off the Pacific coast of Chile sits Easter Island, one of the world's most isolated—yet still inhabited—lands. The island forms one tip of the great Polynesian triangle, with Hawaii and New Zealand forming the other points. Archaeologists believe the island may have been settled as early as AD 300, with broader colonization around AD 1200.

The most intriguing aspect of Easter Island is the fact that its population, a people called the Rapa Nui, all but died out by the end of the 1700s. Anthropologists suspect overpopulation depleted the island's natural resources, leaving insufficient stock for later generations. But there is another, perhaps equally significant factor that caused the islanders' near extinction: unchecked manmade deforestation that set off a chain reaction. Without the huge palm groves that once dominated the island, wind eroded the soil on a massive scale. Without the proper nutrients, many edible plants died out. Large flocks of seabirds, a food source, disappeared because their nesting sites went unprotected. The lack of trees also meant the Rapa Nui couldn't build wooden fishing boats, further reducing their food supply. Over time, perhaps a century or more, the island's ecosystem failed, bringing on famine, sickness, and death to large swaths of its population.

Why did the Rapa Nui denude their forests? Anthropologists surmise that it may be because of their practice of carving *moai,* massive stone monuments to honor their ancestors. You may have seen photos of these giant human heads with their elongated blank faces standing in long rows along the coast of the island. Evidence indicates that the island once had more than 1,000 of these statues. Only a few remain today, resurrected for tourists from the ancient ones that toppled over long ago. Archaeologists believe the Rapa Nui razed the island's palm groves to mine the rock quarries beneath for the stone to build the statues. They also used the trees to construct lattices on which to drag the stones to their installation sites.

The story of Easter Island is a classic case of unsustainable development, one of the clearest examples of man's tendency toward short-term decisions that prove self-destructive in the long term. One could argue that the Rapa Nui did not have the scientific knowledge to understand the consequences of their deforestation, or the historical perspective to notice the patterns of increasing erosion and food-supply failure. Or perhaps they had a political system in which their leaders insisted on building the monuments despite the obvious signs of impending doom.

The same accusations could be leveled at our own capitalist society. We can be equally ignorant and shortsighted when it comes to denying the unsustainable effects of our own economic behaviors and choices. Although the collapse of the Rapa Nui happened long ago, it should serve as a lesson to us about our own destiny if we allow free market capitalism to mask the fact that we are depleting resources, impoverishing most of our populations, and undermining our progress toward building the great society we imagine. Without a significant change in our mindset, our world may very well be left with little more than rows of long-faced statues honoring the titans of Wall Street.[1]

## TODAY'S NARROW APPROACH TO SUSTAINABILITY

Most of us are familiar with the concept of sustainable development, although we usually think of it as exclusively related to the environmental movement. Companies throughout the world are starting to implement sustainable practices in their sourcing, manufacturing, distribution, and disposal of products and services. "Minimizing one's footprint" and using "cradle to grave" thinking are becoming widely accepted standard operating procedures. Corporations are reflecting on the changes they need to make to address the worldwide scientific community's warnings about global climate change caused by burning fossil fuels. Consumers are likewise altering their habits to shop more consciously and purchase from companies that implement sustainable practices, such as more efficient packaging, the use of recycled materials, or other green initiatives.

Environmentalism and sustainability seem completely logical and rational to most of us now. But when environmentalist thinking originally began, it was viewed with derision and skepticism, just as it is now among those who deny global climate change. The modern environmental movement goes back to the 1970s, when a small stratum of environmentalist thinkers began questioning the consequences of rapid economic development and its potential impact on the Earth's natural resources and the environment. In the late 1980s, the United Nations World Commission on Environment and Development issued a longitudinal study (often referred to as the Brundtland report) that challenged businesses to acknowledge the unsustainability of their practices and find ways to "[meet] the needs of the present without compromising the ability of future generations to meet their own needs."[2]

In the decades since, the business world has inched along, requiring constant pressure from environmental groups to adopt major changes in their business practices that often require upfront costs or a reduction in profits. Meanwhile, a vast field of research has emerged to study and develop new methods to reduce the conflicts between business growth and environmental sustainability. The Green Tech sector, for example, consists of numerous start-up companies seeking to adapt emerging technologies to contribute to a healthier environment.

If you are in business or government, you may be familiar with Andrew Savitz's book, *The Triple Bottom Line,* which posits that the public and private sectors must measure their outcomes based on the three *P*'s: people, planet, and profit. The "bottom line" in the title refers not only to the accounting of an entity's financial results, but also to the social and environmental impact of its operations. In the private sector, the notion of the triple bottom line encourages businesses to adopt practices that benefit all stakeholders, not just the investors and shareholders seeking financial gain.

According to this philosophy, profit must be evaluated in a much larger context than the standard measures of return on investment (ROI) and earnings figures. True triple bottom line math subtracts from net profits the costs to society that the business's practices create, such as environmental, health, or social ills. To offset these costs, however, companies can add back the value of economic benefits that the business brings to society, such as increased tourism, more retail business, bigger tax revenues, and so on.[3]

While some companies and governments are embracing elements of triple bottom line accounting, our overall progress at integrating sustainability into the fundamental principles of free market capitalism has been irresponsibly slow. It has taken 40 years to get to where we are today, requiring nearly an entire generation of corporate leaders to rethink their business strategies and recognize that the long-term consequences of unsustainable practices are potentially disastrous for the planet.

As an example of how slowly corporations have responded to sustainability issues, consider this passage from the report of a 2010 survey of CEOs conducted by the United Nations Global Compact, a group that convenes business leaders with U.N. human rights, labor, and other agencies to review business practices:

> We have witnessed a fundamental shift since the last Global Compact survey in 2007. Then, sustainability was just emerging on the periphery of business issues, an increasing concern that was beginning to reshape the rules of competition. Three years later, sustainability is truly top-of-mind for CEOs around the world.[4]

What is striking about this passage is that it oddly asserts that in 2007, *sustainability was just emerging on the periphery of business issues for CEOs.* This is shocking. How is it possible that CEOs were just starting to wonder about sustainability in 2007 when the rest of the world has been attuned to the issue for more than a decade?

It is tragic that only a select group of major corporations has truly begun to provide the necessary leadership for deep and broad changes in their sustainable business practices. These include Walmart, profiled later in this chapter, as well as Nike and PepsiCo (profiled in later chapters). The majority of corporations, however, continue to move slowly or merely pay lip service to meaningful efforts at achieving sustainability.

But this chapter is about more than environmental sustainability. Free market capitalism suffers from unsustainable behaviors on many fronts other than the environment. Brands and consumers alike must expand the definition of sustainability—without a more profound and comprehensive vision of sustainability, capitalism will die an untimely death.

*We badly need leaders inspired by sustainable values, not situational ones. Without that, we'll just be digging our hole deeper and making the reckoning, when it comes, that much more ferocious.*

—Thomas Friedman, *New York Times* columnist
and Pulitzer Prize–winning author

## A DEEPER UNDERSTANDING OF SUSTAINABILITY

Our first task is that we must come to recognize a deeper meaning to sustainability in that it needs to encompass two distinct connotations. The first is the concept that today's development must preserve resources for future generations. In this context, the term "sustainable" conveys a sense of "enduring and lasting"—i.e., that our business practices today must ensure that we leave enough resources for future generations. This meaning is critical to recognizing our need to stop utilizing the Earth's resources as if their depletion does not matter.

But it is not deep enough to correct another significant flaw in capitalism. Corporations can change—and are changing—their practices to become more environmentally sensitive and resource efficient for future generations, but they are still failing to serve the greater good in other ways. To be truly sustainable, we need to accept a second meaning of the term: *life giving.*

If capitalism is to remain an effective and productive economic system in a world of nearly 7 billion people, business must help people survive and thrive *today.* If capitalism doesn't help create a sustainable world that accommodates a population of up to 9 billion by 2050, we will face such results as chaos and terrorism—anti-capitalist and anti-government actions that could alter the course of history and end our hopes for a more peaceful world for our children. In this context, capitalism must become sustainable by spreading prosperity around with greater equality, allowing more people to support themselves and their families so they can live for today.

## EXPANDING SUSTAINABILITY ON FIVE LEVELS

Beyond that deepening of its meaning, we also need to expand the application of sustainability, as we can no longer restrict it to being just an environmental term. While the triple bottom line seeks to address sustainability through the three elements of people, planet, and profit, the framework I propose encompasses five domains of activity: economic, moral, ethical, environmental, and social. These five domains are interconnected and interdependent. The lack of sustainable practices in any one of them weakens all others. They must work in tandem, with businesses and consumers partnering to ensure they become the new operating principles of capitalism.

Let's look at each of these domains of activity.

## ECONOMICALLY SUSTAINABLE CAPITALISM

There are several aspects to making capitalism economically sustainable. The first is learning how to control its boom-and-bust cycles. One of the major factors working against capitalism's sustainability is its propensity for crashes, meltdowns, recessions, depressions, and inflation. American economic history is marked by numerous periods of high unemployment and stagnation. Economists have gotten better at predicting such "anomalies," but the fact is, no one has found the magic formula for preventing them. Even the venerated former chairman of the Federal Reserve, Alan Greenspan, failed to foresee the Great Recession, and admitted that the Treasury's economists did not predict the subprime mortgage collapse.

Our manifest inability to control the engine of capitalism is a serious threat to sustainable economic growth over the long term. In researching their book *This Time Is Different,* the economists Carmen M. Reinhart and Kenneth Rogoff spent years analyzing the data associated with financial crashes throughout the world since the 1400s. The authors believe that economists constantly rationalize these failures, making it seem as if they can indeed forecast them. Reinhart and Rogoff chastise this fallibility among economists by concluding, "The lesson of history, then, is that even as institutions and policy makers improve, there will always be a temptation to stretch the limits. Just as an individual can go bankrupt no matter how rich she starts out, a financial system can collapse under the pressure of greed, politics, and profits no matter how regulated it seems to be."[5]

To prevent these types of destructive economic swings in the future, proponents of free market capitalism must admit that we need to find new answers to ensure capitalism's stability and ultimate sustainability. One of these must be that we need to think more farsightedly about economic trends, perhaps 10 or 20 years ahead, and take steps to be prepared to deal with recessions with enough capital reserves to last through the lean years.

We must also learn to manage globalization more effectively. Governments can no longer protect their national markets from the effects of what happens elsewhere in the world. As the world's national economies merge into a single seamless network of trade, investment, capital flow, and workforces, state sovereignty over finance has been effectively eclipsed. The challenges of globalized capital are complex and have not yet been mastered among leading multinational corporations. And as globalization expands, it forces companies to make difficult decisions, sometimes yielding a positive impact in one location while producing a negative impact in another. In the coming decades, all corporations and consumers will be forced to decide if they prefer to defend their national interests or become global citizens sharing one world supported by the practice of sustainable capitalism.

## WALMART: A COMPANY IN TRANSITION

Walmart is a case study in why sustainability must be applied across five domains. Founded in 1962 by Sam Walton, Walmart is the world's largest retailer, accounting for 11 percent of all retail sales in the United States. In the fiscal year ending January 2010, it had worldwide sales of $405 billion and profits of about $15 billion. Its mind-boggling size makes it one of the few companies that can singlehandedly shift the direction of the world economy. As of the end of 2010, it has 8,747 stores— among them are 2,300 "supercenters" spread over 20 to 30 acres of land—operating under 55 different brands (including Sam's Club, Asda in Britain, Líder in Chile, Seiyu in Japan, Walmex in Mexico, etc.) in 15 countries. It serves its customers more than 200 million times per week, employing 1.4 million associates in the United States and 2.1 million worldwide. It has been growing by more than 300 stores per year. It utilizes more than 60,000 suppliers around the world, creating millions of other jobs. Many suppliers are national brands, but some are local companies for whom Walmart's endorsement is the ticket to survival. It is also proactive in supporting women- and minority-owned businesses, purchasing more than $9 billion worth of inventory from these enterprises.

Long reviled for the harsh conditions it demands from its supply chain, Walmart has lately become a global leader in championing environmental sustainability. The company has vowed that it will work only with suppliers that fulfill its ambitious environmental goals, including powering its stores and headquarters with 100 percent renewable energy, keeping net waste to zero, and selling products that sustain people and the environment. The company has moved quickly toward these goals, becoming the largest private producer of solar power in the United States. Its trucking efficiency increased nearly 40 percent between 2005 and 2008, and it is designing new stores to use 25 to 30 percent less energy.

Walmart is also the initiator, funding source, and lead player in creating the Sustainability Index Consortium, a group composed of Walmart, universities, suppliers, non-governmental organizations, and other retailers whose mission is to develop an easy-to-understand and comprehensive sustainability index that consumers can use to evaluate every product's history and compliance with sustainability standards. Walmart has effectively leveraged its size—formerly its chief source of criticism—to begin advancing similar environmental practices around the world, cascading down through its supply chain.

Walmart shares its success through numerous charitable gestures. It provides financial and volunteer support to more than 100,000 charities and community organizations. In 2010 the corporation gave $467 million in cash and in-kind gifts, while its U.S. customers and associates donated an additional $76 million, and its international customers and associates another $35 million. Walmart and the Walmart Foundation have agreed to fund $2 billion in cash and in-kind supplies to fight hunger in America between 2010 and 2015.

But Walmart is still a company in transition, as it has yet to begin applying sustainability concepts to the ethical, moral, social, and economic aspects of its business practices. Its management still draws criticism for tight-fisted labor policies. Although it pays its workers more than minimum wage, its wages are slightly below the national average for retail employees. The company's health plan is so expensive that only 47 percent of its workers sign on, compared with a national average of 67 percent. As a result, taxpayers end up covering the costs for many Walmart workers who resort to their state's Medicaid plans for their healthcare needs.

The pressure to constantly push retail prices lower comes at a severe cost to Walmart's suppliers and the overall U.S. economy, as many suppliers are forced to move production overseas to lower-wage nations. Critics also cite how the company's stores have added to traffic problems in many cities and to soil and water pollution from its gigantic parking lots, where rainwater mixes with toxic residues. The company's constant store moves have also dotted the landscape with empty properties. Many claim Walmart also created the economic conditions that have forced thousands of small businesses to close.

Walmart is a study in how challenging it is to balance sustainability on all fronts with capitalism's drive for profit and consumer demand for low prices. While Walmart's investors may be pleased and its customers might believe that its low prices help keep their budgets in check, the company is still transitioning to a true model of sustainability in the way We First proposes.

## MORALLY SUSTAINABLE CAPITALISM

If we are to be honest about capitalism, we also need to admit that this economic engine is not morally sustainable. The poverty of the developing world, in particular, represents not just the failure of capitalism to help those nations but the failure of human morality to have allowed billions of people to be so neglected in an era of so much growth.

Western-style capitalism is not to blame for many of the causes behind the lack of prosperity elsewhere. In many developing nations, totalitarianism, political conflict, corruption, and war are responsible for halting economic growth or stealing the resources needed to improve the quality of life for their populations. However, it is undeniable that poverty in some of these areas is perpetuated by capitalist economies seeking cheap labor. The sweatshop scandals of the last 30 years, featuring many of the world's most famous brands, illustrate how the hunger for profit often diverts our moral compass.

Political, educational, and financial efforts by the World Bank, along with grants and loans from individual nations and generous donations from private philanthropists, have made a dent in eradicating the poverty of the world. But in many instances, the disbursement of goods and funds has not directly benefited the poor. In *Dead Aid,* the economist Dambisa Moyo argues that the more than $1 trillion in aid transferred from rich countries to Africa over the past 50 years has inspired greed and corruption, engendering even greater poverty. She points out that countries such as China, which never received Western aid, have fared far better than any African nation in increasing their productivity and GDP.

Moyo recommends that Africa's developing nations begin refusing free aid and instead begin participating in the bond and investment markets, learning better business management skills, and starting to compete for business with the great corporations of the world. Some of her recommendations fit the category of what Bill Gates would call creative capitalism, such as "conditional cash transfers," payments made to the poor that give them an incentive to attend school, work a certain number of hours, or see a doctor—all actions that can help break the poverty cycle. More research like Moyo's is needed to begin new conversations about how the richest nations can apply the expertise and resources of the private sector to improving the unconscionable economic conditions of billions of people in the developing world.[6]

*These unhappy times call for the building of plans that rest upon the forgotten, the unorganized but the indispensable units of economic power . . . that build from the bottom up and not from the top down, that put their faith once more in the forgotten man at the bottom of the economic pyramid. They become a positive proactive force for change rather than a pawn in the game of depletion.*

—Franklin Delano Roosevelt

Corporations can make capitalism morally sustainable by beginning to apply triple bottom line accounting to any commerce they undertake in the poorest of the developing nations. While doing so may not produce the level of profit they are used to, they will gain from the added public awareness of their good deeds, as Bill Gates suggested at the World Economic Forum's annual meeting in Davos, Switzerland, in 2008 when he talked about "recognition" as being a viable form of profit. As we will see in the later chapters, what brands gain in terms of consumer loyalty and goodwill through their socially responsible actions can become a critical factor in their success, proving that the future of profit is purpose.

Finally, there are also certain social advantages to making capitalism morally sustainable. In *The Moral Consequences of Economic Growth,* Benjamin Friedman explains how growth tends to foster open societies that function better, are more tolerant, and are more interested in further advancing themselves. In contrast, periods of economic failure tend to undermine these social attributes. If we can transform capitalism into a morally sustainable economic system, the world could very likely become a more positive, future-oriented, and innovative place.

## ETHICALLY SUSTAINABLE CAPITALISM

Any examination of capitalism as a system must face up to another undeniable reality: capitalists are prone to behaviors that collectively make for an ethically unsustainable economic system. This refers to the thousands of people in the business world who stretch the boundaries of acceptable and legal practices for their personal gain. Often such people start out as honest practitioners of capitalism, but along the way, they lose sight of ethical principles and begin to cheat, steal, or embezzle their way to greater riches.

At some point, ethical violations are nearly indistinguishable from moral failures, with the sole difference being that society and corporate governance can attempt to issue laws to dictate ethical business practices while they cannot dictate personal morality. But the distinction is ultimately moot, as both types of behaviors detract from the practice of sustainable capitalism.

Many ethical and/or moral abuses can be traced to a buildup of wealth and power. This is a readily observable dynamic, because, in a world of conflicting self-interests, the people with the most money wield disproportionate power over the political and economic decisions of a society. They have the political clout to push advantageous regulations and tax laws through national and state governments, often enshrining in law unfair advantages for themselves. The

---

### UNILEVER: A STUDY IN SUSTAINABILITY

Unilever is an Anglo-Dutch multinational corporation with operations and factories on every continent. It is the parent company of such brands as Dove, Lipton, Vaseline, Best Foods, and a bevy of other food, personal, and home-care brands. Its experience in complying with sustainability guidelines is a prime example of the turnaround that multinational corporations have had to make to their entire range of operations.

Consider packaging alone. Unilever is one of the world's most voracious packagers. It sells more than 60 million products every single day across 170 nations, requiring more packaging than almost any company in the world. Learning how to become sustainable has been no easy task, but Unilever has nevertheless emerged as one of the global leaders in sustainability.

One of the first things Unilever did starting in 2008 was to design a system by which it measured the waste footprint of its products, including the weight of leftover product and packaging that cannot be reused, recovered, or recycled. This analysis helped them review their packaging designs early in the manufacturing process. Unilever's goal, unique within its sector, is to have 100 percent of its paper and board packaging come from sustainably managed forests or from recycled materials by 2020.

Yet on the other hand, only 44 percent of Unilever food products are in line with internationally accepted guidelines for saturated and trans fat, sugar, and salt. Only 15 percent of its tea leaves and palm oil come from sustainable sources. From 1995 to 2009, it achieved only a 40 percent reduction in its emission of greenhouse gases.

In 2010, Unilever captured the number-one spot in the food-and-beverage supersector of the Dow Jones Sustainability Index for the twelfth consecutive time, with an overall score that is nearly double the industry average. Impressive, but is it good enough for consumers who want to build a better world?

wealthiest also have the social power to influence others and manipulate decisions to benefit their own companies.

In the hands of unethical corporate leaders and their political bedfellows, bad behavior easily becomes more than a personal failing, because their decisions have such wide financial and social impact on others. Their failures are multiplied exponentially through their positions of influence, power, and wealth. For example, we have seen many CEOs and executives whose greed led them to insider trading, stock manipulations, and improper decisions—all at the expense of innocent investors, their employees, or in the case of the Great Recession, workers and families all around the world.

If capitalism is to be a sustainable economic engine, we need to develop ways to prevent unethical people from destroying the hard work, wealth, and prosperity of millions of other people.

## ENVIRONMENTALLY SUSTAINABLE CAPITALISM

We have already covered some of the issues involved in making capitalism environmentally sustainable, but here are some additional thoughts. First, we cannot pretend that environmental concerns are not complex, often requiring difficult choices about priorities and weighing the lesser of two evils. Nor can we claim that modern human beings can easily change our evolutionary heritage as foragers, meat eaters, home builders, family makers, and consumers of the Earth's resources in an effort to improve our lives.

Yet we must ultimately face the challenge of balancing useful, if not necessary, capitalist growth with the risks of further damaging the environment. For decades, we have consumed as if our natural resources were unlimited. According to the Global Footprint Network, for three decades humans have consumed so much that we are now living beyond nature's capacity to supply us with resources and absorb the impact of our existence. Measuring diverse data, the group estimates we are producing $CO_2$ emissions at a rate 44 percent greater than what nature can regenerate and reabsorb. In their calculations, it now takes the Earth 18 months to regenerate what we use in a year. The group refers to this deficit as "ecological overshoot," which it recalculates every year based on population and the utilization of resources (cropland, pasture, forests and fisheries, and space for infrastructure).[7]

Using this concept, the London-based New Economics Foundation devised the concept of Ecological Debt Day, an exact date they calculate each year to signify "when we, as a global community, begin living beyond the means of what the planet produces." That date has moved forward each year for decades. In 1986, it was December 31; in 2006, it was October 9; in 2009, September 23; and in 2010, it was August 23.[8]

The second problem we must address is related to the consequences of our enormous consumption, in that our living habits are leading to unsustainable conditions for the planet. We need to begin figuring out how we can reverse the forward march of global climate change. Scientists know that average temperatures across the world have climbed 1.4 degrees Fahrenheit (0.8 degree Celsius) since 1880, much of this in recent decades. Global warming is causing Arctic ice to rapidly disappear, and it is predicted that the region may have its first completely ice-free summer by 2040—or earlier.[9] In addition, industrialization, deforestation, and pollution have increased atmospheric concentrations of water vapor, carbon dioxide, methane, and nitrous oxide—all greenhouse gases that trap heat near the Earth's surface—thus reinforcing global warming. Meanwhile, according to the Carnegie Institution for Science, developed nations are outsourcing from one-third to one-half of their carbon emissions outside their own borders to the developing world by virtue of the fact that the goods and services consumed by people in the developed world are now produced in the developing world.[10]

To date, our solutions to these problems are inadequate. We have to learn how to halt the loss of the Earth's natural "bio-solutions" to global warming, especially the loss of rainforests that once covered 14 percent of the Earth's land surface but which now cover a mere 6 percent. The international carbon cap-and-trade system established by the Kyoto Protocol recognizes only industrial projects and programs to actively reforest land already cleared, but not programs that prevent global deforestation.

Human activity is also endangering many other species on the planet. Experts estimate that we lose 50,000 plant, animal, and insect species a year due to rainforest deforestation.[11] In addition, a 2010 report examined the status of 26,000 animal species on the planet and estimated that one-fifth of all vertebrates and as many as one-third of all sharks and rays are now facing the threat of extinction, largely due to human activity that converts ever-larger swaths of their natural habitats into areas for human food production.[12] Meanwhile, the U.N.'s Green Economy Initiative reported in 2010 that the world's oceans could be completely depleted of fish within 40 years if action is not taken.[13]

As dire as these facts are, the cost to human sustainability is even graver. About 25 percent of Western pharmaceuticals are derived from rainforest ingredients, but fewer than 1 percent of the world's rainforest trees and plants have been tested by scientists. The loss of those species may deprive the world of many possible cures for life-threatening diseases.

The most troubling part of the environmental consequences of Me First capitalism is that the corporate world is seldom asked to pay for it. The Earth's resources are provided free to the corporate world, yet the public pays the price in damage to our planet. If capitalism is to become truly environmentally sustainable, the private sector must recognize the detrimental environmental effects of their actions. The solutions necessitate a partnership

---

### PATAGONIA'S COMMITMENT TO SUSTAINABILITY

Patagonia is one of the leading producers of sport clothing and gear, founded by Yvon Chouinard in 1965 as a mountain-climbing equipment producer. It is a company that lives and breathes the Earth's natural wonders and works diligently to ensure that, as a company, it contributes to sustainable business practices. To demonstrate its commitment, Patagonia has undertaken an extensive review, measuring the resources and energy used throughout its entire supply chain for every one of its products.

Called "The Footprint Chronicles," the inward-looking study examines Patagonia's choices for all the primary components, materials, energy, and waste that go into each of its garments. The company challenged itself to account for 95 percent of a garment's weight through such production metrics as energy consumption, carbon dioxide emissions, waste generated, and water usage (as of 2009). The company measures these data all along its supply chain, starting at the origin of the primary material—be it the agricultural field for cotton, the ranches where its wool and leather are produced, or the lab for synthetic polymers—and continues through each step in the production process, ending when the garment reaches the distribution center in Reno.

Patagonia takes the further step of boldly displaying the "Good" and the "Bad" of each product on its website so that consumers can make their own choices. The company also has an informative three-part video series that examines the challenges of global sourcing from social, environmental, and product-quality vantage points.

Patagonia has taken sustainability to its logical extreme. It just launched its Common Threads program, which endeavors to make all of its products adhere to the four R's—Recyclable, Reusable, and Repairable, so as to Reduce consumption. The company goes so far as to encourage its customers to buy less of its clothing; repair broken zippers for free; help them resell, trade, or donate used clothing; and conscientiously dispose of those products, some of which will soon be nearly 100 percent recyclable.

between corporations, consumers, and governments all acting on the shared belief that we no longer have time for uncertainty regarding environmental sustainability.

> *We say, stop hiding and start leading: businesses have the capacity to innovate and therefore to cope with the cost of carbon. Don't tell us business can't reduce emissions and improve profits—we have, and many other leading companies in a variety of industries have.*
>
> —Jeffrey Swartz, CEO, Timberland

## SOCIALLY SUSTAINABLE CAPITALISM

Capitalism's demand for constant development and expansion fails to account for the social damages this rapid growth can cause. These include urban blight, dysfunctional families, stress, psychological turmoil, mental and physical illnesses, gangs, and crime.

Such issues are a critical factor in the long-term social sustainability of capitalism. Companies need healthy, educated staff; safe environments for their offices and factories; attractive cities in which workers want to live; and a high quality of life to keep employees and their families happy and well adjusted. Without social well-being, capitalism falters or has to move elsewhere.

Ultimately, the corporate world must be held accountable for its contributions to social problems. Many governments are overwhelmed by the social services they are asked to provide, while lacking the funds to do so because the corporate world does not pay through taxes a proportional share relative to the social ills it contributes to creating. Many large corporations simply fail to pay even their fair share of taxes, using foreign tax shelters to reduce their revenues. According to a 2009 Government Accountability Office study, 83 of the 100 largest publicly traded companies in the United States had units in multiple tax havens (legally speaking, "financial privacy jurisdictions") in 2007 which allow them to evade taxes.[14] The *New York Times* reported in March 2010 that the federal government estimates corporations fail to pay $30 billion in taxes through abusive offshore schemes—which leaves the shrinking middle class to make up the shortfall.[15]

## INTEGRATING SUSTAINABILITY IN CAPITALISM'S PURPOSE

As the United States and other hard-hit nations struggle to recover from the Great Recession, they must seek a new, sustainable vision for capitalism that incorporates this wider understanding of the five domains of sustainability. We cannot return to old selfish habits, continued callousness toward the rest of the world, and neglect of the environment. We must recalibrate the fundamental tension between the healthy pursuit of profit and the purposeful exercise of capitalism for the greater good.

> *This generation's overarching challenge is sustainable development: the ability to live together peacefully, prosperously, and sustainably on a crowded planet of nearly 7 billion people. The challenge is global, not local. It requires a perspective of decades, not years. It is a shared task, not the efforts of individuals interested only in getting ahead of the pack and the rest be damned.*
>
> —Jeffrey Sachs, economist and director of the
> Earth Institute at Columbia University

## CHAPTER TAKEAWAYS

- The majority of corporations in the world continue to move slowly or pay only lip service to meaningful efforts at achieving sustainability.
- Sustainability must mean both *enduring* and *life-giving*.
- Corporations need to extend sustainability into five domains: economic, moral, ethical, environmental, and social.

# 5 INSTILLING WE FIRST VALUES INTO CAPITALISM

In this newly connected world, nothing is simple—not even a chocolate bar. Consumers wanting a better world taught this lesson to two of the biggest confectioners in the world, Cadbury and Nestlé. Using boycotts and social media to embarrass and pressure the companies, consumers forced Cadbury and Nestlé into agreeing to live up to higher values. Here's how it happened.

In 2008, Greenpeace, one of the most visible non-governmental watchdog agencies in the world, launched a campaign aimed at persuading corporations not to buy palm oil sourced from Malaysian and Indonesian suppliers involved in cutting down precious rainforests to build palm plantations. At the heart of the issue was the threat that this deforestation posed to the extinction of orangutans which relied on the rainforests for their habitat.

Greenpeace first targeted Unilever, which uses palm oil in soaps and toothpaste, and successfully pressured the company to buy the palm oil only from sustainable sources. But Cadbury and Nestlé, which use palm oil in their chocolate formulas, did not acquiesce as quickly. As a result, Greenpeace stepped up its campaign against the two companies, and over the next year, their protests went viral. New Zealand consumers started a Facebook page to collect names on a petition and publicize a boycott of Cadbury. The Auckland Zoo refused to sell Cadbury products. Finally, after a year of consumer pushback and Greenpeace protests, Cadbury announced it would no longer use palm oil in its candy bars produced for the New Zealand market, though this decision did not affect Cadbury chocolate made for other countries.

In press releases, Cadbury insisted it was a responsible company and only purchased palm oil from sustainable plantations that adhered to a certified "GreenPalm" program created by the newly formed Roundtable on Sustainable

Palm Oil (RSPO), of which Cadbury was a founding member, along with Nestlé and Unilever. But critics shot back that this was a ruse, as RSPO member companies had only to pay a fee to receive their certificates. The whole enterprise, according to critics, was little more than greenwashing.

In March 2010, Nestlé, too, attempted to assuage Greenpeace activists and consumers, saying it would stop purchasing from any companies involved in deforestation by 2015. But environmental critics were not satisfied with Nestlé's claim that it needed five years to make the change. They noted that Nestlé would still be purchasing much of its palm oil from Cargill, a global supplier of food and agricultural products that itself buys from Sinar Mas, which owns the largest plantation accused of deforestation.

Both Greenpeace and consumers found Nestlé's response unacceptable and so continued their campaign. In April activists dressed up as orangutans picketed and performed disruptive antics at Nestlé's annual shareholder meeting in Frankfurt. But the most effective tactic was begun a month prior. In March Greenpeace posted a satirical video on YouTube mocking Nestlé's "Take a Break with a Kit Kat" television commercials. In it, we see an office worker opening a Kit Kat wrapper and taking out and then eating a bloody orangutan finger. Nestlé managed to get the video removed from YouTube within a short time, but consumers had by then copied it and kept reposting it on other sites. It garnered over 180,000 video views in 24 hours; a few days later, that number was 700,000. The British tabloid *The Sun* called the battle a "Kitkatstrophe," and *Forbes* labeled it a "Kat Fight." Consumers began tweeting about Nestlé killing orangutans and covered the company's Facebook page with angry comments. The fiasco demonstrated how little Nestlé understood about the power of social media and its demands for transparency, authenticity, and accountability. And in the end, Nestlé's reputational damage was extensive.[1]

Today, Greenpeace continues to gather evidence that proves deforestation continues in the name of expanding palm oil plantations. In August 2010, independent auditors investigating Sinar Mas as a result of Greenpeace allegations found it had cleared peatlands and rainforests without the required Indonesian permits. In a counterattack, a nonprofit association called World Growth, whose pro-development website states it aims to "bring balance to the debate over trade, globalization, and sustainable development," countercharged that Greenpeace fabricates its evidence of rainforest destruction.[2]

This case is a perfect example of the two key dynamics of We First capitalism, *Consumers want a better world* and *The future of profit is purpose*. It demonstrates the growing potential of consumer power to influence companies, and it confirms that purpose can be a driver of profit. But it also points to another element that capitalism must change: the loss of values to guide businesses in their decisions.

## THE VALUE OF VALUES

So far this book has lobbied for three shifts in our thinking about capitalism: one, envisioning a new kind of self-interest that emphasizes mutual benefit; two, finding ways to ensure that profit is always merged with purpose; and three, instilling an awareness that our activities must be sustainable economically, environmentally, ethically, morally, and socially.

To those components of We First thinking, we must add a fourth—the need to re-instill values in capitalism because *technology is teaching us to be human again.* Consumers, connecting through social media, are sharing their common concerns, wants, and dreams. They are empathizing with each other around universal values that are becoming the currency across social media. If corporations are to become true partners in transforming capitalism and building a better world, they must align their thinking and behavior around these same universal values that can serve as a new foundation for sustainable commerce.

But what are those universal values? Who decides what they are?

## THE ROLE OF *WE* IN VALUES

The answer lies at the root of the term "We First." The "we" in We First capitalism has links to traditions as old as humankind. It reflects the concept of reciprocity epitomized by the Golden Rule—"Do unto others as you would have them do unto you"—which has existed in every culture in recorded history. It was present in the empires of Babylonia and Egypt, and it also existed in the ancient Eastern cultures of India and China. The belief that we should act toward others in the same way that we want to be treated is clearly a deep-rooted human formula for peace and harmony. It emanates from our natural inclination to be social animals, to share our lives with other people and to build communities with them. The power of We is thus profoundly human, and We First thinking seeks to embed this timeless wisdom within capitalism.

Ironically, it is technology that now drives us back toward this Golden Rule by renewing the connections between people. The social fabric of our society is literally being rewoven into a vast synaptic network of humans connected through the online world. The Internet, social media, and smartphones are giving people the opportunity to connect, communicate, and share values on a scale that before was unimaginable.

Those same tools are radically changing the way companies and consumers must interface. Companies can no longer dictate to consumers what to buy, wear, eat, or think. They can no longer cover up their track records on safety, human rights, and sustainability, as those truths increasingly affect consumers' decisions about where to spend their money. Communities of concerned citizens can now instantly and globally expose companies that sell bad products, unhealthy foods, or fraudulent information. Thousands of smartphone applications have been created to help consumers share and connect, exchanging information on those businesses that hope to win their loyalty as customers. In short, our constantly advancing technology is helping society at large morph into a We First culture, making it impossible to abide by values that fly in the face of We First thinking.

As a result it will become increasingly difficult to remain a Me First leader or corporation. To put business on a path to meaningful, long-term progress, we need corporate leaders, experts, and public figures who are willing to take a stand as proponents of We First values. These people should inspire other corporate leaders and public figures to join them, as the only way to combat the fear of isolation in change is through collective action. Consumers, too, must accept and apply this set of values to their own behaviors.

## INTRODUCING THE WE FIRST VALUES

Given these parameters, We First proposes seven values to guide capitalism into the future.

### 1. SUSTAINABILITY

We have already reviewed sustainability in detail, as it is perhaps the most fundamental value that capitalism must start to uphold. As the first We First value, sustainability implores businesses and consumers to use the Earth's resources intelligently, to reduce further degradation of the planet's condition, to seek renewable sources of energy that do not contribute to greenhouse gases, and to use cradle-to-grave methodologies that eliminate waste and reuse our resources.

The concept of sustainability also incorporates the need for corporations to respect human capital as a resource as precious as any other. In its lust for profits, Me First capitalism too often destroys or neglects so many key human qualities: dignity, self-esteem, intelligence, independence, and even happiness. In the same way that biologist, author, and innovation expert Janine Benyus noted, "Life creates the conditions that are conducive to life," We First capitalism seeks to create the sustainable conditions of life that are necessary for sustainable We First capitalism.[3]

## 2. FAIRNESS OF REWARD

Notice that this value is not just the word *fairness* but *fairness of reward.* The former is abstract and immeasurable, while the latter is visible and measurable. Fairness of reward encompasses the wide range of incentives companies give. This includes rewards for suppliers, employees, and investors. Fairness in paying suppliers helps spread the prosperity of business success to a wider group of people. This is the thinking behind the growing movement toward fair trade—with companies like Starbucks and Patagonia committing to fairly paying their suppliers in developing nations to help them prosper. The fairness of these rewards can be measured using trackable information that compares payments made to suppliers versus their expenses of production and the cost of living in their communities.

Fairness of reward in paying employees means recalibrating the serious disproportion between CEO and senior executive pay packages and those of average employees within a company. It requires restructuring a bonus system that incentivizes executives to make decisions that emphasize short-term profits and replacing it with a system based on rewarding long-term results. Fairness of reward for investors, meanwhile, must be balanced by the fairness of rewards for suppliers and employees and by the need to recognize that a fair profit comes to them not just in monetary terms but also through the corporation's contribution to building a better world for everyone.

## 3. FISCAL RESPONSIBILITY

The term *fiscal responsibility* is most often used in accounting to refer to a company's need to balance its budget, but in the context of We First capitalism, it refers to a company's responsibility to shoulder the impact it has on the environment and on society. This involves agreeing to pay its fair share of taxes, to redress its negative impact on the environment, and to support its community proportional to any harm it causes.

All too often, corporations take advantage of the social license they have to operate in society by failing to pay the costs of the negative externalities they create. These costs include a wide range of harms that are seldom allocated to companies, such as higher healthcare costs in populations affected by the activities of a company and higher infrastructure costs for highways and roads their trucks need to use. Fiscal responsibility prompts questions like: Should a coal-mining company pay a larger share of health insurance costs or make a contribution to combat diseases like asthma within the region it operates? Should fast-food restaurants fund research about how to prevent obesity?

Another plank of fiscal responsibility dictates that companies, especially those in the financial services industry, should take responsibility for their own mistakes. For example, in the wake of the financial crash of 2008, some governments proposed that banks be required to have their own "living will" to protect the public from absorbing the costs of their risky ventures. Instead, the bank's creditors would be at risk if they condoned the bank's behaviors, and even stockholders and management would not be protected in the event of a liquidation to pay off the bank's debts.

One recommendation for how consumers might insist on fiscal responsibility reflects the use of social media to influence annual corporate board meetings. Writing for *Slate*, former New York governor Eliot Spitzer even suggested this possibility: "For decades, shareholders have abandoned their responsibility to use their votes to shape corporate behavior. But perhaps technology can revive democracy on Wall Street. Could shareholders, gathered by an emergency Twitter message, soon converge on a shareholder meeting to demand a claw-back for ill-gotten bonuses?"[4] This would be an ingenious deployment of the concept of the "flash mob"—a sudden surprise assembly of people at a specific site triggered through instant messaging.

> *Today's great competitive challenge isn't going from Good to Great.*
> *For people, companies, and countries, it's going from great to good.*
>
> —Umair Haque, director, Havas Media Lab

### 4. ACCOUNTABILITY

The We First value of accountability is what builds trust between institutions and the public and between brands and their consumers. In today's world, trust is declining rapidly. According to the Edelman Trust Barometer, trust in American companies fell to an all-time low of 36 percent in 2009, although it rose to an unimpressive 54 percent in 2010. The study also found that companies headquartered in the United States tend to be trusted less than companies headquartered in Canada, Germany, and Sweden.[5]

Only in the past few years have companies started to understand that they cannot buy or impose trust; it must be earned and renewed. In an open, transparent, and connected world in which millions of consumers have a video-enabled smartphone, a Facebook page full of friends, and Twitter-happy fingers, it's easy to expose companies that fail to live up to their promises.

Trust has become the new social currency for businesses, and in this connected and globalized marketplace, it is also the only currency that will pave the way for the partnerships we need to build a better world. Only with trust can there be cooperation and collaboration between governments and businesses, as well as among the companies involved in the vast global value chains that multinational businesses are using today.

In the same way that companies and people must earn the trust of others, they must also earn goodwill, another component of accountability. Goodwill is the quality of having others be favorably disposed to you, whether as a brand or an individual. Trust makes people want to buy from your company; goodwill makes them want to recommend your company to others. The way to earn trust is to be honest and forthright. The way to earn goodwill is to give of yourself. In the eyes of the Millennial generation, the masters of goodwill are those people who blog, tweet, talk, and share ideas and information for free. As a result, this is the same disposition they expect from We First companies and brands.

The final element of accountability is transparency. Transparency requires that individuals and companies operate with honesty, credibility, and congruency between their words and deeds. This must now be a given, since all actions and records can now be viewed from outside the organizations. Transparency works against backroom deals, hidden agendas, false pretenses, and unethical conduct. It holds boards and executives responsible for telling the truth to consumers and investors. While some might argue that transparency will have the opposite result, forcing companies to guard and disguise their actions even more, the WikiLeaks scandal that erupted at the end of 2010 is an example of how even the most closely guarded information can now be subject to public exposure and cyberattacks.

## 5. PURPOSEFULNESS

Purposefulness, the most foundational We First value, forms the key premise of this book. In We First capitalism, we must seek to ensure that our business efforts do more than build wealth; they must add meaning and purpose to life. This value is antithetical to Me First capitalism's pursuit of wealth for its own sake. As such, it is a reminder for companies and brands that their true business is building relationships with customers, rather than simply coercing them to buy their products. Such an approach can generate enormous and rapid success, as exemplified by Zappos, founded by Tony Hsieh. The priority Zappos places on employee and customer satisfaction, described as "Delivering Happiness," has become the new benchmark for corporate America.

The true meaning of purposefulness extends beyond the common admonition that a brand must discover a mission or purpose for itself. For a truly We First purpose, a company must articulate and demonstrate a consistent contribution to others. Take Nike. Perhaps no other company in the world so epitomizes long-term effective marketing. Yet what makes Nike a We First company is not its consistently successful branding but its commitment to world-changing ideas and causes.

For example, Nike is a leader in collaborating with other companies to share information on sustainability. It is one of the five founding companies of Business for Innovative Climate & Energy Policy (BICEP), which was started in 2008 and includes among its members Starbucks, Levi Strauss & Company, Sun Microsystems, and Timberland. BICEP is committed to lowering the risks of global climate change by developing new ideas to reduce greenhouse gases and increase the use of renewable energy.

Nike also launched the GreenXchange, in which the company and several corporate partners, including Creative Commons, nGenera, Salesforce.com, and 2degrees, have agreed to create a web-based marketplace that Nike expects will help companies collaborate and share intellectual property in a way that can lead to new sustainability business models and innovation. In addition, Nike released in December 2010 an open-source application that helps apparel manufacturers design their clothes in a more sustainable manner. Called the Environmental Apparel Design Tool, it allows designers to more effectively evaluate waste, energy, and toxins found in their manufacturing processes and to make real-time decisions from the start of the product creation cycle to minimize environmental impacts.[6]

Finally, Nike consistently engages itself in the service of meaningful causes. The company's collaboration with Lance Armstrong's Livestrong campaign during the 2009 Tour de France is a prime example. Cancer sufferers and their families were invited to send SMS and Twitter messages of hope to Nike. The phrases were then spray painted in large lettering on the road in front of the cyclists using a special chalk printer vehicle called the Chalkbot developed for this purpose. Helicopters covering the race for TV picked up the messages while filming the road and broadcast them for the world to see. In this way the heartfelt personal messages of those touched by cancer received international exposure through the media focused on the tour and Lance Armstrong. This innovative campaign raised both awareness and donations for cancer research and demonstrated the brand's commitment to ideas and causes beyond its own success. By the end of the race, the Nike Chalkbot printed more than 23,000 user-generated messages and triggered a 46 percent increase in sales for Nike's Livestrong Collection. Nike then donated $4 million to the Livestrong Foundation.[7]

How does a company measure its purposefulness score? There are a variety of ways, such as conducting consumer surveys targeted at reputational sentiment analysis, or by using one of the emerging consumer-sentiment tracking technologies, such as Radian6, Visible Technologies, and Sysomos, among others, that track in real time social conversations taking place online to assess whether what consumers are saying about a brand is positive or negative, and if it is achieving the desired effect.

*If you have a product adding value to the world, you have a product that can add to the fight against poverty as well.*

—Jeffrey Sachs

## 6. ENGAGEMENT

In a social-media-driven world, brands must engage deeply with consumers. It is the cornerstone of brand-consumer communication, and without it, the We First dynamic cannot exist.

Ever since the advent of modern advertising, brands have believed they are in "dialogue" with consumers. Historically, however, this has not been true; brands have conducted little more than monologues with consumers, whom they imagined as being receptive. Brands were in charge of the media and the messaging through their broadcast advertising campaigns, while consumers could barely respond.

But now consumers not only have access to almost all kinds of media; they control much of it themselves. Through the Internet, social networks, smartphones, and mobile applications, consumers can now talk amongst themselves. Armed with these tools, every person can be a content creator, producer, distributor, and curator—positions that allow consumers to reverse the polarity and drive the conversation about and with brands.

Engagement must become a deeply integrated value in any organization that wishes to participate in We First capitalism. Any company that wants to keep its customer base must recognize this power shift and acknowledge consumers' shared stewardship of the brand. Most significantly, companies must also realize that the connections they seek with consumers cannot be dictated by autocratic methods. We First capitalism cannot be conducted, as it was for decades, from a top-down model that is deaf and monolithic.

In the first signs of a substantive shift, a few leading companies are starting to talk to consumers where they live: on Facebook pages, Twitter streams, and blogs, using crowdsourcing to engage them in the products, services, and futures of their brands. For example, Mars, Inc. invited consumers to help choose a new M & M color; PepsiCo let Mountain Dew customers choose the next three flavors, design the packaging, and approve the marketing; Levi's let Facebook users choose the next faces of the brand. But these campaigns are primarily driven by Me First interests that serve the brand, rather than the community at large.

To be truly We First, engagement must be used in the service of the brand's broader purpose. That means having conversations or content exchanges with customers about meaningful issues that can affect their lives or that can contribute to a better world.

British Petroleum's handling of the Gulf of Mexico oil spill in the spring of 2010 is a great example of how *not* to conduct engagement. In July 2000, BP had positioned itself at the forefront of the green movement and launched a $200 million PR and marketing campaign to reinterpret their name as "Beyond Petroleum." They created an appealing flower logo and described themselves to the public as the most environmentally sensitive oil company. Yet when the oil spill occurred, BP's evasion of responsibility and distortion of the truth alienated the public to such a degree that its brand image is now in tatters.

## 7. GLOBAL CITIZENRY

This last value of We First capitalism is closely related to that of purpose. As technology increasingly connects us, it also makes us *aware* of our interconnectedness. Twenty years ago, it was hard to know what was happening on the other side of the world, but today, we can know in real time when people are dying, suffering, or celebrating anywhere on the planet. It's virtually impossible to ignore the crises in our world, or deny the contributions we can make through our thinking, actions, and behaviors.

As such, corporations need to act like global citizens. Many of the problems our world faces are too severe to be ignored, and too big for any single company or nation to manage alone. In his 2009 TED address, former U.K. prime minister Gordon Brown put it this way:

> Climate change cannot be solved in one country but has got to be solved by the world working together. A financial crisis, just as we have seen, cannot be solved by America alone or Europe alone; it needs the world to work together. Take the problems of security and terrorism and, equally, the problem of human rights and development: they cannot be solved by Africa alone; they cannot be solved by America or Europe alone. We cannot solve these problems unless we work together.
>
> So the great project of our generation, it seems to me, is to build for the first time, out of a global ethic and our global ability to communicate and organize together, a truly global society . . . and make for a different future.[8]

Global citizenry is the antithesis of the Milton Friedman philosophy of capitalism, wherein the sole function of corporations is to make money for their shareholders. If capitalism is to become sustainable and succeed, companies must begin to acknowledge a human side, including the ability to demonstrate compassion, understanding, and empathy. Indeed, these goals are no longer at odds with business realities, as companies now need these human qualities to form the type of emotional connections with their customers that drive loyalty and profits. By acting as a responsible global citizen informed by universal values, companies ensure that they remain relevant to consumers' lives—and that their meaningful projects are sharable within the online social world.

Perhaps one of the clearest demonstrations of a personal commitment to global citizenry is "The Giving Pledge"—the notion created by Bill Gates and Warren Buffett that asks the world's wealthiest people, most of whom have made their money as CEOs or entrepreneurs of capitalist companies, to give the majority of their fortunes to philanthropic causes or charitable organizations either during their lifetime or after their death. As of December 2010, an impressive 57 of the world's wealthiest people have signed on. Even though these pledges are not a legal contract and donors can change their minds, they act as a powerful example that illustrates the meaning of global citizenry wherein all Me First capitalists recognize that they need to more fairly share the spoils of wealth that capitalism has provided them.

*We make a living by what we get, we make a life by what we give.*

—Winston Churchill

## WE FIRST AND THE HUMAN CONDITION

To begin the transition away from Me First capitalism, corporations need to institutionalize these values of We First thinking. They provide a solid foundation for a new practice of capitalism that has the purposefulness and sustainability necessary to repair the damage done in the past and to build a brighter future.

I have no doubts that plenty of skeptics will think many companies would never implement these values. Their executives would be laughed out of the boardroom for proposing values such as fairness of rewards (for suppliers and employees especially) or global citizenship. But recent research suggests that human nature is predisposed to many of these values. Rather than being selfish, people are actually empathic creatures.

In a 2009 study, for example, researchers at the University of California Berkeley found evidence that humans are successful as a species precisely because of our abilities to nurture and be altruistic and compassionate. Dacher Keltner, a U.C. Berkeley psychologist and author of *Born to Be Good: The Science of a Meaningful Life,* wrote: "Because of our very vulnerable offspring, the fundamental task for human survival and gene replication is to take care of others. Human beings have survived as a species because we have evolved the capacities to care for those in need and to cooperate. As Darwin long ago surmised, 'sympathy is our strongest instinct.'" Another U.C. Berkeley social scientist, Robb Willer, conducted research that showed that the more generous we are, the more respect and influence we wield. As Willer summed it up, "The findings suggest that anyone who acts only in his or her narrow self-interest will be shunned, disrespected, even hated. But those who behave generously with others are held in high esteem by their peers and thus rise in status." In other words, compassion and empathy are the hallmarks of great leadership, a necessary element in solving the world's problems at this time.[9]

These values can no longer be considered antithetical to business. They are increasingly evident in today's marketplace, where the stewardship of brands is being shared with large communities of consumers. As such, companies no longer have a choice; they must adjust their mindset and practices accordingly. They can no longer deceive or persuade customers to like their brand or their products; they must do something meaningful to earn consumer goodwill.

Implementing these We First values is, in many ways, no more complicated than any corporate change management process. It can be done through the company's standard change management steps. Indeed, several of these values have already found their place among accepted new business practices, proving that change is already under way. Sustainability, for example, has been on the table for two decades now—it is finally starting to change business practices in many companies and industry sectors. Engagement is also seeping into the corporate consciousness, as a function of the brand interaction across social networks in order to reach consumers, and in the growing number of social business networks. The same process of acceptance, understanding, and integration can happen for each and every one of the other We First values.

*We need to use the Internet to get off the Internet and form a twenty-first-century civil society.*

—Scott Heiferman, CEO and cofounder of Meetup

## WE FIRST—A PARADIGM WHOSE TIME HAS COME

Ultimately, all the changes that We First advocates are reflections of Joseph Schumpeter's theory of creative destruction, as we discussed in Chapter 1. The fact is, Me First capitalism is an old business model that reflects the economic, moral, ethical, environmental, and social goals of a now-past era—a period that never had to question self-interest, sustainability, purpose, or how to act in a globalized world of 7 billion people.

In *The New Capitalist Manifesto: Building a Disruptively Better Business*, Umair Haque characterizes the old form of capitalism as being in a crisis of ideals inherited from the industrial age. His position is that the old capitalism produces what he calls "thin value," meaning short-term economic gains (that largely accrue to a small class of people and ultimately fail to make them truly happy). This old capitalism depletes our resources, causes global conflict, and brings on economic stagnation. He, too, proposes to replace the old capitalism with a version based on new ideals, thereby demonstrating the growing awareness of the need for a values-based practice of capitalism.[10]

The advantage of capitalism is that it is a flexible system, able to accommodate change while surviving largely intact. This flexibility has made it easy, for instance, to propagate new industries while destroying obsolete ones.

But now capitalism must change in a larger way than ever before. We must adopt an expanded definition of self-interest that accounts for the globalized, technologically advanced, consumer- and citizen-driven world that we live in today. We must think longer term to ensure our own survival and the well-being of the planet that sustains us. And we need new values to guide us through the process of building a better world and future.

This will be no small feat, and so we will need to set goals and establish milestones to achieve it. It is possible to make significant strides in the next ten years, but looking further on, we can imagine transformative improvements in 20, 50, and 100 years. Why not commit to making the twenty-first century the period that will go down in history as when humankind created a monumental change in how it ran the world, equivalent to the agrarian revolution, the Industrial Revolution, and the digital revolution? It will be the We First revolution.

### CHAPTER TAKEAWAYS

- Technology is teaching us to be human again. Consumers, connecting through social media, are rediscovering their shared concerns, hopes, and dreams.
- Corporations must commit to a set of values consistent with their authentic brand narrative and share them with consumers; shared values are the universal currency for communicating across social media.
- We First capitalism's values are: sustainability, fairness of reward, fiscal responsibility, accountability, purposefulness, dialogue, and global citizenship.
- We are undeniably empathic creatures, and research shows that human nature is predisposed to the values of We First capitalism.
- Implementing We First values is a change management process. Even though some of the values are already accepted, all of them need to be integrated into corporate thinking and behavior.

# 6

## WHY THE WORLD NEEDS A RESPONSIBLE PRIVATE SECTOR

On January 12, 2010, at 4:53 P.M., a 7.1-magnitude earthquake in Haiti toppled not just thousands of buildings but decades of hope that governments and private charities could help the world's least prosperous people. Haiti is the poster child of a failed nation-state, suffering under the weight of enormous poverty, unemployment, and lack of optimism for the future. The country has a population of 10 million, of which roughly one-third is crowded into its capital, Port-au-Prince. This is typical of the rapid urbanization that occurs in developing countries when desperate rural dwellers flock to cities for jobs. When the quake hit, the overcrowded housing conditions contributed to an unimaginable loss of life. With more than 250,000 houses and 30,000 commercial buildings destroyed, the natural disaster killed an estimated 230,000, injured 300,000, and left 1 million homeless.

News of the quake was available instantly, largely thanks to people using social media. Twitter and mobile phones proved themselves to be the most reliable technologies to transmit on-the-scene information to aid and news organizations. With the collapse of traditional channels of communication, citizens tweeted and used their cell phones to send SMS messages and shoot videos. Bloggers posted reports. Ushahidi, an open-source technology that uses crowdsourcing to geo-tag and map incoming SMS messages during crisis situations, received 10,000 text messages within hours. In the days that followed, both Google and Facebook were used to create missing-persons lists, and Twitter groups established the tag "#rescuemehaiti" to direct rescuers to locations where trapped survivors could be found and "#relativesinhaiti" for Haitians living in the United States to help locate their relatives.

For weeks after the quake, mobile phones and social media became the primary tools of charity. Millions of people around the world donated money to Haiti through various charities using a simple SMS message authorizing a donation charged to their cell phone account. In the United States alone, an estimated $600 million in private charitable contributions poured in, much of it through cell phones. International governments and corporations pledged another $2 billion. The world's biggest celebrities advocated for charity: former U.S. presidents Bill Clinton and George W. Bush; Bono; scores of Hollywood movie stars; famous musicians; and athletes.

But it will take more than money to repair Haiti. Its problems are deep and its despair wide. *New York Times* columnist David Brooks offered a perceptive insight into the tragedy: "This is not a natural disaster story. This is a poverty story."[1] Despite an estimated $3 billion in U.S. foreign aid sent there since 1992, as well as hundreds of millions more from other prosperous nations, Haiti remains the poorest country in the entire Western hemisphere. Roughly 56 percent of Haitians live under the "extreme poverty line," meaning less than $1 per day, and 78 percent of the entire country lives on less than $2 per day. Inequality defines the country, with the top 20 percent of citizens receiving 68 percent of all income.[2]

More than two-thirds of Haitians do not have steady jobs, instead eking out their livings as day laborers and street vendors. The country produces very little in the way of exportable goods or food supplies. Most of its farms are unproductive since the soil has eroded away because the forests were cut down for cooking fuel. Its manufacturing capacity is negligible. Fifty percent of the population is illiterate. Only one child in five attends secondary school. Only about one-fourth of the population has access to safe water.

Given all its civil problems, Haiti has been unable to attract much private investment. The World Bank reports that the investment/GDP ratio in Haiti is only about 10 percent, less than one-third of countries like Chile. The World Bank called the interplay between government and the private sector in Haiti a "poverty trap . . . from which there frequently appears no exit nor hope."[3]

Most crucially, Haiti's government has been universally recognized as dysfunctional. It has a long history of corruption, instability, and political infighting. The government is poorly staffed; misuse of public funds is uncontrolled. Before the earthquake hit, the country's engineering standards were so subpar that the mayor of Port-au-Prince himself acknowledged that 60 percent of the city's structures were unsafe. After the earthquake, it was obvious that the Haitian government was helpless to save its own people.

For decades, Haiti has relied on the generosity and knowledge of thousands of non-governmental organizations (NGOs) to provide any semblance of progress. Nearly every major global NGO has had a presence in Haiti. Some are global and funded with donations from around the world; others are small and funded by members of churches or religious groups in the United States and other nations. The sardonic refrain about NGOs is that the more of them there are working in a country, the more the host government has abdicated its responsibility to govern. In Haiti's case, more than 10,000 NGOs were already working to improve conditions there when the earthquake struck. Despite the valiant efforts of so many NGOs working to fix healthcare, education, housing, and infrastructure, lifting Haiti out of its persistent poverty has seemed impossible.

Haiti tragically illustrates what happens when the prosperous fail to spread wealth around, but it also demonstrates the power of what we can achieve through global empathy. The dire conditions in Haiti are a shrill wake-up call to the entire world that we need to turn the tide on human misery. We need new thinking and solutions to match the scale of crises facing us. Living as modern, rational human beings in this twenty-first century, we need to break out of the mindset that allows our planet to be bifurcated into a small world of Haves and a large one of Have-nots.

## WHO WILL SOLVE THE PROBLEMS OF THE WORLD?

Currently, we are trying to fix the problems of the world by relying on only two agents of change: governments and philanthropies. Is that enough? And, if not, *who else can help?* This is the key question of social transformation in our era. Let me explain.

Broadly speaking, as a society, we tend to put our faith in government to be the first pillar of support in dealing with poverty, malnutrition, epidemics, and unemployment. If you grew up in the United States or Europe, you know well how government has long played the major role in alleviating domestic poverty through programs like welfare, unemployment insurance, and food stamps. For decades, the United States, like many other developed countries, has also contributed billions of dollars in foreign aid to scores of countries in an effort to alleviate the poverty of their populations and to build their infrastructures in an attempt to provide the conditions for capitalism and democracy to flourish.

Meanwhile, since the end of World War II, professional aid experts and citizen volunteers have created a massive network of thousands of private non-profit philanthropies and charities devoted to solving specific crises around the world: saving children, eradicating starvation, providing clean water, improving sanitation, educating against illiteracy, teaching business skills, and supporting women's rights. In effect, such charities and philanthropies have become the de facto second pillar of social transformation. They are especially common in the United States, a testament to the American spirit of charity and the Judeo-Christian religious traditions of "helping thy neighbor."

Many charities and philanthropies are as familiar as brand names, thanks to their extensive advertising and celebrity spokespeople. Most people know and respect the Red Cross, United Way, Oxfam International, Save the Children, and Doctors without Borders (Médecins sans frontières). They have become today's major players in social justice, with small numbers of paid staff and thousands of volunteers who perform the charitable work that governments are simply unable to perform. We count on them to go into the poor areas of our cities and rural communities, and into beleaguered foreign nations, with food supplies, tents, medical care, infrastructure-building skills, professional management techniques, education and teaching capabilities, and most of all, hope.

In recent years, we have begun to see the emergence of a third pillar: corporations that are starting to make an effort to support governments and philanthropies. But this is a new trend. Between the 1930s and 1980s, corporations played almost no significant role in addressing the crises of the world. They made charitable donations, but many of these were to support cultural institutions (like museums and symphonies) rather than causes devoted to alleviating human suffering.

In the past 20 years, however, we have seen the start of a sea change in corporate behavior. Corporations have become more involved in funding significant national and global causes through cash contributions, in-kind gifts of their products and services, and by providing some of their expertise and management capabilities to governments and philanthropies that need assistance. With cause-related marketing (CRM), more and more companies are also inviting consumers to partner with them to make targeted donations to many of the major causes consumers care about.

But are corporations doing enough meaningful work to create a better world? Are they becoming a true third pillar of global change?

I do not believe so. The fact is, corporations have yet to fully transition from a mindset of Me First to We First. Despite the generous increases in corporate charitable contributions to causes, and the growing movement to embed social responsibility into their business practices, the majority of companies still practice business according to an archaic paradigm of profit first and purpose later.

So *who* will build a better world?

## WHAT WE NEED FROM THE PRIVATE SECTOR

We First thinking posits that we as a society need to construct a new paradigm of cooperation among governments, philanthropies, and corporations to achieve the scale of meaningful social transformation required to build a better world against a ticking clock. Each of these institutions is a vital pillar of our fast-moving and complex global society. We cannot generate effective and widespread solutions unless *all three* of these social institutions agree to work together in unison toward the same goals and objectives. These are the three fundamental institutions that form the glue of our modern societies—and we cannot build a better world without their collaboration.

It will not be easy to align these three pillars, but it can be done by shifting to a We First mindset. Each pillar has distinct strengths and advantages, but each also has its own drawbacks and challenges that the other institutions must compensate for. Cooperation, collaboration, and creativity form the dynamic of a new paradigm in which all three agents of change strive to build a unified vision of a better world. In this new paradigm, we need to replace the traditional silos of responsibility that have divided governments, philanthropies, and private enterprises with vast collaborative networks working together to create a globally prosperous society.

This cannot happen, however, unless the private sector shifts from serving only itself to serving the greater good. If the purpose of government is to serve the people, and the role of philanthropies is to aid people in need around the globe, the private sector must adopt that same outward focus in order to be their true partner. Solving the problems of the world cannot happen if governments and philanthropies spend their time and resources cleaning up the inequalities and injustices that capitalism's corporations leave in their wake. We need as many private-sector corporations as possible to accept a far higher level of responsibility for the impact of their business practices on society.

*The time for the corporate world to embrace a new role as purveyors of progress, rather than preemptors of profit, is* now. Governments and philanthropies have been seriously weakened by the Great Recession. Burdened by historic debt and losing substantial tax revenues due to the economic downturn, federal and state governments are grappling with how to continue funding services for the poor and unemployed as well as provide essential programs like schools and public transportation, from which all citizens benefit. And while U.S. foreign aid has not yet declined, it may at some point need to be reduced. With millions of people out of work or just worried about the future, philanthropies, too, have lost millions in funding from donors large and small.

To understand how this new paradigm links governments, philanthropies, and the private sector together, let's take a look at each sector to understand the challenges facing each and then examine how they might come together to fill in the gaps.

## GOVERNMENT AS THE FIRST PILLAR OF CHANGE

In the course of the twentieth century, government effectively became the social insurance for the poor and the disadvantaged in a rapidly growing industrial society. Today, government is the primary driver of social change in the United States and in most Western nations, but it was not always that way. In fact, the U.S. government played no formal role in providing assistance to the poor until the early twentieth century.

The modern concept of government as the first pillar of support is actually the product of the broken capitalism that brought on the Great Depression. The almost instantaneous spread of poverty to more than 15 million people in the early 1930s was considered an economic injustice of such magnitude that President Franklin D. Roosevelt could not allow government to stand aside and let the social and economic fabric of the country unravel. His New Deal program, in which the federal government provided relief for the millions of poor families, set the precedent for the 80 years that followed. In the same vein, the massive destruction of Europe during World War II and the sense of global responsibility that the war had bestowed on the Allies instigated decades of U.S. government-sponsored foreign aid in the postwar era.

But my goal here is not to explore the history of domestic social welfare programs or foreign aid. The purpose is to identify the factors that make government an effective first pillar of support, as well as the challenges that keep it from eradicating domestic and international poverty, malnutrition, and other problems of the disenfranchised. In short, we need to understand what government can contribute to a new paradigm for change, and where it falls short.

## STRENGTHS OF GOVERNMENT

On the positive side, there are five strengths of government when it comes to combating poverty and social problems in the best of conditions.

- *Executive power.* Chief among the advantages of government is that the executive branch can throw the weight of its authority into legislation to help people in need. Every American president has an agenda on how to deal with domestic poverty and foreign aid that he can press Congress to enact.
- *Authority to create legislation.* Government efforts to alleviate poverty carry the rule of law behind them, and this imbues them with an imprimatur unrivaled by private enterprise. The government alone can pass laws and regulations on financial issues such as minimum wage, unemployment, and social welfare.
- *Tax-funded.* The constancy of tax dollars adds stability to funding antipoverty and foreign-aid efforts; levels of funding tend not to swing wildly from year to year.
- *Experience and learning.* With more than 80 years since the New Deal and 50 years of foreign aid under its belt, the government has extensive experience in the management and execution of relief efforts.
- *Infrastructure.* Government has existing infrastructure at local and federal levels to support relief efforts through the many departments and offices that oversee domestic and foreign aid.

## LIMITATIONS OF GOVERNMENT

On the other hand, it is also clear that government efforts to deal with problems like poverty face significant roadblocks. Critics contend that government efforts over several decades have not proven to be as effective or lasting as they should be, given the advantages they ostensibly bestow. Some of the challenges government faces in providing relief are:

- *Lack of public enthusiasm.* Nearly all Western civilizations struggle with unsympathetic attitudes toward poverty and helping the poor. Social scientists remain deeply divided by the causes of poverty, adding fodder to political objections. Some believe that poverty results largely from individual failings, such as laziness or lack of motivation and drive, while others see poverty as a structural failure of society to provide people with jobs.
- *Belief that private charity is superior.* In many countries, especially the United States, there is a pervasive belief that families and churches are the appropriate channels to provide charity, rather than the government using taxpayer money.
- *Bipartisan politics.* Because control of the legislature swings back and forth between parties, governmental priorities are not consistent across decades. From administration to administration, philosophical differences and politically motivated grandstanding often result in weak, underdeveloped, or ineffective legislation.
- *Disagreement about where to draw the poverty line.* The official poverty line was created in the 1960s, but there is controversy over whether its formula holds true today, blurring the lines of who should qualify for aid.
- *National self-interest vs. global humanitarian agenda.* The government must sometimes choose between allocating resources to its national self-interest and allocating them to its aim of providing humanitarian aid.
- *Bureaucratic inefficiency, fraud, and corruption.* Critics insist that government has no incentive to improve efficiency, since there are no measures of profit and no real consumers to serve. This, they say, can lead to manipulation, fraud, and corruption within the process.

## PHILANTHROPY AS THE SECOND PILLAR OF CHANGE

The number of philanthropies, nonprofits, charities, and NGOs has exploded in the 80 years since the New Deal. There are now more than 1.5 million organizations registered in the United States whose missions are to complement or supplement government and private good works. For purposes of this book,

I will refer to all of them as philanthropies or NGOs, but there are legal and tax distinctions between them to understand.

- *Nonprofit* refers to any organization that is tax-exempt according to the U.S. tax code.
- *Charities* are a subcategory, specifically nonprofits that are eligible for Internal Revenue Code 501(c)(3) status. There are two types of charities: public charities, which receive broad public support and tend to provide charitable services directly to the intended beneficiaries; and private foundations, which are usually tightly controlled, receive significant portions of their funds from a small number of donors or a single source, and make grants to other organizations rather than directly carrying out charitable activities.
- *Philanthropy* typically refers to an individual or a trust set up to fund a cause. The private foundations described above are philanthropies.
- *NGO* refers to any nonprofit, voluntary citizens' group that is organized on a local, national, or international level to perform a task that supplements government efforts, usually in the health, environment, or human rights arenas.

NGOs may receive funding from governments, but governmental representatives are barred as members. Some NGOs, such as Amnesty International, are membership-based and refuse to accept money from governments or political parties. Many obtain their funds from governments that contract them to perform services on their behalf. For example, CARE International, Oxfam, World Vision, and Doctors without Borders all receive large portions of their budgets from governments.

The world of philanthropies, charities, and NGOs is vast and includes organizations like hospitals, churches, museums, labor unions, arts and cultural organizations, animal-rights organizations, and many other areas. My focus is those philanthropies and NGOs working to help the poor in the United States or globally, as these comprise the second pillar of social change.

The United Nations Charter recognizes NGOs that assist in humanitarian projects and grants some of them status to provide consultative expertise to its Economic and Social Council (ECOSOC). Those NGOs that obtain a formal

U.N. accreditation can attend conferences and events where they can participate in discussions and lobby for their causes in informal sessions with General Assembly members. NGOs also host their own parallel conferences, called the NGO Forums, which, like a trade show, feature booths, main events, and workshops. In 2009, there were 3,289 NGOs in consultative status with ECOSOC.

Some NGOs function purely as think tanks, providing advice, research, and ideas to governments, which then implement the work. Other NGOs are "operational," meaning they have people on the ground working to provide direct relief to those in need. In the past two decades, the general trend has seen increasing numbers of operational NGOs moving into the most severe hot spots of poverty in developing nations. Nigeria is said to have 600 NGOs, but the world leader is clearly India, which estimates to have more than 2 million.

## STRENGTHS OF PHILANTHROPIES

Like government, NGOs offer several benefits as agents of social transformation, both within the United States and among developing countries.

- *Credibility and neutrality.* NGOs are viewed as neutral organizations whose goals are to serve the public good without hidden political agendas. The "big-brand NGOs" are well known worldwide and operate with extensive credibility—more than the host government, in many places.
- *Motivated employees and staff.* Employees are usually motivated not by money but by caring about others and a commitment to social change. This makes for warmer receptions and greater goodwill from relief recipients.
- *Field expertise.* NGOs working on the ground often employ specialists and experts that governments cannot provide, such as Doctors without Borders. They can often accomplish change at a faster pace than governments.
- *Ability to attract big contributions.* More and more of the world's most affluent are using their wealth to effect social change, and they often choose to go through NGOs, viewing them as more efficient than government. The Bill and Melinda Gates Foundation is the world's wealthiest NGO, with an endowment of roughly $35 billion, plus significant annual contributions of Berkshire

Hathaway shares pledged by Warren Buffett. Many successful entrepreneurs and businesspeople establish their own charities or fund existing ones.

- *Limited infrastructure and staffing.* NGOs often operate with little overhead and avoid bureaucratic red tape and regulations. Most don't maintain big offices or have large administrative costs so they can devote the lion's share of their funds directly to their causes.

## LIMITATIONS OF PHILANTHROPIES

Just as with government, NGOs face challenges to provide solutions to the world's crises. Despite the respect they engender and their history of accomplishments, their efforts are frequently encumbered with challenges.

- *Chronic and acute funding problems.* The single most critical barrier preventing NGOs from achieving greater results is *chronic* funding difficulties. But disasters often cause an *acute* problem as people rush to donate to disaster relief but then halt their usual contributions to long-term aid providers. Successive disasters can also lead to donor fatigue, as we witnessed in summer 2010 with the Pakistani flood relief efforts coming so soon after the earthquake in Haiti. As Bill Drayton, Ashoka founder, told *Bloomberg BusinessWeek,* "The financing system for nonprofits is one of the biggest bottlenecks holding back change in the world."[4]
- *Policy conflicts among NGOs.* NGOs are not immune from disagreements and policy conflicts among themselves. Major differences often exist between NGOs headquartered in or representing Western industrialized nations and those based in the developing world.
- *Corruption and fraud.* Like government, NGOs are not immune to corruption and fraud. Some have proven to be little more than fronts for their directors to steal money from unsuspecting donors. In other cases, NGO money is often stolen and channeled to corrupt politicians, oligarchies, and even warlords.
- *Lack of coordination.* Some countries have thousands of NGOs in the field without any communication among them. This can lead to duplications of effort, wasted resources, or NGOs working at

cross-purposes. A lack of open-source technology and cooperation is also detrimental. This last problem is so acute that the 2006 TED Prize was awarded to Cameron Sinclair, founder of Architecture for Humanity, whose mission was to create a global open-source network where architects, governments, and NGOs could share design plans and expertise to help build emergency housing in developing nations.

- *Subject to donor or host government political agendas.* NGOs may be viewed with skepticism if they are perceived as purveyors of a political or religious agenda. NGOs with a clear political agenda at odds with that of their host country may also face such problems as restrictions and intimidation.

## WHY TWO PILLARS OF CHANGE ARE INSUFFICIENT

For all their merits, governments and NGOs alone are not achieving the scale of social transformation that participants in both sectors deeply desire. We need more support—a third pillar—to assist governments and philanthropies in the work of developing sustainable solutions to these crises.

The private sector is the best hope, as it alone can offer all the elements that governments and philanthropies need—a perpetual flow of money, worldwide resources, extraordinary talent, cutting-edge technology, managerial skills, global coordination, preexisting distribution channels, and global bricks-and-mortar infrastructures. But the only way that the private sector can participate is if it replaces its Me First mindset with a more holistic and purposeful system of capitalism embedded in We First thinking.

## CAN THE PRIVATE SECTOR TRULY BE A THIRD PILLAR?

Many proponents of capitalism and defenders of the corporate world will argue that corporations have already come a long way in adopting corporate social responsibility. They will point to the increasing acceptance of CSR among the world's major companies setting an example for other companies to follow. They will cite the generosity and largess of thousands of companies donating to support NGOs working on the ground to save lives and educate children.

But this tells only half the truth. Although corporations have improved in supporting causes and accepting greater responsibility for their actions, their overall commitment to CSR remains too self-interested, inauthentic, and in-sufficient. We can see why this is so if we examine the history of corporate in-volvement in socially responsibility.

The shift away from the purely self-focused thinking of Milton Friedman's policy toward corporate social responsibility began in the 1980s, inspired by the likes of management guru Peter Drucker and his strategy of "enlightened self-interest." This gave rise to charitable actions like cause-related marketing.

But the idea that corporations could act as a real partner to government and philanthropies is relatively recent, dating from only the 1990s. One of its chief results was an enormous increase in the size of corporate donations. Cor-porate sponsorship of nonprofits went from $200 million in 1980 to $2 billion in 1994 to $9.6 billion in 1999. By this time, some companies also began doing more than giving out cash. They donated in-kind gifts, such as products or services. Some loaned out their management expertise, technological support, and the use of their marketing and distribution channels to NGOs. Compa-nies also began allowing employees to take paid time off for volunteerism, and some firms partnered with external charities and NGOs to participate more directly in relief efforts. For example, LensCrafters' foundation teamed up with Lions Clubs International to solicit used glasses from citizens, which were then delivered by LensCrafters employees to impoverished countries, where they gave eye exams and handed out free glasses.

Many firms began funding public service announcements and advertise-ments to raise consumer consciousness about issues, such as Anita Roddick's successful health-and-beauty chain, the Body Shop, which promoted animal-rights awareness. Other companies promoted behavioral change, like en-couraging people to stop smoking, drinking, using drugs, or being absentee parents. Procter & Gamble, maker of Pampers, assisted the National Institute of Child Health in a campaign against Sudden Infant Death Syndrome (SIDS) by imprinting on its diapers a reminder to parents to put their babies to bed face-up.

The 1990s also marked an expansion of corporate interest in issues. Most of their donations prior to this period were directed at only local or national causes. Few companies donated to or supported global problems, until Reebok virtually reinvented CSR by sponsoring Amnesty International's Human Rights Now! concerts featuring Sting and Bruce Springsteen in the late 1980s. The commitment was still too great for most companies; only a few others followed suit.

The late 1990s and early 2000s, however, marked another evolution of CSR, as corporations began applying it more holistically to their internal structures. The primary motivation was a slew of corporate scandals, including Enron in 2001 and WorldCom in 2002, which unleashed a tremendous public outcry demanding that companies impose a higher level of ethical conduct on their behavior. Those scandals pushed government to enact strict guidelines that set new accounting standards (the Sarbanes-Oxley Act of 2002), and new environmental laws as well.

Many leading companies finally agreed to adopt more sustainable manufacturing and packaging processes to reduce waste, lower their energy use, and obtain supplies from sustainable sources. Since 1999, The Home Depot has ordered most of its wood products from sustainable logging operations, thanks to consumer pressure. The fast-food chains began yielding to consumer requests that they offer healthier foods. Companies began to set more concrete goals at the start of their CSR campaigns and measure results at the end so they could assess whether their strategic missions were being accomplished.

One of the most significant CSR funding changes of the '90s and early 2000s was the use of cause-related marketing campaigns that, as discussed earlier, utilize consumer purchases to trigger corporate donations. The number of companies touting CRM campaigns skyrocketed, and they became increasingly inventive and creative. In the past decade, hundreds of companies have experimented with cause-marketing campaigns. A few of the most notable have been:

- Ben & Jerry's "One Sweet Whirled" campaign in 2002, which sought to raise awareness about global warming.
- Subway's "America Heart Walk" campaign in 2003, in which the company sponsored five-kilometer walkathons in 750 cities to support the American Heart Association.
- Whirlpool's ongoing "Habitat for Humanity" campaign, in which the company donates a refrigerator and range for every house built by Habitat for Humanity.

A surface reading of this account might suggest that there has been a steady upward progression of socially responsible corporate behavior. We can see how, from a starting position of almost no effort in the early 1900s when corporations were legally barred from making charitable contributions, companies moved in the 1950s from supporting the arts and culture to the 1960s and 1970s when they gave to civic causes, and ultimately to the 1990s and early 2000s when they began supporting national and global issues related to poverty and social injustice. We can see their cash contributions grow from zero to about $14 billion in 2009. And we can take heart in how companies are now incorporating sustainable sourcing, manufacturing, and distribution practices and a commitment to ethical conduct.

Yet questions remain.

## WHY CSR NEEDS CONSUMERS

Despite the fact that governments and philanthropies desperately need help, the history of private-sector assistance suggests that corporations are not yet motivated to play the role society needs them to play. There are two reasons.

First, CSR is still a second thought in most companies and operates with many deficiencies.

- *Giving is disproportionate to profits and salaries.* Corporations currently donate $14 billion to charities, but this amount is small when compared to the billions reserved for investors and the salaries and bonuses of individual CEOs and executives.
- *Top executives are uninvolved or insincere.* There is a revealing gap in what corporate leaders say about their commitment to sustainable business versus how they enact it. In a 2010 McKinsey survey of nearly 1,800 respondents, more than 50 percent of the executives consider sustainability to be "very" or "extremely" important. However, only 25 percent agree it is a top priority for their CEOs, and only 30 percent say their companies invest in sustainability or embed it in their business practices.[5]
- *Companies fail to understand CSR.* The private sector still claims to be confused about the meaning of sustainability. The McKinsey survey cited above shows that 20 percent of executives say their company has no definition of sustainability. Their impressions are revealing: 55 percent think sustainability has to do with the management of environmental issues; 48 percent think it relates to governance issues (ethics, compliance, and regulations); and 41

percent believe it concerns social issues such as working conditions and labor standards. This lack of understanding is odd, given decades of government efforts at passing regulations, pressure from consumers, media attention, and entire MBA programs devoted to the topic.

- *CSR efforts are just "window dressing."* Despite the evolution of CSR, the vast majority of companies still use it only to enhance their corporate reputations. Even the conservative *Economist* magazine criticized the corporate world for using CSR as little more than a public relations ploy.

> For most companies, CSR does not go very deep. There are many interesting exceptions . . . practices that work well enough in business terms to be genuinely embraced; charitable endeavours that happen to be doing real good. . . . But for most public companies, CSR is little more than a cosmetic treatment. The human face that CSR applies to capitalism goes on each morning, gets increasingly smeared by day, and washes off at night.[6]

- *Companies spin their CSR and CRM.* Many companies have been exposed for greenwashing, cause-washing, or local-washing, in effect using CSR as a marketing scheme.
- *CSR results and measurements are scattershot.* Few corporations measure their results, leaving it to watchdog agencies to rate and rank the most socially conscious companies. There are no standards of achievement in social causes comparable to the U.N. Millennium Development Goals.

All these issues are indicative of a strategic failure in corporations to see CSR as a necessary and purposeful component of their business. But the most alarming reason that we might believe that corporations are not yet in a position to become the third pillar of change is that the history of CSR reveals a single, all-encompassing truth: *Corporations have adopted socially responsible behaviors only when citizens or government pressured them to do so or when there is money to be made in doing so.*

This is because profit, not purpose, has been the only motivation in the modern history of corporations. It was not benevolence that compelled companies to donate to charities to support war families following World War I in the early twentieth century; it was citizen pressure. During the Great Depression, public outrage and Roosevelt's courage to stand up to corporations pushed companies into greater charity. In the 1950s and 1960s, charitable contribution was an opportunity for companies to enhance their reputation with consumers. In the 1980s, it was enlightened self-interest that led companies to invent CRM, which guaranteed them a sale for every donation they made. In the early 2000s, it was public outcry over unethical behaviors that nudged companies into adopting new internal standards of ethical conduct. And since the 1970s, it has been environmental groups and citizens who have forced corporations to finally recognize the greater savings they could obtain from adopting sustainable manufacturing and energy utilization processes.

Amid all those changes, however, the single most important driver of corporate responsibility has been the global adoption of the Internet. The most significant developments in CSR have occurred only with the advent of the digital age, when consumers began logging on to the web to research and communicate information about corporate transgressions, fraud, and manipulation. Starting in the late 1990s, the web has made it difficult—if not impossible—for companies to operate without transparency. Thousands of chat rooms and activist bloggers opened the door for consumers frustrated by irresponsible companies to spread the word to thousands of others.

The Internet birthed a new class of professional citizen activists and watchdog agencies devoted to identifying and exposing corporate malfeasance and irresponsibility. Web tools enabled them to coordinate their actions directly with NGOs, using their collective power to document proof of how many corporations failed to live up to ethical and environmental standards—as in the famed Kathie Lee Gifford child-labor clothing scandal in 1996 and Nike's and Gap's low-wage scandals at their plants in several developing nations.

The power of "citizen media" continues to grow stronger as more consumers tap into social-media tools and new smartphone apps are developed. In the Nestlé case already discussed in Chapter 5, we saw how consumers flocked to Nestlé's Facebook page to leave critical comments. Today, apps for mobile devices are helping consumers shop mindfully by tracking the treatment of employees, the size of carbon footprints, and the CSR track records of companies from which they are considering buying.

In effect, were it not for the steady and committed actions of citizens and consumers, one might wonder if corporations would have embraced consciousness of their social responsibility at all.

## FOUR SCENARIOS OF THE FUTURE: WHICH DO YOU WANT?

The Committee Encouraging Corporate Philanthropy is an association of CEOs founded by Paul Newman. To better understand whether social responsibility really matters to the future of corporations, it commissioned McKinsey & Company to do a study projecting ten years into the future.[7] The report, *Shaping the Future,* predicted five transformative trends between now and 2020. They are: one, a rise in the power of China and other emerging economies; two, a shrinking labor force and talent shortage due to demographic changes; three, a continuing global integration of capital markets, trade, and technology; four, natural resource scarcities; and five, competition among nations to attract work.

But more important, the report also determined that there are four possible scenarios for corporations depending on how extensively they become involved in improving their social responsibility.

### SCENARIO 1

In this scenario, society places greater demand for social responsibility on corporations, which react positively. As a result, consumers begin to trust that businesses will agree to do good. Corporations and consumers collaborate to create positive world change, and governments allow companies to voluntarily meet social expectations.

### SCENARIO 2

Companies try to adopt socially responsible practices, but citizens fail to trust them. As a result, governments and NGOs also stop partnering with companies, and we end up with a patchwork of international laws and standards, as well as a bifurcated system of capitalism.

### SCENARIO 3

Society's expectations of business rise, but companies refuse to work proactively for global change. Governments are forced to regulate corporations, adding to their expenses and reducing their capital for productive uses. Consumers do not trust businesses, setting up a dangerous mismatch of expectations.

### SCENARIO 4

Society and corporations cannot match their expectations and engagement levels, creating a downward spiral of social responsibility. Trust in business declines to the point where the economy suffers, leading to further social and environmental deterioration around the globe.

The report concludes that, of course, only the first of these scenarios—corporations voluntarily becoming socially responsible, thereby gaining the trust of consumers, governments, and NGOs—is the logical solution for the future. None of the other scenarios provides a beneficial outcome for the corporate world. The report represents yet another respected voice calling for a new relationship between the corporate world and society.

*Earnest concern for the common good is not a dangerous illusion; it
is the cost of doing business in a connected society.*

—Scott Henderson, managing director, CauseShift

## PROPOSAL FOR A NEW MODEL OF CORPORATE CITIZENSHIP

In order to become a real third pillar, corporations must accept four new truths. First, when investors demand profits, they have to allow governments to deduct the costs that corporations directly or indirectly impose on society. This includes the thousands of negative externalities that are never counted or calculated into the corporation's tax burden, such as pollution, traffic, defense expenditures, dysfunctional families resulting from overworked employees, obesity from sedentary office lifestyles, crime resulting from a society of disenfranchised, unemployed people, and many others.

Second, corporations must recognize that they can truly succeed only in healthy societies. Profits can be sustainably generated only when a society is functional and stable; this much is proven by how the Great Recession decimated entire industries in a chain reaction that spread across the globe. On the flip side, the undeveloped world is a gold mine of potential future customers whose prosperity, if corporations help develop it, could deliver even more profit.

Third, corporations must accept, as Bill Gates suggests in his vision of "creative capitalism," that they need to look for new ways to profit from helping to find solutions to the world's crises and building a better world. CSR and profit are not mutually exclusive.

Finally, corporations must wake up to the reality of today's globalized world. The network of interconnections that now exist among and between nations, corporations, and consumers disrupts the old paradigm that boards and shareholders have control over their companies' profits. Emerging competitors in developing nations, new tools of communication and connection, and the growing power of citizens and consumers are all altering the corporate landscape. Make no mistake: Those corporations that fail to embrace a new paradigm for capitalism will be overpowered by new companies willing to redefine it.

Many defenders of capitalism still resist this notion. As recently as 2010, an article in the *Wall Street Journal* reiterated the same arguments on which traditionalists have relied for decades—that a corporation's only task is to make money for its shareholders and that it doesn't owe society anything. The *Chronicle of Philanthropy* published a rebuttal to this, which nicely summarizes the new global reality that can no longer be denied. As its author, Scott Henderson, wrote,

> [This] essay has exposed the futility of an ideological debate pitting the free market against the common good as if they were wholly separate entities. This is not a hypothetical conversation. The world is full of real problems that threaten the corporate sector. . . . Effective corporate social responsibility recognizes the importance of strengthening and buttressing the community, which makes profit and enduring value possible. The savvy corporations understanding their refocused role will not settle for lip service and lukewarm commitments. Rather, the vanguard will raise the standards of success to new heights, thereby opening the doors to exponential growth of profit and shareholder value.[8]

Henderson's argument reiterates the same rationale that We First suggests for a new world for capitalism. It is based on a growing consciousness—or perhaps *vision* is the more appropriate word—of a world in which corporations understand that they must function as an element of society as integral as government. In *The Triple Bottom Line,* Andrew Savitz posits that companies need to find "the sweet spot," where their maximum economic, environmental, and social interests meet. He writes,

> It could be said that the truly sustainable company would have no need to write checks to charity or "give back" to the local community, because the company's daily operation wouldn't deprive the community, but would enrich it. Sustainable companies find areas of mutual interest and ways to make "doing good" and "doing well" synonymous, thus avoiding the implied conflict between society and shareholders.[9]

Savitz's notion that corporations cannot first deprive society of social justice and then give back to it using charity parallels a criticism of capitalism often raised by noted European philosopher Slavoj Žižek, who points out that there is a glaring hypocrisy in how corporate attempts at social responsibility try to save with one hand what the other hand has destroyed. Both Savitz and Žižek say that corporations must endeavor to always do good rather than to profit from harm and then use some of the money to repair it with good works.

*We First* endorses Savitz's and Žižek's visions but seeks to build upon them. In a We First framework, it is not just the task of corporations to find their CSR sweet spot, but the work of all capitalist societies to reengineer this economic system and transform it into an engine of global prosperity that works in partnership with governments and philanthropy to build a better world. Every capitalist corporation and its brands need to endorse a set of new principles to replace the anachronistic paradigms of supply and demand, opportunity costs, single bottom line, return on investment, and other narrow parameters of profit.

These new principles of We First capitalism emphasize the four concepts of the previous chapters.

- One-sided self-interest is no longer compatible with the new realities of a complex, interdependent, and connected global community. In its place, business must think in terms of mutual self-interest.
- Profit must merge with purpose, because consumers want a better world, and the future of profit *is* purpose.
- Capitalism must seek to implement sustainability in five domains: economic, ethical, moral, environmental, and social.
- Companies must conduct business according to a universal set of values that together foster a positive, trusting environment in which commerce contributes to society.

These principles are not abstract. They mandate very clear behaviors and practices that corporations and brands can begin implementing immediately. A growing cadre of forward-thinking CEOs have already started adopting elements of this new framework of corporate citizenship. Theirs are the companies that are undertaking and funding meaningful CSR programs to address major humanitarian issues. These firms see how corporate responsibility pays off in motivating and retaining employees, creating a positive image among customers, and contributing to building a better world.

The Committee Encouraging Corporate Philanthropy, an association of 100 CEOs committed to changing how their companies utilize philanthropy as a central element of corporate social responsibility, published a document that synthesizes this very shift. Entitled "Business's Social Contract: Capturing the Corporate Philanthropy Opportunity," it demonstrates the type of We First thinking that all corporate CEOs need to adopt worldwide.

> Business has always had a contract with society—expectations from a variety of stakeholders that a company must fulfill in order to earn its freedom to operate and achieve success. Today, companies are facing tectonic shifts in social expectations. Customers have more ability to put pressure on companies to meet their expectations for contributions to the public good. Shareholders are exerting pressure to increase companies' social presence; and increasing attention is being paid to indirect stakeholders, such as lawmakers, regulatory agencies, the news media, community activists, and nonprofit organizations. All of these groups can influence, and may even redefine, the social contract and what it means to a company to fulfill or exceed it. . . .
>
> The practice of corporate philanthropy of many companies must be redefined. Successful philanthropy today is not simply writing checks to the local charity. Philanthropic pursuits are becoming an important way for most corporations to communicate with stakeholders, gauge their interests, and satisfy their elevated expectations. By choosing the right philanthropic programs—those that yield social benefits and address stakeholder interests—companies can build a good corporate reputation. And a good reputation is both a source of tangible value and a reservoir of good will.[10]

According to Rakesh Khurana, a professor at Harvard Business School, the pendulum is swinging toward a model in which corporations will be regarded more often as social organizations whose obligations extend well beyond Wall Street.[11] To that I add an even more exciting prospect: By embracing social business and building loyal communities of customers using social-media technology, corporations will not only serve the need for social transformation; they will be rewarded with the opportunity to become "brand nations."

### CHAPTER TAKEAWAYS

- We tend to put our faith in government to be the first pillar of social transformation, while charities and philanthropies have become a de facto second pillar.

- The private sector is our best hope for a third pillar, as it alone has all the elements and resources that governments and philanthropies need.
- We need to construct a new paradigm of cooperation among governments, philanthropies, and corporations to meet the scale of meaningful social transformation that is needed.
- Corporate social responsibility is still an afterthought in most companies. There is a glaring hypocrisy in how CSR attempts to save with one hand what the other hand has destroyed.
- Corporations have adopted socially responsible behaviors only when citizens and government pressured them to do so.
- It is not only the task of corporations to find their optimized CSR "sweet spot," but the work of all capitalist societies to reengineer capitalism and transform it into an engine of global prosperity.

# 7
## HOW BRANDS BUILD THEIR BUSINESS AND A BETTER WORLD

For 23 years, Pepsi and Coke were the leading brand rivals at the Super Bowl. The two companies typically pulled out all the stops for this one game, each spending millions of dollars for just a few minutes of commercial airtime spotlighting their products and featuring America's top celebrities. To most people, this battle of the brands epitomized traditional advertising—exactly what they had come to expect on Super Bowl Sunday.

Until 2010, that is. That's when Pepsi turned the tables on consumers, dramatically reversing its approach to marketing and advertising. Instead of its usual TV spots during the Super Bowl, Pepsi used the money to fund the Pepsi Refresh Project, in which the brand invites consumers to its website, where they can nominate a social cause they want Pepsi to support. Anyone—an individual, a business, or a nonprofit—can list any cause they like. All they have to do is fill out an application to explain the cause and select one of the four award categories: $5,000, $25,000, $50,000, and $250,000. Each month, Pepsi accepts up to 1,000 entries on a first-come, first-served basis.

Rather than Pepsi executives deciding which causes to fund, the brand uses crowdsourcing to select the winners. Visitors to the website are allowed to vote for up to ten of their favorite projects a day. A leaderboard updates the rankings every 24 hours to display the top vote-getters. By the end of the month, it is the community that has selected the final 30 winning projects totaling up to $1.3 million in grants—two $250,000 winners, ten $50,000 winners, ten $25,000 winners, and nine or ten $5,000 winners.

Compared with any previous cause-marketing campaign, the Pepsi Refresh Project differs by an order of magnitude. It demonstrates how a major brand has opted to tackle social responsibility head-on, using an unquestionable commitment of its resources and brand image. Pepsi not only gives away $1.3 million each month in grants to the winning projects, but it also throws the imprimatur of one of the world's best-known brands behind the effort to inspire consumer-led social change.

The credit for Pepsi Refresh goes to its adverting agencies TBWA/Chiat/Day, Los Angeles, but it is PepsiCo's CEO, Indra Nooyi, who is responsible for the vision that has transformed the company into a corporate leader in new social thinking. PepsiCo is not a perfect company; it still makes mistakes. Yet under Nooyi's direction, it is leading the way to a new interpretation of capitalism. In her speaking engagements, she espouses an enlightened corporate mindset with such statements as "Companies can no longer perform and toss costs to society" and "We believe that every corporation operates with a license from society, and as a company, we owe society a duty of care."

Under Nooyi, all business units in PepsiCo adhere to a philosophy she calls "Performance with Purpose." This has translated into numerous pioneering innovations. The Frito-Lay division, for example, introduced for its SunChips product line the first 100-percent compostable snack-size bag. Made entirely from plant-based materials, the bag will decompose in about 14 weeks when placed in an active compost pile or bin. The Frito-Lay plant in Modesto, California, uses a solar concentrator field to capture energy to power its SunChips manufacturing.[1] PepsiCo's potato-chip (crisps) brand in the U.K., Walkers, is working on capturing water extracted from potatoes during their processing to purify and use in the plant, and even to feed back into the city where the factory is located.[2]

In addition, PepsiCo helped develop, in partnership with Waste Management, a "reverse" vending machine. Called the Dream Machine, it lets consumers recycle cans and bottles to earn reward points for travel or Pepsi products—or they can donate the cash value of the recycling deposit to charities. The partnership hopes to boost the national recycling of cans and bottles from the current national average of 34 percent to 50 percent within the next few years.[3]

PepsiCo also created what it calls the "i-crop" technology, developed in conjunction with the U.K.'s Cambridge University Farms to help Pepsi farmers reduce their water usage by 50 percent in five years. The technology uses web-based software that pulls together information from soil moisture probes and local weather stations to avoid over- or under-watering, which in turn reduces excess energy use and carbon emissions from the water pumps. The i-crop technology is currently in use at 22 farms in the U.K. and will expand in continental Europe by 2011, and then in India, China, Mexico, and Australia by 2012.[4]

The advertising industry was shocked when it heard about the Pepsi Refresh idea. Trade-magazine headlines trumpeted their disbelief: "Pepsi Abandons Super Bowl" and "Pepsi Ditches the Super Bowl." In reporting on Pepsi's decision, some national media outlets, including the *Wall Street Journal,* CNN, and *Good Morning America,* questioned the risks it posed to Pepsi to miss out on the biggest audience of the year. Pundits saw it as a shortsighted tactic to attract young people using faddish social media. Some fellow Fortune 500 executives thought it was just an example of Pepsi jumping on the cause-marketing bandwagon.

But Pepsi Refresh has been proven successful beyond even its own expectations. Pepsi's advertising agency estimates the Refresh site received more than 1 billion impressions in its first three months. In mid-2010, Bonin Bough, global director of digital and social media at PepsiCo, announced that "more people have voted for projects pitched to Pepsi Refresh than voted for the last U.S. president."[5] Pepsi's Facebook page grew by leaps and bounds, from 225,000 fans to more than 1 million. The website has become so popular that Pepsi executives now see it as a valuable media property, attracting more page views than many of the companies that solicit Pepsi to advertise on their sites.

By September 2010, the company decided that not only would it keep the program running through 2011, but it would also expand it to Europe, Asia, and Latin America, offering each its own set of grant monies. "When you look at the powerful movement that we are creating, there's no question that we have on our hands something big," Ami Irazabal, marketing director at Pepsi, told *Advertising Age.* "Good ideas need to expand. They cannot be encapsulated, especially when something is working for the brand."[6]

PepsiCo also announced it was returning to the Super Bowl: this time with user-generated ads chosen by an online crowdsourcing selection process. PepsiCo's departure from traditional advertising and return with consumer-generated ads within two short years serves as a powerful example of how quickly even large brands can seize the opportunities presented by the shifting marketplace.

Above all, Pepsi Refresh reveals the real undercurrent of desire among consumers to build a better world. Rather than rehashing the language of selling soda, Pepsi has tapped into an ocean of consumer empathy seeking purpose and contribution. The Pepsi Refresh website has effectively become a "shared space" where people can gather, nurture their common interests, and express their mutual concern for the planet. It is also an exceptional example of a visionary CEO who deeply understands the benefits of community engagement for the brand and for the world at large. Little wonder that in 2010, *Fortune* magazine named Nooyi the most powerful woman in business for the fifth year in a row. Under her leadership, Pepsi Refresh has become perhaps the brightest beacon pointing the way to a new era of We First capitalism.

> *A business that makes nothing but money is a poor business.*
>
> —Henry Ford, founder of Ford Motor Company

### BRANDS AND CONSUMERS AS THE THIRD PILLAR OF CHANGE

Can you imagine a world in which the majority of the world's leading corporations move along the same pathways as PepsiCo, creating innovative cause campaigns that transform their profit-making businesses into engines of growth and prosperity? Can you imagine the progress that could be made if thousands of corporations began partnering with their customers, governments, and NGOs to establish and reach specific goals in alleviating poverty, malnutrition, infant mortality, illiteracy, and the other crises humanity faces?

This is the vision that We First holds out: for corporations, consumers, and citizens to start acting in concert to create the powerful third pillar of social transformation that governments and philanthropies so desperately need. Often ambitions like this are seen as naïve and impractical, but companies like PepsiCo prove it is both possible and beneficial to a brand. In this vision, both sides carry equal weight in the change process. Each depends on the other to fulfill their obligations in a new social contract. Together, they are instrumental in legitimizing social business and making transformational global change popular, aspirational, and increasingly achievable.

This chapter and the next hold the keys to putting We First principles into action. These two chapters explain how brands (this chapter) and consumers (next chapter) must each begin changing their behavior. The value of We First as an economic model relative to other proposals that have been made to change capitalism—such as ethical capitalism, constructive capitalism, philanthrocapitalism, and so on—is that it is based on pragmatic and actionable steps that brands and consumers can take as partners enabled by social media.

## BECOMING SOCIALLY RESPONSIBLE IN THE AGE OF SOCIAL MEDIA

There are many ways that corporations can begin practicing capitalism to serve the greater good. But let us get down to specifics and identify the most critical shifts brands need to make to implement the We First model of capitalism.

There are two courses of actions corporations must take. The first consists of *unilateral* changes—purely voluntary decisions to revise the old models of corporate thinking and to put into operation a higher level of responsibility, accountability, and sustainable business practices. These actions are largely internal, but they also serve to demonstrate to the outside world of consumers that the brand understands their expectations. The second course consists of actions that companies and their brands need to initiate in an effort to draw consumers into their sphere of influence, where they become partners in social transformation.

In other words, one set of actions reflects a commitment made by corporate leaders and addressed to employees—to revise core strategies around purpose, sustainability, and values. The other set of actions aims to build a following of loyal fans of the brand who are eager to use the tools of social media to co-create the change the brand seeks to make. Both sets of actions turn on the transformative technology of the Internet, social media, and smartphones. Like many technologies, these tools are neutral and nonpartisan; they can be used either in the service of consumers to connect with one another or to brands, or in the service of brands to converse with and market to their consumers—or both.

At present, consumers are more sophisticated in their use of social-media tools because corporate culture is more difficult to change than individual behavior. But by following the example of a growing number of case studies featuring Pepsi, Starbucks, Nike, Coca-Cola, and Ford, all brands can learn how to harness social media to further their corporate interests and goals *within the context of becoming a socially responsible organization.*

### UNILATERAL BRAND ACTIONS

#### LEADERSHIP COMMITMENT TO SOCIAL RESPONSIBILITY

As with any major corporate change, the first action any company must take is to enlist leadership to create and promulgate a vision for the future. Naturally, the endorsement of the most visible players in the corporation is a key element to ensuring any shift in an organization's groupthink. To achieve it, leaders must reject the false approach that pays lip service to corporate social responsibility while in reality relegating it to an afterthought.

There are a growing number of leaders who are models of this thinking. Indra Nooyi's chief competitor, Coca-Cola CEO Neville Isdell, is another example of this new corporate leader. In 2009, for example, Isdell organized a conference of executives from leading corporations headquartered in the Southeast, along with several NGOs like CARE International, the United States Agency for International Development, and delegates from Georgia State University's J. Mack Robinson College of Business. The group discussed how they could help change capitalism for the betterment of business and society. As Isdell told the group, "In business, you must lead change or else change leads you. . . . If capitalism fails to re-mold itself, the global recession, increased government intervention, social issues and changing social mores will fundamentally alter the free market."[7]

One of the challenges here is that most leaders fail to understand how social media can assist them. A 2010 survey conducted by global public relations firm Weber Shandwick found that the majority of CEOs frown on social media. A full 64 percent of CEOs at the world's 50 largest companies do not engage in any social media, and only 28 percent perform simple actions such as posting a letter to a corporate website. Only 18 percent of these CEOs have appeared on YouTube, and fewer than 10 percent use Twitter, Facebook, or LinkedIn.[8]

While CEOs must be careful when making public statements, shying away completely from social media robs them of the tremendous potential benefits. Social media can easily become one of the most valuable tools a leader has to persuasively communicate his or her vision and passion for a better world to both employees and the public. In the survey above, Leslie Gaines-Ross, Weber Shandwick's chief reputation strategist and an online reputation expert, stated, "In this increasingly digital age, CEOs should embrace the value of connectivity with customers, talent and other important stakeholders online. With 1.96 billion Internet users around the world, CEOs should be where people are watching, reading, chatting and listening."[9]

There is a wide range of messaging that CEOs can create using social media. They can appear in videos on the company's intranet and in public videos on YouTube, for example, where they can state and reiterate their corporate commitments. They can blog, both internally for employees and for consumer-facing media. They can authorize the company's intranet to become a collaborative space in which the employees share content, ideas, and feedback informed by the company's core values.

Lastly, CEOs should endeavor to speak directly to consumers and listen to their concerns about the brand and its meaning in their lives. From the consumer point of view, nobody in a company better epitomizes the brand's values than the leader at the top. Erik Qualman, author of *Socialnomics*, puts it this way: "If done correctly, social media enables CEOs to hear raw, candid feedback from real people—people who aren't afraid of being fired because they CAN'T be fired. The truth is, leaders with their egos in check are already fully aware that they work for the customer."[10]

*The whole corporate social responsibility idea is trying to graft something onto the old profit maximization model. What we need is a transformation. . . . People want businesses to do good in the world. It's that simple . . . we need a deeper, fundamental reform in the essence of business.*

—John Mackey

## EXPANDING THE SOURCES OF THOUGHT LEADERSHIP

Ideally, every business executive should become actively involved in new thought-leadership groups such as TED where they will find the inspiration, ideas, and courage to push for change in their organizations and in the world. Fueled by the Internet and social media, these groups solicit the best new ideas from world leaders, experts, and visionary thinkers in many fields and present them to the public in an effort to drive government, business, and citizen-driven social action.

TED is an acronym for Technology, Entertainment, and Design. Founded in 1984 by noted designer Richard Saul Wurman and now led and expanded by thought leader Chris Anderson, TED strives to drive innovation in nearly every field of human endeavor and become a force for transformational change. Under its signature banner, "Ideas Worth Spreading," the organization sponsors numerous conferences and special-interest workshops. It has a rich website, where more than 850 videos of thought-provoking talks, translated into more than 80 languages, are available free of charge.

The value of thought-leadership groups like TED cannot be underestimated. Any corporation that sets its sights on becoming a world leader in social responsibility should use these groups as invaluable goldmines of information and wellsprings of inspiration for its leadership. They offer a fresh source of innovation and solutions, while enabling brands and consumers to learn and evolve together, thus accelerating the opportunities for partnerships and collaborations that can advance social change on a global scale.

## EMBED PURPOSE INTO YOUR CORE BUSINESS STRATEGIES

It is no longer credible for brands to claim to practice social responsibility by donating to charities while still conducting business as usual. Such a pretense is especially problematic in brands whose business is unhealthy, unsustainable, or unfriendly to the planet. Obviously there are shades of gray, and brands will need time to migrate their businesses away from unsustainable practices, but transforming the core of one's business requires an absolute commitment to We First purpose. Today's consumers want and need to see how a brand contributes concrete solutions to human problems: how the company makes its products, whom it hires and how well it treats employees, what steps it takes to reduce its carbon footprint, and how it shares its profits—in short, everything that the brand does to contribute to a better society.

Brands should use social media to inform consumers of how they have embedded purpose into their core. The websites of companies such as Patagonia, TOMS Shoes, Starbucks, Unilever, Zappos, and Nike all go to elaborate lengths to market their purpose as clearly as their products. Using narrative techniques, they weave a tremendous amount of meaning into their websites, sharing images of their employees and production sites, explaining the intimate details of how they source their products, and prominently noting which agencies and NGOs they work with to ensure the integrity of their fair-trade and sustainability policies.

> Nothing seems more obvious to me that a product or service only becomes a brand when it is imbued with profound values that translate into fact. . . . Everybody appreciates being treated decently. Everybody wants excellence and value. Everyone likes to have fun and to feel part of something bigger than themselves.
>
> —Sir Richard Branson, chairman, Virgin

## ENGAGING EMPLOYEES *AND* MANAGEMENT IN THE COMPANY'S PURPOSE

A powerful statement to demonstrate a brand's commitment to social transformation is giving employees paid time off to volunteer for causes. A growing number of responsible companies allow employees to support their favorite cause on the company's time. An impressive example of this occurred in October 2010, when Kraft Foods conducted its Delicious Difference Week, in which 20,000 of its employees in 56 countries performed volunteer work. The efforts ranged from 3,000 employees in Brazil working in 40 cities helping the elderly and poor to 1,000 employees feeding the homeless in the U.K. to 1,500 employees building new playgrounds from start to finish in one day in 8 states in the U.S. (in conjunction with the nonprofit KaBOOM!).

Volunteering, however, needs to go beyond the efforts of individual employees. The complexities of our global crises often mean that government and NGOs lack the professional skills and management necessary to overcome hurdles and bureaucracy. We need more companies to willingly agree to loan out their professional talents, including senior executives, trainers, accountants, legal staff, engineers, and researchers, whose knowledge and skills can make a profound difference to a cause-related effort.

Here again, social media can enhance the effectiveness of corporate volunteerism. There are now a number of specialized platforms and networks to which companies can subscribe to help match employees to volunteer opportunities. Causecast, for example, helps companies in the United States develop cause campaigns that include volunteering efforts. In the U.K., LeapCR offers companies access to a large database of one-off daylong volunteer assignments from which employees can choose.

Social media can also be used to amplify the reputational value of employees donating their services to causes. For example, employees can take photos or videos and post them online so other employees and even the public can see how the brand's commitment is being accomplished. Companies can also use social media to challenge their consumers to volunteer—Coca-Cola, for example, encourages its customers to volunteer at their local charities as a way to fulfill their slogan "Live Positively."

*A funny thing happened when we actually communicated [our purpose] to our employees. We found that suddenly employees were a lot more passionate about the company, a lot more engaged, and when customers called they could sense the personality at the other end of the phone wasn't there just for a paycheck.*

—Tony Hsieh, CEO, Zappos

## REFOCUS ON SUSTAINABLE BUSINESS, NOT SHORT-TERM PROFITS

The overall level of corporate consciousness has improved in the last decade, but the number of corporations committed to sustainable thinking and behavior is small relative to the scale of change the world needs. The sustainability initiatives most corporations undertake remain inconsistent and incomplete.

Consider two surveys done in 2010. One of them was a McKinsey survey of executives that showed that only 25 percent of them say sustainability is a top priority for their CEOs, and only 30 percent say their companies invest in sustainability or embed it in their business practices. Meanwhile, the other survey, sponsored by the U.N. Global Compact and Accenture, which interviewed CEOs directly, showed that while a full 96 percent of CEOs say they believe sustainability issues will be critical to the future success of their business, only 54 percent have implemented sustainability in their own supply chain.

The two studies illustrate the huge gap between CEO beliefs and actions. As we have noted, their priorities, not surprisingly, are still focused on meeting short-term quarterly earnings expectations. In a responsible company, however, corporate leaders emphasize instead business practices that further sustainable behaviors in all five We First dimensions—economic, environmental, moral, social, and ethical.

> *Successful brands are not cold: they have a soul, a character. But thanks to the power granted to consumers by the Internet, brands that betray their character risk getting slapped around.*
>
> —Lee Clow, Worldwide Director of Media Arts, TBWA/Chiat/Day

## EARN PROFITS, BUT BUILD PROSPERITY

Socially responsible companies must begin reversing the disparity of incomes they have created, as well as undertaking a concerted effort to reduce the gaps in the overall wealth between the developed and developing nations of the world. The basis for this principle is less a moral argument than an economic reality: without a reasonably prosperous middle class in any society, the engine of capitalism falters.

One of the hardest—but most important—tasks that corporations must tackle is fair compensation. This is not merely a moral issue; it is pragmatic public-relations issue, in that CEO and senior executive salaries at public companies are by law reported, and consumers will increasingly punish companies that spend disproportionate amounts on executive compensation, relative not only to the ranks of their workers, but also to their philanthropic and social contributions. Internal income inequality negatively impacts employees' motivation to work hard and be active proponents of the brand.

Corporations must also start developing a stronger commitment to spreading prosperity globally. The crucial nature of this task is synthesized in a single question: *Can the world wait yet another generation to achieve the goal of shared prosperity, lifting two to three billion people out of poverty and transforming them into vibrant, productive citizens and consumers?*

Demographics dictate that for any major brand to substantiate its global citizenship, it must make worldwide prosperity a strategic priority if it wants to cultivate new consumers and convince existing customers that they truly share the vision of a better world. The door is wide open for corporations and brands to innovate new ways to spread prosperity throughout the world.

Social media is already enabling progress in this regard. I've cited how the spread of mobile phones is playing a huge role in connecting impoverished areas to the Internet, providing opportunities for poor rural populations to start businesses. Following the 2010 World Economic Forum meeting in Davos, nonprofit thought leader and blogger Beth Kanter reported that social networks are especially useful for women in developing countries to get training and learn new skills. She noted that the CEO of the executive management firm Manpower, Jeffrey A. Joerres, envisions a day when such networks will provide job opportunities for these women as part of local project teams at major Western companies. Kanter concluded, "Although social networking technologies are not the solutions to the world's ills, they are solution-finders with enormous potential."[11]

*Ethics is the new competitive environment.*

—Peter Robinson, CEO, Mountain Equipment Co-op

## COLLABORATE TO ACHIEVE GREATER RESULTS

Creating a better world requires teamwork, partnerships, and collaboration, as we need an entire army of companies to work together to build a better world within the next few decades. This means corporations must embrace the benefits of cooperating with one another. This is not to say that brands should not compete for business or seek to attract the largest number of customers. But when a larger goal can be established, companies can benefit from working together to breed innovation and arrive at the most effective solutions. The corporate world is full of intellectual-property and research departments that remain unnecessarily proprietary when they could be helping each other solve problems. There are four ways that companies can seek to collaborate.

### Across Industry Sectors

An example of this is the Business for Innovative Climate & Energy Policy (BICEP), jointly founded in 2008 by Nike, Starbucks, Levi Strauss & Company, Sun Microsystems, and Timberland. Together, these five companies have crafted several proposals to reduce greenhouse gases through renewable energy and fewer coal-fired power plants. To express their commitment to the proposals, each company has also vowed to reduce its energy consumption or emissions.

### With Competitors

Since most corporate competitors have the same problems with sustainability and social reputation, it's worth trying to solve them together. For example, in March 2010, Safeway became the first American grocery chain and manufacturer of private-label merchandise to join the Sustainability Consortium, which already includes such grocery-store staples as General Mills, Procter & Gamble, and PepsiCo, which fund scientific research on creating a more sustainable global supply chain for the entire industry.

### With Supply Chains

More and more companies are reaching out to their suppliers and contractors to work jointly on issues of sustainability, environmental responsibility, ethics, and compliance. Walmart has notably led the way in helping to educate its vast chain of suppliers in sustainable business practices.

### With Government

Corporations often partner with government after natural disasters, as many companies did in the aftermath of Hurricane Katrina in 2005. As a rule, however, long-term civic-corporate partnerships are still rare. But this need not remain the status quo, as many opportunities are available for such partnerships. The Healthy Weight Commitment Foundation, for instance, is a new consortium formed at the behest of First Lady Michelle Obama to require 80 of the leading U.S. food and beverage manufacturers—including Campbell's Soup, Kraft Foods, Kellogg, General Mills, and PepsiCo—to take collective action against the rapidly rising rates of obesity in America, especially among children. In a major transformation of their practices, these manufacturers have agreed to cut the calorie counts in their products by 1 trillion in 2012 and 1.5 trillion by the end of 2015.[12]

There are many ways that corporations can collaborate.

- Offer their intellectual property as open-source when it might help other industries.
- Share development expenses and research leading to advances beneficial to all.
- Co-fund or cosponsor emerging ideas of common value.
- Co-conduct seminars and learning workshops for employees and management.

---

## TIMBERLAND'S COLLABORATION ON SUSTAINABILITY STANDARDS

The footwear industry has an inherent disadvantage when it comes to sustainability, given the raw materials and manufacturing processes it uses—leather, rubber, toxic dyes and chemicals, and energy-heavy production. Yet from the beginning, the Stratham, New Hampshire–based Timberland has tried to set itself apart as a leader in ecologically sensitive practices—the company is now discovering that collaboration provides even greater benefits.

One example is the Green Index label initiative. Timberland is in the process of gathering data on all its products, which by 2012 will inform consumers about three measures of its product sustainability:

- Climate: the amount greenhouse gas emissions produced from raw material extraction through manufacturing
- Chemicals: the presence of hazardous substances such as solvent adhesives and PVCs used in the production of products
- Materials: reports on the use of organic, recycled, and renewable materials used in each product

While it believes the Green Index is an effective stopgap, Timberland is taking this commitment one step further by collaborating with the 200-member Outdoor Industry Association to create an industry-wide "footprinting" standard, The Eco Index, because such an index is far more valuable for consumers. As Betsy Blaisdell, senior manager of environmental stewardship for Timberland, notes, "Individual efforts . . . are good options for now, but to truly empower consumers, we knew we needed a commitment from the entire industry. First-mover companies only get so far—collaboration is integral to achieving a consumer-friendly, industry-wide standard, which is why we applaud the launch of the OIA Eco Index as a positive step in the right direction."[13]

- Cohost events to raise awareness and funds for research or causes.
- Combine employee volunteer activities to generate greater awareness and impact.
- Lobby jointly for new legislation to improve efficiencies and reduce environmental damage.

Social media is, by definition, a tremendous enhancement to collaborative efforts. It gives people the space and tools to form virtual "communities of practice" focused on shared goals and values, as well as the ability to share white papers or webinars for information exchange and training, among many other benefits. The momentum for corporate collaborative efforts is building, and a growing number of websites are tracking trends in cooperation, collaboration, and co-creation. Industry leader CSRwire, for example, tracks what companies and groups of companies are doing to bring about more responsible and sustainable business practices, while international nonprofits like Net Impact serve to inspire, educate, and equip corporate executives and business students for operating in a more socially and environmentally sustainable world.

## ENLISTING CONSUMERS AS PARTNERS

Companies should take the actions reviewed above solely in the context of their *own* commitment to change. Beyond those, however, there are also several steps companies can take to solicit consumers to become their partners in change efforts.

There are many reasons this second group of actions is necessary. First, it removes the us-versus-them mentality, which corporations know is antithetical to the social business world we live in. Since consumers now have the power to reward or punish brands, companies gain little by pretending they can maintain the old balance of power. Second, corporations that take the leap toward social responsibility typically encounter numerous obstacles. Some of these are internal, such as reluctant board members and senior executives, who might see their perks, salaries, and profits in jeopardy. Others may be external, such as Wall Street brokers who predict doom and gloom for the company, or leading investors seeking to dump the stock. Reaching out to consumers for support during the transition can be a counterweight and calming force to such reactions. And of course, the best form of protection is proof that a company's brands are gaining in popularity because of its corporate commitment to greater social responsibility.

Finally, consumers provide a brand's best hope for research and development—the ignition of sustained growth—in today's world. By energizing their consumer base and drawing new consumers into their communities, companies gain valuable insights about customers' needs and wants. They ensure their own future by reaching out to consumers for the new ideas they need to keep innovating.

The next actions to be examined are therefore oriented toward attracting consumers to brands and persuading them to congregate around the vision of the world that informs their services and products. These actions are voluntary but essential for any company that takes its mission of building a better world as seriously as it takes its mission of delivering profits to its shareholders.

Before examining them, it should be noted that all of these actions reflect a paradigm shift that has already transpired at the core of marketing and branding: *Pull has replaced push in capturing eyes, minds, and hearts.* Due to the voice and power that social media has given consumers, brands can no longer monolithically force their products onto consumers or dictate why they should buy. The only way to reach consumers in the age of citizen media—what I call "Wedia"—is to pull them in with messages imbued with meaning and purpose.

In their insightful book, *The Power of Pull: How Small Moves, Smartly Made, Can Set Big Things in Motion,* the noted co-chairs of the Deloitte Center for the Edge, John Hagel III and John Seely Brown (along with executive director Lang Davison), outline the strategic explanation of why pull is replacing push. Push, they contend, is not useful in a world that is no longer predictable, stable, or constant. Forecasting has lost its value. Corporations instead need to be flexible, nimble, and quick to respond to changes in markets and consumer needs. Technology, globalization, the interconnected world, and the volume of information available also mean that knowledge changes rapidly.

This impacts work environments in profound ways, from how companies approach learning and training, to how they go about recruiting and staffing.

According to these authors, pull is about learning to utilize three practices: *accessing* information, resources, and people when you need them; *attracting* the necessary sources of connection, inspiration, and talent needed in the moment; and *achieving* new levels of performance that increase our individual, institutional, and collective potential. Pull moves us toward new knowledge, innovation, and advancement. It takes us away from the core, out to the edges, where people begin connecting to discover the new ideas, innovations, and business strategies that will earn them praise and profits of the future.[14]

The shift from push to pull thinking holds the key to how corporations and brands need to attract consumers today. Companies must begin moving away from the old core of traditional push ideologies, still dictating to consumers what to buy, and move toward pulling consumers in by offering them innovative new ideas about how their brand makes a meaningful contribution to the world.

The marketing strategies and actions enumerated below all seek to maximize this type of pull on consumers. They recognize both the redistribution of power that allows consumers to share in the stewardship of brands, and also the ability of brands to create meaningful connections with consumers that drive their long-term loyalty and daily purchasing decisions.

*We are not really embracing technology, we are embracing the consumer.*

—Robert A. Iger, CEO, the Walt Disney Company

## ALLOW CONSUMERS TO CO-CREATE YOUR BRAND'S STORY

The most effective way to attract consumers today is to invite them to share and help shape your brand narrative. Brands are finally starting to notice that loyal consumers *want* to be part of their brand's storytelling. They are open to offering their creativity and networks to support and publicize when brands they like are doing good work. Crowdsourcing works because consumers are sincerely interested in the creative advantages and potential of collaborating with the brands they admire.

The smartest brands will acknowledge this desire and provide consumers with a platform to contribute using some form of social media. What consumers bring to the brand must be respected and treated as credible, so that they really feel the brand is allowing them to participate in its stewardship. The successes of Dove's "Real Beauty" campaign, Ford's Invisible People, Nike's Livestrong partnership, and Patagonia's Footprint Chronicles testify to the profound motivation consumers have to imbue their favorite brands with altruistic intentions.

## INVOLVE CONSUMERS IN MEANINGFUL CAUSE INVESTMENTS

Many corporations already make charitable donations or conduct cause-based marketing campaigns that link their contributions to product sales. But, as we know from the *Chronicle of Philanthropy* surveys, the median corporate cash donation to charitable causes is just over 1 percent of profits. In comparison, eleven American companies widely considered to be authentically socially responsible donated 5 percent to 24 percent of their profits in 2009. Seventh Generation, for instance, makes it a policy to donate 10 percent of its profits. This disparity raises the question: What is the bar by which corporations should measure their responsibility? We First thinking suggests that corporations need to reassess their priorities in the face of our ever more daunting problems in the world.

Beyond the dollar-amount issue, though, is how companies are supporting charitable efforts through cause-related marketing campaigns. Consumer interest in CRM is now a given. CEOs would do well to heed these results from the 2010 Cone Cause Evolution Survey measuring consumer interest, especially among Moms and Millennials, in cause marketing:

- 81 percent of consumers say they want companies to give them an opportunity to buy a product that supports a cause.
- 90 percent believe companies should tell them how they support causes.
- 61 percent say they would try a new brand if it supported a cause.
- 83 percent of consumers want more of the products, services, and retailers they use to benefit causes.
- 81 percent believe companies should continue to provide financial support for causes at the same level or higher during an economic downturn.

Cause marketing is now a serious business-building opportunity. As Alison DaSilva, executive vice president at Cone, told *Philanthropy Journal*, "When price and quality are equal, we know most consumers will choose the product benefiting the cause. But cause alignment can have an even bigger influence on consumer choice, pushing them to experiment with something different and unfamiliar. Cause branding is a prime opportunity for companies to extend beyond their traditional market and increase exposure to potential new consumers."[15]

## ATTRACT CONSUMERS BY BUILDING SOCIAL CAPITAL

To pull consumers in under this new dynamic, brands need to redirect their thinking from building profits to building social capital. Consumers are increasingly drawn toward brands that convey a larger social meaning, not just an emotional attachment, as the old advertising paradigm went. Thought leader and blogger Stowe Boyd characterized this shift as "Meaning is the new search."[16]

Focusing on social capital in addition to financial capital is necessary because what consumers expect and want from brands is changing. They are more probing, making an effort to discern the "real" truth of what their brand stands for in terms of its values, ethics, and character. Tom LaForge, Coca-Cola's director of Knowledge & Insights, has suggested that we are in fact witnessing the evolution of a new type of consumer—a sort of hybrid who is simultaneously a consumer, citizen, environmentalist, and community member. In his view, the most successful companies will be those that transform themselves into what he calls "social construction brands," which allow consumers to merge their various identities into one persona. To attract this new class of consumers, however, brands need to become storytellers, stewards of the planet, cultural leaders, and skillful designers.[17]

The tools of social media are perfectly tailored to helping brands maximize their social capital, because what consumers ideally seek to do with social media is share their values and opinions with the people they know. Brian Solis, principal of FutureWorks and author of *Engage!*, describes several recent studies confirming that consumers use social media to talk to one another about their brands. In one study, ROI Research found that one-third of Twitter users share their opinions about companies or products at least once per week. Another study, conducted by Chadwick Martin Bailey along with iModerate Research Technologies, found that people who follow brands on Facebook and Twitter are 51 percent and 67 percent respectively more likely to buy a product post-connection. That study also found that Facebook and Twitter users are 60 percent and 79 percent more likely to recommend a brand as a result of engaging with them online.[18]

Millennials, especially, are drawn to companies that build social capital. In a 2010 study entitled *For Millennials, Taking Action Is a Core Value*, published by Edelman, the world's largest PR firm, it was shown that 70 percent of global Millennials and 80 percent of American Millennials said that once they find a company or product they like, trust, and respect, they will keep

## FOUR EXAMPLES OF COMPANIES BUILDING SOCIAL CAPITAL

Just a few decades ago, many companies would simply donate their dollars to a cause. But today, many brands are investing their reputation and money in far more profound social initiatives to build their social capital. These are examples of corporate social responsibility that are *not* dependent on a consumer purchase. Rather, they are straightforward corporate efforts intended solely to demonstrate a company's desire to make a contribution to the world.

### FAST RETAILING

The owner of the popular Japanese clothing chain Uniqlo, Fast Retailing, has launched a subsidiary in Bangladesh whose mission is to "help solve social problems, including those related to poverty, sanitation and education issues." The subsidiary will be aimed at getting cost-effective clothing production facilities up and running to boost the local economy. In Japan, Uniqlo actively encourages the recycling of used clothing, which is then sent to poorer parts of Asia and Africa, or to disaster victims around the world.

### STARBUCKS

Starbucks sets the standard for Fair Trade–certified and sustainable coffee- and tea-growing practices. The company works closely with Conservation International, which created certification standards called Coffee and Farmer Equity (C.A.F.E.) Practices. These guidelines establish environmentally sustainable growing conditions, workers' rights and acceptable working conditions, child labor laws, and accountability procedures to track and confirm what percentage of what Starbucks pays for green coffee beans has been paid to farmers. The company established two Farmer Support Centers, in Costa Rica and Rwanda, to help educate growers about how to raise their yields and lower their costs. The company has provided $15 million to organizations that make loans to farmers during the growing season to give them income until the beans fully ripen. Starbucks also leads ethical tea production by supporting Mercy Corps' Community Health and Advancement Initiative, which provides tea- and spice-growing communities with economic development and health services.

### PROCTER & GAMBLE

P&G launched the Children's Safe Drinking Water Program in 2004 to distribute 4 billion liters of clean water in 57 countries around the world. The program distributes packets of PUR, a water-purifying technology the company developed with the U.S. Centers for Disease Control and Prevention (CDC). As part of P&G's global Live, Learn, and Thrive initiative, the clean-water program focuses on eradicating the diseases and deaths caused by contaminated water sources. Each packet cleans 10 liters of water. The company hit its 2 billionth liter of clean water following the Chilean earthquake in March 2010, with 2 billion more to go.

AMERICAN EXPRESS
The American Express Open Forum is an example of building social capital using value-added content, information, and insights to create a unique bond with its small business customers that goes far beyond the usual goodwill. The company has built an entire network and ecosystem, including a mobile phone app, to share the expertise of top industry minds with every small business customer at no cost. In this way, American Express seeks to earn social capital by making a meaningful contribution to the wider community of small business owners.

coming back. Further, the study found that 90 percent of American Millennials are willing to take online or off-line action every week on behalf of their favorite brands, including 68 percent who recommended the products to their family and friends; 44 percent who "friended" or followed a brand on their social network; 33 percent who posted something about the brand on their social network; 35 percent who volunteered to test new products from the brand; and 32 percent who wrote an online review of the brand or product.[19]

Social capital will offer far better returns over the long term than its previous short-term equivalent, profit alone. For example, IBM reports that it now receives a roughly $3 return on investment for every $1 it invests in corporate-citizenship initiatives.[20] The drive to build social capital is critical for companies that want sustained profits and increased shareholder value. As Jeffrey Hollender, founder of Seventh Generation, states, CEOs need to recognize that "we are entering an age in which business valuation will be determined not just by profits but also by a company's positive and negative societal and environmental impacts."[21]

> *What has happened is that social media has become one of the biggest mass changes in global behavior in a generation (since the advent of the Internet itself).*
>
> —Dion Hinchcliffe, senior vice president, Dachis Group

## GIVE CONSUMERS A CHANCE TO "ELECT" YOU EVERY DAY

Since social media lets consumers talk about their brands at any time, companies would be wise to give them something to talk about. Rather than resisting or ignoring the dialogue, engage with consumers and let them "vote" on you every day. One way to do this is to create an online space where consumers can connect to your brand and the causes it supports. A recent study from the leading digital firm Razorfish's FEED blog found that of the thousands of consumers surveyed, 65 percent said an online experience with a brand had changed their opinion of that brand, and 97 percent said that experience influenced whether or not they would purchase an item or service.

Another study, produced by WetPaint and Altimeter Group, found that brands that engaged in seven or more channels of social media experienced an 18 percent growth in revenues in the 12 months prior to July 2009.[22] The study also cited specific examples of how a company's growth in social-media engagement translated into visibility and profit. For instance, Starbucks already had a Facebook page that attracted 200,000 people, yet when it offered to run a fan page and post exclusive content for its members, its Facebook fan base swelled to 5 million people, one of the largest groups of its kind.

The return for brands on conscious reputational management is beyond question. Reputations Corporation, a Vancouver-based consultancy group, reports that 72 percent of consumers say reputation influences their buying decisions. A remarkable 80 percent of employees will accept less pay to work with a company with an excellent reputation, while a full 89 percent say that a company's reputation is a tiebreaker between equal products.

Companies must also recognize that consumers' ability to commend or criticize them is increasingly facilitated by the rapid growth of new online tools that deliver information about brands and corporate behavior. One of these is Brandkarma.com, which collates information from consumers about a company's social responsibility and carbon footprints, treatment of employees, and other factors. Scores of mobile-phone apps are also available to put information about brands and their products into the hands of consumers in the shopping aisle. These apps are socially oriented and detailed, containing not just pricing information but a wide range of context about a brand's social and environmental track record, giving consumers motivation to buy—or not. For example, the GoodGuide app for iPhones provides instant product and company information for more than 50,000 personal care, household chemical, toy, and food products right in the shopping aisle.

GoodGuide and many other new smartphone technologies are based on two-dimensional "quick response" (QR) bar codes that enable consumers to use their phones' cameras to get instant information about the manufacturers' social responsibility. Interest in this technology, already prevalent in Asia, is skyrocketing in the United States—one bar code technology provider, ScanBuy, reported an astounding 700 percent increase in consumer bar code scanning in 2010 over 2009. Another survey from ABI Research found that 80 percent of American consumers surveyed have an interest in scanning mobile bar codes.[23] There are now dozens of companies in this field, including BarcodeHero, CheckPoints, Microsoft Tag, RedLaser, Shopkick, ShopSavvy, Stickybits, Tecca, SnapTell, and the recently updated Amazon Mobile. QR codes are an example of a technology that could easily be used on behalf of mutual self-interest—brands could deliver coupons and product discounts to socially conscious shoppers who, in turn, would reward the most responsible companies with their purchases.

The future of QR codes promises to turn shopping into a social experience and the store aisle into a conversation space between brands and their customers. For example, the mobile bar code reader from Stickybits links users to the Internet, where they can have multimedia conversations about brands featuring videos, creating a "social graph" around products. This gives brands and marketers a chance to engage with fans in product-related conversation chains. Pepsi, for instance, signed on with Stickybits and arranged for users who scan Pepsi cans to see an entertaining sponsored message from Pepsi.

Beyond QR code scanning, there are also many new "augmented reality" (AR) applications that provide additional layers of geographically specific content to conscious consumers. With an AR app, consumers can look through their smartphone camera and see labels or tags on products with details about their manufacture: photos of where they came from, who made them, and their impact on the planet. One of the most popular of these apps is Layar, which lets consumers choose specific data layers or experiences. Brands can use AR apps to add information that demonstrates transparency and builds trust.

And finally, there are numerous "check-in" apps, like Facebook and Twitter Places and Check-ins, Foursquare, and Gowalla, that use location-identification GPS software. These originated as ways for users to tell their friends where they are, but they are being quickly integrated into sophisticated marketing campaigns in which brands engage their consumers in loyalty-based purchasing. Location-based services allow brands to target customers specific to a location or store, offering them unique coupons or discounts as incentives to buy.

Given the potential of all these technologies to create social shopping experiences, companies are also beginning to invest in consumer sentiment-tracking platforms. This is an entirely new industry emerging to provide Chief Marketing Officers, Chief Listening Officers, and brand executives with a wide variety of tools to monitor and measure consumer dialogue and sentiment across popular social-media platforms. These include desktop toolboxes like TweetDeck and Hootsuite, brand reputation and social-media listening software like Radian6 and Nielsen BlogPulse, and virtual "command centers," like the one PepsiCo built for Gatorade, which oversees monitoring, marketing, and crisis management. The relevance of these platforms is swiftly taking hold in the corporate world; in fact, the Winterberry Group estimates that companies will more than double the amount they currently spend to get online data—as much as $840 million by 2012.[24]

Sentiment-measuring technology will also have predictive capabilities. Compass Labs, for instance, says it can gather information about people from the patterns of their social network and web usage and make predictive guesses about their future purchasing interests and intentions.[25] Meanwhile, Google's Eric Schmidt postulates a near future in which Google search evolves into a "serendipity engine," wherein queries run constantly in the background based on one's activity on various devices.

Armed with this data about their present clients, brands can begin to engage with potential customers on the basis of what they care about and want to buy well in advance of their actual contact with them. Such changes are happening so fast that the New York–based consulting group PSFK predicts that brands will soon need to invest in new "infrastructure, knowledge, and discipline to mine, analyze, and identify opportunities to better meet the evolving needs of a changing consumer market—lest they risk losing a consumer that has moved onto other brands that better met their changing needs."[26]

If brands think of every day as Election Day, they must seek to win over their audiences, not only through their products, but also through their behaviors. Any slippage in a brand's social capital can cause damage, while broken promises or outright betrayal can erase years of loyalty and effective marketing. In order to achieve this, *brands must become day traders in social emotion,* constantly seeking to amass, manage, and monitor social capital by making meaningful contributions to their customers' lives.

## GENERATE FAN ACTION, NOT JUST FAN ACQUISITION

Though many brands are rushing to embrace social media as a marketing strategy, many assume the key to success is quickly generating a sizable social footprint, as measured by the number of fans and followers they can gather across multiple social networks.

This approach mistakes the map for the territory. One million Facebook fans are not helpful to a brand if they are not engaged, whereas one thousand fans that share the same core values as the brand and who are willing to do, say, or buy something on the brand's behalf are extremely valuable. In fact, if a brand measures its success by the numbers of fans rather than their engagement, the dynamics of social media will work *against* them. When brands treat Facebook as yet another broadcast medium and Twitter like direct mail, they demonstrate a lack of understanding of social-media dynamics inciting rejection and consumer criticism. If a brand displays genuine engagement with the community, then that is the feeling that consumers will share with their friends and peers.

## THE BENEFITS TO BRANDS

By implementing the two groups of actions described here, corporations and their consumers will begin the journey from Me First to We First capitalism. Many may still question that the transition to We First capitalism will pay off, but there are numerous advantages.

The following is a powerful list of benefits that becoming a socially responsible company will deliver to any organization. I collectively call these benefits the "return on contribution"—or ROC—reflecting the shift from Me First's profit orientation to We First's focus on sustainability and social responsibility. These benefits apply to every aspect of the organization, including human resources, public relations, research and development, and the all-important profit and loss. Collectively they are the value proposition We First makes to corporations and their brands.

## HUMAN RESOURCES BENEFITS

From a human-resources standpoint, a responsible company is a magnet for dedicated employees, who become your first and best line of support and marketing. Satisfied employees who believe in their company are more motivated and passionate about work. Starbucks, for example, cites its salary policies and efforts to promote fair trade as critical reasons why their annual employee turnover is only 50 percent, compared with the usual industry standard of 200 percent. The reduced turnover saves the company $1,000 per lost employee in training costs.

## NIKE: THE COMPLEXITY OF CORPORATE SOCIAL RESPONSIBILITY

Engaging in social media and corporate responsibility does have some caveats. Nike, one of the world's best-known brands—and often considered among the most socially responsible—recently experienced how difficult even the most well-intentioned social efforts can be.

Nike made an agreement with the local government of Tokyo's fashionable Shibuya district to fund the redevelopment of a small park in its ward, Miyashita Park. The famous sports retailer had offered to spend $5 million to reconstruct the park, turning it into a pay-for-use rock climbing and skateboarding area. The company would also pay an annual fee of about $200,000 for the naming rights to the park for ten years. Local businesses backed the ward's plan.

As it turns out, however, Tokyo has thousands of homeless street people, and Miyashita Park was home to about 30 squatters, some of whom are artists. Park officials offered to help all of them find a new place to live, but the fact of Nike's involvement kicked the dispute up into a form of class war over who owns the rights to a park.

When word spread about the plan, anti-Nike grassroots activists, supporters of the homeless, and artists all around Japan picketed Nike's flagship store in Tokyo. The protests spread to other Nike stores around the world as activists used social media to rally the masses. One of the park's homeless artists blogged the events, and others used Twitter to update sympathizers. Our Planet TV filmed a documentary video and posted it to YouTube. Slowly but surely, the demonstrators' rallying cry "Just Doite" (a coincidental Japanese pun on Nike's famous slogan, meaning "Just move") transformed a local affair into a global battle. Sure enough, other consumers around the world began launching boycotts against Nike. As of this writing, Nike is proceeding with its plan to rebuild the park, but protesters remain on the construction site.

The Miyashita Park affair is a testament to the poverty that capitalism creates in the world, allowing millions of people to fall through the cracks of prosperity. Was Nike wrong in attempting to name and clean up the park, or were the squatters too entrenched in protecting the land they had come to consider their home? Unfortunately, tackling many of the planet's problems will force the same difficult choices, which can only be resolved through sincere and transparent partnerships among governments, nonprofits, and the private sector.[27]

Satisfied employees also become your most vocal word-of-mouth (WOM) advertisers, which translates into a stronger reputation and increased sales. Keep in mind that today's WOM now extends into all the social-media tools that employees use in their personal lives. A single happy employee sharing your brand's good deeds can connect with several hundred friends or colleagues, who in turn connect with hundreds more of their own. That same employee may also read or write blogs and comment on your company's innovative social outreach programs, or on the volunteering efforts he or she has completed under the auspices of the brand.

The 2010 Cone Cause Evolution Study provided numerous findings to back this up. For example, 76 percent of employees would like their companies to give them paid time off for volunteering, and 76 percent would like their company to help them find opportunities to do so. The survey concluded, "Just like consumers, employees want to feel vested in their employers' programs and are willing to roll up their sleeves to have an impact. For companies, the investment is well worth it. Employees who are very involved in their company's cause program are 28 percent more likely to be proud of their company's values and 36 percent more likely to feel a strong sense of loyalty than those who are not involved."[28]

## PUBLIC RELATIONS BENEFITS

From the PR perspective, corporations that commit to social responsibility earn consumer goodwill and strengthen their reputational value. For example, Holding Associates and its client sponsor, CoreBrand, KLD, examined how much of a brand's value is attributable to its socially responsible actions, and learned that a positive profile in this regard has a measurable impact on a company's value. Analyzing data gathered between 2003 and 2006, the study found that CSR was more responsible for increasing a company's value than other contributing factors such as advertising, market cap, and how that company competes in an otherwise flat market.[29]

> *Profits are not always possible when business tries to serve the very poor. In such cases, there needs to be another market-based incentive—and that incentive is recognition. Recognition enhances a company's reputation and appeals to customers; above all, it attracts good people to the organization.*
>
> —Bill Gates

## RESEARCH AND DEVELOPMENT BENEFITS

Socially responsible companies that attract consumers gain tremendous potential R&D benefits. A vast audience of customers becomes an ideation community to help with product development and marketing research, potentially saving millions of dollars that would have been spent on outside consultants or developers. The online thought-leadership platform TED, for example, enlisted its community to make its website and videos of speakers accessible in more than 40 languages. Wikipedia, founded by Jimmy Wales, was built by unpaid community members who have so far devoted the equivalent of 100 million man-hours of time to create and update its free content on a daily basis.[30]

## BOTTOM-LINE BENEFITS

Numerous studies have shown that socially responsible companies fare better according to traditional measures of success, such as stock appreciation. Ethisphere, an independent agency that ranks and rates companies according to strict criteria, performed a study of the 100 corporations it selected for its list of the World's Most Ethical Companies. The study found these firms to have outperformed the FTSE and the S & P 500 indexes, delivering, between 2005 and 2010, a 53 percent return on investment (ROI) to shareholders. Compare this with the FTSE 100 return of only about 15 percent and the S & P's 4 percent shareholder *loss* over the same period. Furthermore, Ethisphere pointed out benefits beyond stock price: "In addition to improving a company's bottom line, a strong ethics program has shown to lead to increased consumer loyalty, regulatory leniency in the event of a transgression, and stronger employee retention rates."[31]

Bottom-line success can no longer be viewed only in the narrow context of ROI. As the adoption of social media is rising, so is the range of tools and formulas by which brands need to begin examining the benefits to their bottom line. In fact, the returns on social-media marketing challenge conventional business measures, because they engender many new types of engagement that are as valuable as increased sales and stock appreciation.

For example, Brian Solis notes in his book *Engage!* that Best Buy measures ROI in terms of lower employee turnover; the National Association of Manufacturers measures the ROI of its blog by greater access to Capitol Hill; Dell measures the success of its IdeaStorm community in terms of lower support costs and the number of new ideas generated; and SeaWorld measures lower outreach costs as well as tickets sold.[32] Solis goes on to propose three formula categories that can be used to measure the success of a social-media campaign. All of these focus not on profits but on the measure of *increased influence* that a brand earns through the performance of a campaign. The three formulae are:

- *Volume:* Frequency and amplification of brand mentions (CPM—cost per impression)
- *Engagement:* Time spent with the brand either individually or as a community (CPE—cost per engagement)
- *Actions:* Activities that directly contribute to business health and profitability (CPA—cost per action)

Using parameters and variables like these, Altimeter Group found that the most engaged and best-performing brands for 2009 included Starbucks, Google, and Nike, all leaders in socially responsible business practices. But such measures will vary across networks and communities, and so will require comparative analysis to establish benchmarks among like brands.[33]

None of these new measures of success is intended to detract from the importance of profits. But any company looking to improve its bottom line can no longer deny the potential value of spreading prosperity. There are huge emerging markets throughout the world, a function of a growing global middle class. Research from Goldman Sachs and Morgan Stanley points to 70 million people worldwide who joined the middle class in 2009, with incomes ranging from $6,000 to $30,000, especially in the so-called BRIC countries of Brazil, Russia, India, and China.

Many multinational companies overlook the substantial business opportunities in Africa, where, according to new projections from the McKinsey Global Institute, just four groups of industries (consumer-facing industries such as retail, communications, and banking, plus infrastructure-related industries, agriculture, and resources) will be worth a combined $2.6 trillion in annual revenue by 2020.[34] Africa's consumer sector is growing *two to three times faster* than those of developed economies. Walmart, for one, has recognized this opportunity, recently offering to purchase the South African company Massmart, the holding company for a chain of 290 stores in 13 African countries that is the continent's leading retailer of general merchandise, home-improvement equipment, and supplies.

The demographics of the planet are rapidly changing. The former "First World" will soon be surpassed by the emerging world in terms of populations. A Nielsen study estimates that by 2020, there will be 1 billion new people on the planet, *only 3 percent of whom will be born in the developed countries;* the other 97 percent will come from undeveloped and emerging nations. The study noted that the World Bank estimates that 1.3 billion people will enter the middle class by 2020 in the developing economies of the world (where the "middle class" is defined as having at least one-third of their income left over after paying housing costs). Much of that money will be controlled by women, whose earned incomes will grow faster than those of men in the developing world. The study reminds companies that the middle class is typically the leading edge of change, as they are the demographic group with the education, motivation, and interest to adopt new products, especially new technologies.[35]

Add to these facts that the International Telecommunication Union has estimated that there will be 2 billion people connected to the Internet by the end of 2010, and that approximately 90 percent of the world already has access to mobile communication services that are offered in 143 countries. It projects that by 2015, half the world's population will be using a mobile phone.[36] Given this, the potential to grow and build profits is enormous if responsible corporations are willing to implement new strategies and business models based on more than short-term results.

All these studies suggest that building a future of prosperity where it is needed most can contribute enormously to enlarging a global middle class and creating opportunities for new business that will pay off in the short and long terms. At the same time, by integrating profit and purpose in their business plans, corporations can take advantage of the rise in social networking enabled by the billions of digital devices. In short, *the future of profit is purpose, not just because it is well intentioned but because it will be well received in an increasingly socially enabled world.*

## BECOMING A BRAND NATION

There is yet another benefit to the We First approach, and it is one that has never existed before. As brands become increasingly esteemed global citizens, they have the potential to attract millions of consumers around the world to their vision of a better future. These consumers, linked by shared values aligned with those of the brand, become loyal fans. For each advance the brand makes toward becoming a more responsible company or achieving social improvements, its fans spread the word across social networks, spurring new fans to join in.

This dynamic enables a new potentiality: The brands that are most successful under these terms can metaphorically become the equivalent of a *brand nation*.

Let me clarify what this means. A corporate brand nation is not a political organization, but rather a kinship of like-minded consumers throughout the world who believe in "their" brand and the vision it holds out for a better world. A brand nation is not measured by the size of its membership, but rather by the strength of its shared values. It is not defined by geographic boundaries, but by fluid brand lines that are constantly being redrawn to reflect shifting loyalties, platforms, and conversations. Facebook is perhaps the largest association of consumers ever to have been formed—its hundreds of millions of active members would make it one of the largest countries in the world.

What defines a brand nation is the *quality* of consumer loyalty and the *diversity* of its global consumers. In today's world, brands are properties with increasingly multinational markets. Their appeal is no longer based on geographic location or economic bracket. A low-income Millennial in Beijing covets the newest mobile phone, Nike sneaker, or Apple iPad as much as a Baby Boomer corporate executive in Boise, Idaho. Branding, in the sense of capturing audience affiliation and market share, has become globally directed. Even when addressing specific countries or cultures, companies are seeking to maintain a consistent brand voice and set of values.

Becoming a brand nation is the result of achieving the two groups of actions this chapter has described. As brands unilaterally adopt a global mindset and seek to attract more consumers to become partners in social transformation, they pass through seven stages of evolution on the way to becoming a brand nation. Each brand's path will differ for various reasons. For instance, a brand may have a visionary leader who can paint a picture of a better future but struggles to translate that vision and disseminate it across a global workforce. Sometimes employees are crying out for responsible social engagement, yet management will not listen. Or a brand may behave in different ways in different regions according to the conditions in which it finds itself operating, preventing it from becoming a unified brand nation.

As such, the evolution of a company into a brand nation is a gradual and complicated process, but it can be tracked on a stage-by-stage basis according to degrees of integration of We First values.

## STAGE 1: UNSUSTAINABLE CORPORATE SELF-INTEREST

This is the common state of organizations today, one that defines success purely in terms of monetary returns delivered to shareholders. These businesses may perform some philanthropy or cause-related marketing, but it is a small amount relative to pretax profits.

## STAGE 2: SELF-DIRECTED ENGAGEMENT

Many organizations are at this stage today and are just recognizing that change may be worthwhile. But more often than not, their social-outreach efforts are undertaken for public-image management, particularly when they have caught the media spotlight. They act out of fear, motivated by self-interest and the desire to avoid bad publicity. This practice not only strikes consumers as disingenuous; it also robs that brand of authentic outreach.

## STAGE 3: CORPORATE REFLECTION

In this stage, the leaders of a corporation begin to question some of their fundamental assumptions. One or two thought leaders have a vision for the company's future based on a more ethical or sustainable practice of capitalism.

## STAGE 4: CONSUMER-FACING SELF-INTEREST

At this level, the corporation starts to move into a higher level of responsible behavior and announces it through all the channels at its disposal. However, it does not yet realize that *all* outreach must be consistent with the brand narrative and be integrated internally before being communicated publicly. As such, consumers and employees experience a disconnection between what the company says it stands for and its behavior.

## STAGE 5: SELF-DIRECTED REFORM

In this stage, a corporation decides to transform not just its own brand image, but the world around it. It examines the definition of its brand—the core values, purpose, and consistency of messaging. The company makes a few serious changes, such as revising manufacturing processes, changing suppliers, imposing strict ethical standards on its workforce, and hiring new managers. Most of this is unseen by the public.

## STAGE 6: BRANDHOOD

At this stage, corporations embrace the need to share stewardship of their brand with their community. They realize they must offer transparency, accountability, and authenticity if they are to elevate their brand to the highest level. The brand begins to reach its stride as a leader in socially responsible corporate behavior. It gets high rankings from its employees as a place to work, and watchdog groups rate it highly as a responsible company. Influencers talk about the company constantly in their blog posts, tweets, and social networks. The company sponsors numerous philanthropic activities, but more importantly, it adopts a sustainable and socially responsible orientation in all that it does.

## STAGE 7: BRAND-NATION CONSCIOUSNESS

The brand has a dual-sided dynamic and dialogue under way with its consumers. It has struck the requisite balance between transparency and accountability for both good works and unavoidable mistakes. This level of self-awareness is shared at the board level and among employees. The company has a long-term vision of a better world that it seeks to bring into fruition. It does not respond to shareholders who clamor for bigger short-term profits because it puts the general good of the planet and all stakeholders above their myopic demands. The company's brands form a virtuous ecosystem that brings in strong revenues that provide shareholders with substantial returns. Its brand nation of consumers forms a synaptic network that is always communicating in support of not only its products but also its spirit and character, which becomes meaningful in their lives. The company's consumers are its biggest fans, more than willing to offer feedback, advice, and ideas for innovations. They want to see the company succeed because the brand is integral to the sustainability of capitalism and the well-being of the planet.

THE NOTION OF BRANDS AS NATIONS is not far-fetched. Social networks like Facebook are not literally nations, but they have employed similar language as a way to express the relationships and dynamics existing within them. For example, Facebook introduced a "Bill of Rights," called its user-policy page the "Facebook Governance" page, and held virtual town hall meetings to formulate its constitution, which included the "Freedom to Share and Connect," "Ownership and Control of Information," and "Fundamental Equality" for each person. More recently, it introduced its own currency, Facebook Credits, to be used in the sale of both real and virtual goods.

Google took on the same stature of a brand nation in 2010 when it announced it would shut down its censored online service in China. While most countries had yet to articulate their foreign policy for the digital age, Google acted like a nation by exercising its own. As New York University professor and author Clay Shirky stated at the time: "What forces Google to have a foreign policy is that what they're exporting isn't a product or a service, it's a freedom."[37]

The potential for popular brands to become brand nations is clear. Facebook is on its way toward 1 billion users, making it the most likely model for the dynamics at work between brands and consumers. But with mobile handsets rising to meet the world's exploding population, it's easy to imagine a virtual world inhabited by multiple brand nations comprised of loyal consumers. Such virtual corporate entities might exist with populations that effortlessly cross cultural, religious, and commercial divides, free from limits of time, distance, and geography. These brand nations have the potential to become major shapers of our future.

The evolution of brand nations is still in its infancy. It will experience many setbacks as brands learn to compete with one another in the virtual world and manage the commingling of their real and virtual identities. But if we add together the online reach of social-media companies like Facebook and Twitter; the off-line reach of companies like Procter & Gamble, Unilever, Coca-Cola, and Walmart; and the loyalty that companies like Apple, Nike, and Patagonia inspire, it's easy to imagine an Internet-enabled future populated by brand nations.

The next step is to imagine the power that such nations could wield. If we combine the impact of Starbucks's Shared Earth program, Walmart's Sustainability Index, Pepsi's Refresh Project, Patagonia's Footprint Chronicles, and Toyota's push for "Harmony between man, nature, and machine," one can envision how brand nations might become important drivers of global social change.

If we then stir into this mix the visionary leadership of CEOs like PepsiCo's Indra Nooyi, Nike's Phil Knight, Walmart's Mike Duke, and Procter & Gamble's Bob McDonald, plus the philanthropic examples set by the likes of Bill Gates, Warren Buffett, and Mark Zuckerberg—all of whom now donate to social change on a scale previously reserved for governments—there is good reason to believe corporate practices can evolve into We First capitalism.

Such changes are only possible due to the degree by which social media is democratizing information and marketing. As Marc Pritchard, global marketing and chief branding officer of Procter & Gamble, stated at the 2010 Association of National Advertisers' Masters of Marketing conference, "social media gives everyone a microphone," allowing everybody to be "part of the conversations about our brands," which is why "we are at the start of one of the most exciting eras in brand-building history."[38] Any company that declines to transform itself into a socially responsible corporate citizen building a better world will not only miss this opportunity but invite its own creative destruction.

## CHAPTER TAKEAWAYS

- At the core of We First is the principle that brands and consumers will find greater value in working together as a united force for change.
- Corporations must take some unilateral actions and accept a higher level of responsibility, accountability, and sustainable business practices and enlist leadership, embed purpose in strategy, engage employees and management, focus on sustainable business, build prosperity, and collaborate.
- Companies also need to solicit consumers as their partners in change efforts by building social capital, allowing consumers to co-create the brand, involving supporters in meaningful causes, giving consumers a chance to vote on the brand every day, and generating fan action.
- Shifting to We First principles delivers benefits to human resources, public relations, research and development, and the bottom line.
- As brands become increasingly esteemed global citizens and attract millions of consumers, they have the potential to become brand nations.

# 8 HOW CONSUMERS BUILD RESPONSIBLE BRANDS AND A BETTER WORLD

For thousands of years, everyone believed with total confidence that the sun revolved around the Earth. From ancient Greek civilization up through the Renaissance, every astronomer was able to confirm this, even if he had to resort to illogical mathematics to prove it.

Then along came Nicolaus Copernicus, who in 1543 posited that the Earth revolves around the sun. His conclusion was based on years of observation and mathematical calculations that proved beyond any doubt that the heliocentric (sun-centered) model was correct. He published a book announcing his scientific revolution, but those in power refused to listen. The Catholic Church excommunicated him and denounced his theories because they contradicted the "truths" of the Holy Scripture.

Astronomy remained in the dark ages until 1610, a full generation later, when Galileo Galilei performed further scientific observations that confirmed the heliocentric model. But he, too, was denounced and forced to recant his position. Twenty years later, he published his greatest work, *Dialogue Concerning the Two Chief World Systems,* in which he constructed a hypothetical Socratic debate between two philosophers to prove which planetary vision was more rational.

But advancing human knowledge was still out of the question. Galileo's one-time friend and ally, Pope Urban VIII, condemned the book and had the scientist put on trial for heresy in 1633. He was found guilty and sentenced to house arrest for the rest of his life. Galileo died in 1642, having furthered astronomy and mathematics more than any other human up to this point in history—but it hardly mattered. It wasn't until 1687 that Isaac Newton finally put the ancient, illogical view of the universe to rest.

Today, there is an equally significant paradigm shift under way—one that also involves a change in perspective about *what* exactly revolves around *what*. For centuries, corporations have been allowed to operate as if the world revolved around them. But now, owing to the state of affairs on our planet, respected thought leaders everywhere are waking up to the fact that corporations and the creation of wealth must instead revolve around our collective well-being.

Thankfully, this shift will not take 150 years, as it did in the era of Copernicus and Galileo. Through social media, consumers can now play the role of change agents—and they can reverse the dominant paradigm in perhaps as little as a decade or two. We can see this movement already gaining steam in the arenas of sustainability, recycling, climate change, and green technology, and we are now ready for more. This is the era in which consumers can accelerate a major transformation of capitalism using the tools of the digital age.

## SHIFTING PARADIGMS IN THE MODERN WORLD

It is not a fantasy to suggest that consumers have the capability to drive a major shift in corporate thinking and behavior in a relatively short period of time. The pace of technological change—adhering to Moore's law, which predicts the doubling of computer-chip speed and memory every two years—has correspondingly accelerated the ability of consumers and citizens to augment and share their awareness of the planet's dire condition. For each increase in the rate at which the Internet, social media, and mobile telephony speeds up knowledge transfer, there is an equivalent uptick in how fast human thought and action can function. In fact, this process is already under way, albeit in an unstructured, organic fashion. Technology is providing consumers with new tools that offer insights into corporate behavior, while many leading brands are reaching out to consumers with new value propositions using the web, social media, and mobile devices.

The interplay between technological infrastructure and knowledge superstructure has followed this pattern throughout human history. Every new information or communications technology has always triggered a major shift in thought that altered the course of human affairs. In the fifteenth century, Johannes Gutenberg's movable type led to easier and faster book publishing, which spread knowledge and learning throughout Europe, inspiring the Renaissance. In the 1600s and 1700s, advances in printing-press technology paved the way for inexpensive daily newspapers that kept the public informed with emerging ideas about natural rights and democracy. That public awareness eventually helped overthrow the political and social model of government based on the divine right of kings. Later on, the telegraph facilitated dissemination of the Manifest Destiny trope, which spurred the westward movement of millions of pioneers across the United States and has captivated the American psyche since the mid-1800s. And, of course, telephone, radio, and television have each contributed to embedding significant beliefs in the social consciousness of the twentieth century.

The combined consequence of the Internet, social media, and smartphones heralds what is potentially the greatest disruption of accepted belief systems in human history. This is because these tools accelerate the public's access to information, communication, and awareness on an unprecedented scale in terms of how many individuals can be reached, the number of ways they can be connected, and the amount of information they can access instantaneously. In accordance with Metcalfe's law that says the value of a network rises according to the square of the number of users, each of these portals hastens the process by which new models of thought can become popularly shared.

The significance of these digital tools cannot be underestimated. Through them consumers can inform themselves about the impact of reckless capitalism on the world and the dangers of their own overconsumption. At the same time, they empower consumers to exercise real leverage by holding companies accountable for their practices while offering new ways for them to partner with brands that support authentic change. And they provide the infrastructure and human connections crucial to spreading knowledge and new ideas throughout the world.

This chapter is the analogue to Chapter 7's message for corporations and brands. As the other half of the private sector, consumer power is the yin to the corporate yang; it helps balance the drive for profits with the need to fulfill the public good. But this cannot happen unless consumers accept their own responsibility as an equalizing and complementary force for change. They must begin taking constructive actions, individually and collectively, to raise social consciousness about the dangers we face in allowing capitalism to continue on the path it is on. My goal is to add some fresh perspective about why and how *consumers are now in a position to co-create—with corporations—the world we want to live in.*

As with corporations, there are many things consumers can do to get involved in social transformation, using their leverage both on- and off-line. As in the previous chapter, we can divide the actions consumers can take into two groups: one inwardly directed and one outwardly directed. The first set of recommendations focuses on critical shifts in thinking and behavior to change their own purchasing habits as well as how to use their influence. The second set discusses ways consumers can strengthen their collective impact through organized social activism.

## THE ROLE OF SOCIAL MEDIA

Before reviewing the actions consumers must take, let's look at how social media empowers consumers by awakening their collective social consciousness to the possibilities for change. This goes to the heart of how societal change occurs: via knowledge transfer. Social media derives its power, in large part, from the speed at which it can help people transfer knowledge and learn about new ideas. But our understanding of social transformation must go one step further than this if consumers are to understand why these tools can help them effectively achieve significant change in corporate behavior.

For most of human history, the ability to create new knowledge has been limited to a small number of highly educated people, and the ability to spread it around has remained largely in the hands of those in power. These two restrictions impeded the flow of new ideas that are the root of social transformation. The authoritarian control of knowledge and ideas—which always derives from a desire to preserve the status quo—still exists among many dictatorial regimes that practice print and digital censorship. Recall that the reason Google is censored in China is because its product represents not simply access to information, but access to freedom of thought.

In today's world, the Internet, social media, and smartphones disrupt those old barriers. These digital tools democratize information and knowledge, allowing individuals to develop expertise and share ideas easily. The Internet facilitates information search and capture, and provides the connectivity needed to disseminate content across the human landscape. Facebook founder Mark Zuckerberg estimates that the amount of information shared between people doubles every 12 to 18 months.

But the true potential of these digital tools goes even deeper. What empowers consumers using social media to change capitalism is the opportunity to raise the level of "cognitive dissonance." This term refers to the mental state of ambiguity that results when people are faced with two opposing ideas. When people live according to one worldview, such as believing that Me First free market capitalism is the only economic engine, and they encounter a new one, such as We First capitalism, it forces them to question their belief system. Working through that cognitive dissonance can lead them toward a new mindset.

Social-media thought leader Stephen Johnson characterizes the paradigm-change process as the product of exactly this type of public cognitive dissonance. He uses a four-stage model to show how social transformation evolves.

- *Stage 1:* People come into contact with a new idea and recognize it as different from their current worldview.
- *Stage 2:* People reframe their consciousness of that idea in juxtaposition to their current values.
- *Stage 3:* People experience cognitive dissonance between the new idea and the current worldview they hold, which creates a pressing desire to resolve it.
- *Stage 4:* Either people decide they believe in the new idea and change their behavior to align with it, or they reject the new idea and retrench themselves in their current beliefs.[1]

Social media is the perfect technology to create the conditions for cognitive dissonance, helping people to go through these four stages. By plugging tens of millions of people into communities organized around their values and concerns, it offers a shared space where consumers can enter into dialogue about the business practices they see around them. And by providing the infrastructure for millions of people to connect, social media has the power to launch new ideas into widespread public consciousness.

Social media is neutral and borderless. It bridges geographic and political boundaries, ethnicity, income brackets, and even language barriers. Glimpses of the global connectedness it can create have already appeared, such as during the aftermaths of major disasters like the 2004 tsunami in Indonesia, the 2010 earthquake in Haiti, the floods in Pakistan, the rescue of the Chilean miners, and the political revolutions in Tunisia and Egypt. We are obviously still far from achieving a fully interconnected planet, but we are well on our way. The 1 billion-plus computers, soon-to-be 10 billion mobile phones, rapidly rising Internet penetration rates, and mainstream adoption of social-media tools like Facebook and Twitter may soon turn the proverbial "six degrees of separation" into just three or even two degrees.

The democratizing force of social media is also facilitating new types of collaborations and cooperation that contribute to change. Wikipedia, for example, illustrates how people speaking 273 different languages around the world have coalesced around the notion that knowledge resides everywhere and should be available to everyone for free. Another example of cooperation is the rise in international consumer protests, such as those against Nestlé, Cadbury, Unilever, and BP in which people all around the world have participated. These illustrate how economic and social responsibility issues are increasingly relevant to consumers no matter where they are located.

In short, technology is rapidly enabling the creation of a unified, human-made synaptic network. Millions of people around the world can share ideas and opinions, circulate information, propose new models of thinking, and conceivably decide to collectively support a new mindset or worldview. Through this synaptic network, people can develop solutions and collaborate on actions to address the problems they see. Yet such a network must be more than a cultural curiosity, because *the alleged bliss of ignorance has now been replaced by the responsibility of awareness.*

## CAN SOCIAL MEDIA ACHIEVE SOCIAL TRANSFORMATION?

Social-media novices and critics have yet to buy into the power it hands to consumers. They frequently disparage Facebook and Twitter as little more than light-headed entertainment channels, silly tools that allow people to engage in mindless chatter about what they are watching on TV, which Starbucks they are at, or who is famous for those 15 minutes.

Malcolm Gladwell, a respected thought leader and author of *The Tipping Point, Blink,* and *Outliers,* is one such critic who questioned the activist value of social media in an essay in the *New Yorker* in late 2010 where he asserted that these platforms are ineffective tools for serious social transformation.[2] His article, "Small Change: Why the Revolution Will Not Be Tweeted," argued that social media creates little more than "weak ties" between people, as evidenced by the fact that Facebook users can have hundreds and even thousands of friends, most of whom they hardly know. "There is strength in weak ties," Gladwell admits, writing that the Internet is "terrific at the diffusion of innovation, interdisciplinary collaboration, seamlessly matching up buyers and sellers, and the logistical functions of the dating world." But, Gladwell then adds, "Weak ties seldom lead to high-risk activism." In comparison, he cites the strong ties to be found in the social disobedience of the civil rights movement of the 1960s, which required considerable mental strength and mutual commitment among the groups of black protesters who staged restaurant sit-ins and rallies, often under threats of violence and even death.

Other critics of social media have said that it allows people to practice "slactivism"—slacker activism—because it is easy to sign up on a fan page for a cause and do almost nothing. Gladwell commented that the very reason people are so willing to participate in online causes is because it asks so little of them: "Facebook activism succeeds not by motivating people to make a real sacrifice but by motivating them to do the things that people do when they are *not* motivated enough to make a real sacrifice."[3]

For Gladwell, another limitation of social media is that it lacks hierarchy. Without leaders, command structures, rules, and a single central authority, in his view, networks are crippled and ineffective. He writes, "The drawbacks of networks scarcely matter if the network isn't interested in systemic change—if it just wants to frighten or humiliate or make a splash—or if it doesn't need to think strategically. But if you're taking on a powerful and organized establishment you have to be a hierarchy."

There are certainly some hard truths here, but several mistakes negate such critiques of social media. Where the critics are right—and this is an important lesson for consumers—is that much of the current uses for social media do indeed focus on the weak ties between people, and it does enable too many instances of passive activism. If consumers want to empower themselves with enough force to change corporate behaviors, they need to change their use of social media. They must develop new strategies and tactics to engage people actively in causes. They need to merge online power with off-line activism to conduct coordinated, simultaneous campaigns in both the real and virtual worlds. And they need to find thought leaders who can inspire communities of people to take action—sometimes centralized, sometimes decentralized—but always with greater intent and commitment than we currently see.

The critics of social media also overstate its drawbacks. Doubters tend to paint all social media with a single derogatory brush, as if Facebook and Twitter were the only tools available. What's more, they assume the transformative potential of social media is limited to the worst excesses of its current practice, forgetting that the technology and the dynamics it enables among users will mature and grow in sophistication. To answer these critics and demonstrate how rich, diverse, and effective social media can be, here are six levels of potential empowerment it enables.

## LEVEL ONE

At the first level is one-to-one interaction, with individuals connecting with each other via Facebook, SMS, location-based services, or Twitter—and increasingly on smartphones, irrespective of time, distance, or delay. These platforms and tools are constantly integrating, so people can stay in seamless contact as they move between online networks or change locations in the real world.

## LEVEL TWO

At a second level, people use social media to form communities and congregate around shared values, be they their favorite brands, issues, or causes. Groups can be any size, from three people to millions. It is true that these groups can be forged with weak links only, but even those can drive a shift in awareness as weak links are still useful for learning and disseminating ideas to create cognitive dissonance. As Gladwell even admits in that same essay: "Our acquaintances—not our friends—are our greatest source of new ideas and information."

Nearly every major brand has begun to capitalize on consumer gravitation toward these online communities. Thousands of brands have set up their own Facebook fan pages, even multiple and regional pages, to build a community. As of this writing, Starbucks has more than 5 million fans, Skittles has 3.5 million, Zara has 1.5 million, and even *National Geographic* has about 500,000 fans. Many brands employ multiple Twitter streams to maintain dialogue with their consumers. But consumers are also capitalizing on communities, using their fan pages to comment on issues, lobby for causes, propose boycotts and "buycotts," argue political positions, and even create their own unofficial or even renegade versions of fan pages for brands they want to celebrate or punish.

## LEVEL THREE

At a third level are the connections between people across platforms, as conversations around shared values and ideas migrate from one network to another and amongst different groups. Critics fail to note that some of these conversations then extend into the real world, where people relay what they have learned to everyone around them, thus introducing the potential to introduce cognitive dissonance into the workplaces and homes of those who do not use social media. As Henry Jenkins, author of *Convergence Culture: Where Old and New Media Collide,* notes, "We do not live on a platform; we live across platforms. We choose the right tools for the right jobs. We need to look at the full range of tools a movement deploys at any given moment—including some old fashion ones like door-to-door canvassing, public oratory, and street-corner petitions, to understand the work which goes into campaigns for social change."[4]

This diversity of platforms and their shifting user base is precisely why brands have so much trouble keeping track of consumer sentiment. In using multiple platforms for their conversations, consumers often reconstitute themselves into different groupings that espouse different feelings. But many brands continue to think of consumer sentiment as if it were monolithic, which is why reputation-management tools are at a premium today.

## LEVEL FOUR

The fourth level of social media extends beyond the consumer-led platforms into the dialogues that go on between consumers and brands. We see this increasingly happening in Twitter streams between brands and consumers and on websites, like that of Pepsi's Refresh Project. These are spaces where consumers have the ability to publish, curate, and distribute their own content, which can either support or undermine brands, but also where brands have the ability to reach out to consumers.

## LEVEL FIVE

At the fifth level, social media serves as an interface between the private sector and institutions like government or nonprofits. An inspiring example is Lance Armstrong's Livestrong Foundation, which has built the largest Twitter following of any healthcare-oriented organization. Armstrong himself has more than 2.6 million Twitter followers, putting him in the top 30 Twitter leaders. But more importantly, the foundation's CEO, Doug Ulman, has 1 million followers who value his daily tweets about what the foundation's support is doing for cancer patients. In an interview in *Fast Company,* Ulman praised the power of social media to inspire activism for nonprofits. "Social media has changed the not-for-profit world forever," he said. "It used to be how big your [mailing and email] database is. Now it doesn't matter. I'd rather have 10,000 people who are passionate than 3 million who aren't engaged."[5]

## LEVEL SIX

The sixth level of social media is the most complex and involves the commingling of the virtual and real worlds. This refers not just to consumers having online conversations with brands, but to the entire range of parallel universes constructed by social games and virtual worlds in which consumers and brands now interact. For example, McDonald's, H & M, MTV Networks, and Volvo now sell their virtual goods in Zynga's social game Farmville, and more than 1,200 brands advertise within the virtual world of Second Life. The distinction between real and virtual is now so seamless that consumers can earn credit in the virtual world to spend in the real one—and vice versa. This is a level of interaction between brands and consumers that cannot exist without social media.

IN CREATING THESE SIX LEVELS OF ENGAGEMENT, social media provides a complex and rich infrastructure perfect for the activist processes of social transformation, which include information acquisition and knowledge development, transfer, and sharing; ideation and thought leadership; empathy and emotional connection; and the spread of credible ideas that inspire cognitive dissonance. These tools are accessible to nearly everyone, available 24/7, and are infinitely scalable, real-time, and free.

Consumers are clearly in the early stages of adopting all six levels of social media for their activism. But it is progressing quickly, as growing numbers of consumers and citizens are employing social media to publish and distribute ideas, gather audiences, and organize real-world activism, such as protests and demonstrations, boycotts, buycotts (such as those practiced by Carrotmobs), and flash mobs. Twitter cofounder Evan Williams summarized this power in an almost tweetlike format when he responded to Malcolm Gladwell's essay by simply saying, "If you can't organize, you can't activate."[6]

Meanwhile, the other Twitter cofounder, Biz Stone, commented, "'Small Change' dismisses leaderless, self-organizing systems as viable agents of change. A flock of birds flying around an object in flight has no leader yet this beautiful, seemingly choreographed movement is the very embodiment of change. Rudimentary communication among individuals in real time allows many to move together as one—suddenly uniting everyone in a common goal. Lowering the barrier to activism doesn't weaken humanity, it brings us together and it makes us stronger."[7]

No one is suggesting that activism needs to be aggressive. In many ways, peaceful change is the ultimate benefit that social media can offer—to endow millions of people with enough leverage to create change without any violence. With social media, consumers don't need to storm the doors of an irresponsible company; they can simply use Facebook and Twitter to coerce its cooperation. If you look back at Gladwell's essay, he in fact admits that social media is a great tool if consumers just want to "frighten or humiliate or make a splash"—which are often perfectly sufficient actions to damage a company's reputation and shame them into changing their business practices.

Finally, social media is being used in high-stakes activism. In a response to Gladwell, for example, thought leader Maria Popova, blogger and editor of *Brain Pickings,* reminds us that there are numerous citizens around the world who have become "digital refugees" because they tried to use social media to organize democratic protests in countries like China, Uzbekistan, Moldova, Tunisia, Egypt, and Yemen. To prevent their ideas from reaching the larger public, their governments responded using censorship or cyberattacks to shut down their Internet access, as well as putting many of them under house arrest or in prison.[8]

Throughout the world, Twitter has become an important channel for political dialogue. In 2010, all three Brazilian presidential candidates used Twitter to publicize their platforms. The president of Ecuador used Twitter to notify citizens of a state of emergency following political unrest. Russian president Dmitry Medvedev has a Twitter account, as does the Office of the President of South Korea.[9] And in the United States, numerous politicians, including the infamous Sarah Palin, use Twitter to communicate their political positions and motivate their publics.

Even in China, where Google is tightly controlled and Twitter is completely blocked, people have nevertheless found ways to go around the digital barriers. An article in *The Atlantic* published just after the Chinese dissident writer and political prisoner Liu Xiaobo won the 2010 Nobel Peace Prize cited Hu Yong, a professor of Internet Studies at Peking University, as saying that Twitter "invites new possibilities for reshaping China's authoritarian regime." Yong goes on to describe a process he calls "micropolitics," in which literally, bit by bit, the open exchange of information on Twitter helps "push forward real change."[10]

Above all, critics of social media fail to understand its most important power—*its ability to connect people and allow them to show how they care about what happens in this world, and to exercise their innate human empathy.* The true force of social media is in how it can thus amplify cognitive dissonance and initiate the necessary exchanges online and off-line that introduce ideas and a new reality to people around the world.

It is therefore premature to throw our hands up in the air and dismiss social media on the basis of a limited profile of its usage today. Gladwell is right, however, to argue we cannot allow social media to remain a technology used largely to communicate only trivial information. Social media is neutral and should be put to work in the service of building a better world. To that end, it is important to look to the positive role that technology can play and to see how its uses will be increasingly oriented toward meaningful ends.

---

### THE PROTEST POWER OF SOCIAL MEDIA

The political revolutions in Tunisia and Egypt in January 2011 have confirmed that social media empowers social transformation. Although Malcolm Gladwell continued to defend his *New Yorker* essay after the two popular uprisings, reaffirming that, in his opinion, "people protested and brought down governments before Facebook was invented," the events in both countries provide several valuable lessons that bolster the arguments this book has made about the power of social media to build a better world.[11]

1. *Social media provides the communication channel that concerned citizens use to share information and form a community where they can bond and express their opinions.* In Tunisia, the rebellion was launched after a fruit vendor burned himself to death in protest of police actions. This led to public demonstrations that were recorded on cell phones, posted on YouTube, and shared on Facebook. In Egypt, a Facebook page created to honor Khaled Said, a citizen who had been brutally beaten and killed by the police, became the focal point around which 470,000 "fans" organized their dissidence. A YouTube video about his murder was viewed by more than 500,000 people, fueling widespread public outrage.[12]

2. *Social media helps connect thought leaders and activists to ordinary citizens, rapidly expanding the network of people who become willing to take action.* In Egypt, the Facebook page for Mr. Said and YouTube videos allowed human rights activists to connect to the population at large. This

is what I have described as the spread of cognitive dissonance. Brian Solis called it the "density" of connections, writing, "If unity is the effect, density is the cause."[13] Similarly, Stowe Boyd wrote, "Ideas spread more rapidly in densely connected social networks. So tools that increase the density of social connection are instrumental to the changes that spread. . . . And, more importantly, increased density of information flow (the number of times that people hear things) and of the emotional density (as individuals experience others' perceptions about events, or 'social contextualization') leads to an increased likelihood of radicalization: when people decide to join the revolution instead of watching it."[14]

3. *Social media forces the transparency of information and makes it nearly impossible to hide the truth.* In Egypt, the police attempted to cover up the killing of Mr. Said, but cell phone photos of his beaten face appeared on the Internet and witnesses posted contrary accounts on YouTube. Throughout the 18 days of protests that toppled the Mubarak regime, a steady flow of YouTube videos and photos caught using phone cameras told the true story of police violence against protesters, the arrest of journalists, and the aggression of pro-government supporters.

4. *Social media is invaluable as a tactical tool to organize people and schedule events.* The first widespread Egyptian demonstration in Tahrir Square was launched via a posting on the Facebook fan page for the deceased Mr. Said inviting all Egyptians to protest on January 25, 2011. From that post spread the widespread use of Twitter messages, Facebook posts, blogs, email, and SMS to disseminate the need for protest until the Egyptian government shut down the Internet.

5. *Social media helps globalize problems and synchronize our common human reactions and emotions about them.* Social media creates both strong and weak links, which are not opposites but rather complementary dynamics to spread ideas, empathy, and coordinated actions. The first uprising in Tunisia inspired that in Egypt, which then inspired others in Jordan, Syria, Algeria, and Iran, while garnering the empathy of the wider free world. As sociology professor Zeynep Tufekci put it, "Real change will come only if we can make friends we care about everywhere and we bridge ties that cover the world in a web of common humanity."[15]

The events in Tunisia and Egypt are proof positive of the strong functional capacities that social media gives consumers to push back against socially irresponsible corporate behaviors that frustrate or outrage them.

## CHANGES IN CONSUMER BEHAVIOR

To transition from Me First to We First capitalism, consumers need to begin by changing their own behaviors. This includes altering not only their consumption levels and purchasing habits, but also their investing. Change must begin with each consumer assessing the direct impact he or she can have on those businesses he or she supports. Using social media, consumers can then seek to disseminate the information they learn and the tools they encounter so as to encourage others to practice similar mindfulness.

These actions are crucial, because it will almost certainly be up to consumers to take the lead to improve corporate policies and behaviors. The impact of thousands, if not millions, of consumers altering their purchasing and investing habits to reward socially responsible companies and punish irresponsible ones is the only way for their message to reach the brands' bottom line. To build momentum, consumers must organize themselves and begin using their off-line power and online connections to demonstrate what they care about. They should also look to support as much as possible the small regiment of corporations led by forward-thinking CEOs, whose leadership will be invaluable in establishing models of responsible corporate behavior for other companies to follow.

### PRACTICE MINDFUL AND SOCIALLY RESPONSIBLE CONSUMERISM

The most immediate way consumers can reclaim their power over Me First capitalism is to transform their own shopping habits. Of course, the current economic conditions have already put a damper on excessive consumption, and many families are rediscovering simpler pleasures. But consumers still need to become savvier about why they consume and how corporations market to them. They need to be willing to question offers and advertising intended to arouse their desire based on envy or the allure of power or wealth—and to reject purchasing goods that do not support their values.

This is not to suggest that austerity is the answer. A prosperous economy still needs mindful consumerism. Not only do millions of jobs depend on it, but seeking comfort and pleasure are natural human inclinations. But our consumer desires need to be counterbalanced by responsible behaviors that generate sustainable business practices. Through the exercise of our wallets, consumers can powerfully influence how companies make their products, how they practice business, and even how an entire industry functions.

## THE MANY USES OF SMARTPHONE APPLICATIONS

The ways for consumers to use mobile applications are growing daily. Here are just a few of the purposes for which technology companies have created apps.

### CHECKING IN FOR GOODNESS

Checking into stores on Facebook Places or Foursquare to win discount coupons, badges, and mayorships has already proven popular, but imagine the possibilities that checking in for *goodness* can achieve. For example, why not have apps that make checking in at highly socially responsible businesses worthy of special "cause" badges? What about apps that reward points, stamps, or mayorships for civic engagement, such as volunteering at charities? Why not use the badge reward system for more meaningful purposes?

### FINDING GREEN BUSINESSES

Apps such as Yelp and Around Me help us find the usual businesses (restaurants, coffee shops, hotels), but Greenopia has converted its print guides to green living into an app that lets consumers find environmentally sound businesses anywhere in the United States.

### NING FOR RESPONSIBLE PRODUCTS

There are increasing numbers of apps to help consumers learn about the goodness profile of a product and its producer. They can find out where the item was produced, how far it traveled, its chemical contents, carbon footprint, and full life-cycle analysis. Other apps are being developed so consumers can find locally produced goods, including fruits and vegetables, household goods, books, and even electronics.

### GAZING THROUGH AN ECO LENS

Augmented-reality apps offer huge potential. We may soon be able to identify green-rated businesses, LEED-certified buildings, or greenhouse gas emissions through the screen on our smartphones. Using smart meter technology, we could point the camera's lens at a neighborhood and see which homes are utilizing energy the most efficiently.

The tools of social media are already allowing consumers to shop more consciously. Dozens of websites help weed out wasteful or poorly made products. It's never been easier to get information about companies that are exposed for having unhealthy, unsustainable, or unethical practices. Websites like brandkarma.com help consumers research and analyze a brand's "social responsibility footprint" by displaying the aggregate of a company's behavior on a number of qualities, including its carbon emissions, treatment of employees, energy usage, and its overall impact on the environment. Applications like GroceryIQ enable shoppers to share their grocery lists and recommend to each other socially responsible and environmentally friendly products. All it takes is one consumer to do the research to pass on information to hundreds of other shoppers. Consumers can also avail themselves of dozens of watchdog agency reviews, independent rating systems, as well as the recommendations from friends and followers in their networks.

Private shopping clubs are another new online creation organized around socially conscious buying. For example, the Collective is a private online community that aims to connect socially conscious consumers with sustainable brands and causes. Launched by BBMG, a New York integrated marketing agency, the company intends to build a community of 2,000 socially conscious elite consumers who are interested in co-creating the policies, practices, products, and cause-marketing efforts of a variety of socially responsible companies.[16] More consumers might look into joining or starting one of these enterprises.

Without doubt, smartphones, location-based services, and augmented reality technologies are the frontline of the consumer-led revolution in buying habits. With mobile data usage predicted to grow by a factor of 40 within five years, instant product information and social communication will create ever more powerful capabilities to reward and punish brands. These tools will give consumers deep, real-time information right in the shopping aisle about thousands of products and the companies that make them. There is also a new generation of QR code readers that introduces multimedia and two-way conversations to further inform the shopping experience. For example, these tools let consumers tag items as green based on their own experience, rather than on what the company claims.

All these advances are giving rise to what many are calling "social shopping," in which consumers use their networks and communities to share opinions and seek advice from their friends, as well as interact directly with brands to express their satisfaction or scorn. Such consumer-led actions are invaluable in creating change. Collective consumer pressure has already transformed numerous industries including household cleaning products, the auto industry, and now the big-box stores and major multinationals. Keep in mind that changing the practices of one major brand can also impact its competitors—such that consumers can literally alter entire sectors. What's needed now is for consumers to apply the same pressures to other industries such as financial services, energy, agriculture, food production, forestry, and healthcare. Armed with the right technologies and intentions, consumers can truly help to move capitalism into a new age.

*Consuming is a story about us, people, being persuaded to spend money we don't have on things we don't need to create impressions that don't last on people we don't care about.*

—Tim Jackson, economist

## MERGE SOCIALLY RESPONSIBLE SHOPPING ONLINE AND OFF

There are now more opportunities than ever before for consumers to turn *all* their shopping into responsible buying, even among the most traditional mass retailers. Even Walmart, for example, is becoming a leader in providing consumers with products made by companies committed to sustainable practices. But many other off-line solutions for socially responsible shopping exist.

One of these is to shop as much as possible at certified B Corporations— companies that have passed a rigorous set of standards established by B Labs, a nonprofit organization set up to provide an alternative to the traditional C Corporation. The idea behind B Corps is to create a new type of business that is free from the binds of C-corporation legal status that forces them to honor maximizing profit as their primary responsibility to shareholders and to avoid real transparency in their communications. In contrast, the governance documents of B Corporations must clearly state how they will take into account the interests of their community, employees, and the environment. They must also meet comprehensive social and environmental standards. According to co-founder Jay Coen Gilbert, more companies are opting to become B Corps because they respect sustainable business practices and want to help create change in the world.

For consumers who want to demonstrate their own social responsibility, they can conduct their business at any of the more than 330 certified B Corps that exist in about 25 states. The B Corp status is recognized in Maryland and Vermont as a legal form of incorporation, and more states are expected to follow. (Consumers can find a list of certified B Corporations at the B Labs website, www.bcorporation.net.)

*Today, social purpose is the new social status.*

—Edelman Goodpurpose survey, 2009

## GET INVOLVED IN SOCIAL ENTREPRENEURSHIP

Another action consumers can take to effect social transformation is to get involved in social entrepreneuring. The recalcitrance of traditional corporations to change has spurred a vast movement among concerned citizens to find new ways to circumvent Me First capitalism. Driven by passion and a strong vision to change how a sector or an industry works, many people have simply opted to establish their own companies or organizations to provide products and services where they're needed rather than awaiting assistance from government and traditional aid organizations. Their efforts often take the form of a non-profit or low-profit company that employs new technologies and creative solutions to leverage resources and supply markets faster, better, or at lower costs than traditional corporations.

An inspirational example of one individual's foray into social entrepreneurship is the story of Scott Harrison, founder of charity:water, which supplies fresh water to impoverished areas around the world. After spending ten years promoting nightclubs and fashion events, Harrison decided he wanted to contribute to the world and so volunteered his skills as a photojournalist working alongside doctors and surgeons in a humanitarian relief effort in Africa. During that stint, his eyes were opened when he saw the massive lack of clean water in so many villages he visited. Returning to the United States, he launched his own philanthropy in 2006, with a ten-year goal of providing at least 100 million people with clean water. To boost the charity's funding, he also created the Well, an online registry that people can tell their friends to donate to in lieu of a gift whenever they are celebrating a special occasion. Charity:water surpassed supplying its first million people in 2009, just three years after its founding, and is now nearing 1.5 million people.[17]

The fact that so many people are becoming involved in social entrepreneurship speaks volumes about both the frustration and the creativity existing in the world. Recognizing that the corporate market will not bow to change if all we can do is chastise the players, people are taking it upon themselves to educate, fund, and support new kinds of endeavors to supply basic services and spread prosperity in the world.

There are vast opportunities for anyone interested to get involved in social entrepreneurship. College students can join Net Impact, where they can learn about using business to drive change in the world. They can apply to the Compass Fellowship, a program that accepts 15 students at five American universities (and expanding soon to more campuses) who learn personal and business skills and receive mentoring to develop new ideas for socially oriented businesses. College students can also apply to Sparkseed.com, founded by Mike Del Ponte, which selects ten social entrepreneurs each year and provides them with seed money and six months of "high impact" support in the form of mentoring, skills training, technical support, and networking. At the graduate level, many business schools offer courses in social entrepreneurship, some of which are available online.

People with good ideas can also apply to receive seed funding from several organizations that help social entrepreneurs. One of these is Ashoka, which provides three-year stipends that give social entrepreneurs a start at launching a new service or business. Founded in 1981 by Bill Drayton, Ashoka believes "that the most effective way to promote social change is to invest in social entrepreneurs with innovative solutions that are sustainable and replicable, both nationally and globally." Anyone can become a member of Ashoka through a small donation and begin connecting with its network of social entrepreneurs.[18]

Then there is One Billion Minds, whose mission is to link people together in solving global problems. Members participate by offering to work on specific problems listed on the group's website, and mentors help would-be social entrepreneurs develop an idea and find a team to implement it. Their Fellows program invites individuals or companies to "adopt" a project and take it to fruition through advocacy, innovation scouting, and innovation support.

Consumers can also tap into one of several online resources to launch their own charitable project. For example, Crowdrise, an endeavor founded by actor Edward Norton, merges social networking with philanthropy by enabling people to tap their friends and the site's entire community to fund a charitable cause of their choice. Visitors to the site can list and publish a charitable project, then send their friends to the web page to donate to it. Similar to the Pepsi Refresh project, the website ranks the listed charities by popular vote, and the leading ones are awarded points toward prizes.

If you are a business owner, you can participate in social entrepreneurship by implementing your own ideas to generate contributions to causes. Here are a few examples of what creative companies have done:

- *Install an ATM that donates.* A company called Choose Change has created ATMs that retail locations can install. Users pay a small $2 transaction fee, half of which goes to the consumer's choice of one of eight charities listed on the screen.[19]
- *Give customers a chance to participate in selecting a monthly charity.* British grocery chain Waitrose inaugurated a program in

2010 that lets its customers nominate charities to receive grants. Each month, a committee from each store selects three possible charities to sponsor, and the parent company grants the store £1,000. Customers receive a token each time they shop, which they then deposit into one of the three containers. At the end of the month, the piles of tokens determine the proportion of cash that each charity will receive.[20]

- *Coordinate a donation with Foursquare.* In 2010, Foursquare began offering a contribution to the Gulf Coast oil-spill recovery for every member who checks in at selected locations.

The social entrepreneurship movement today is attracting a wide range of creative thinkers who want to use their talents to make a difference in the world. A new study from Sweden's Uppsala University predicts that Facebook will also enable more social entrepreneurship by allowing anyone to start and run their own businesses. The study's author, Håkan Selg, a doctoral candidate in business, notes that "a realistic effect of social media is that many costs of running operations will decline in the long run." He points out that Facebook itself could become the business platform for new social entrepreneuring endeavors.[21]

For those seeking help, there are many resources. The Social Enterprise Alliance offers assistance to early-stage entrepreneurs who need inspiration and knowledge to launch their enterprises, as well as helping mid-stage and advanced practitioners network with their peers. It also serves individual or group investors looking to fund social enterprises. Meanwhile, the Hub is an incubator for social entrepreneurs around the world that offers workspace and meeting rooms, special lectures, meet-ups, and events all geared for people who want to work in social innovation. They have offices in several cities in North America, Europe, Israel, and South Africa.

Finally, numerous for-profit companies are sponsoring competitions focused on social entrepreneurship to solve global problems. For example, Sony and the World Wildlife Fund cohosted a contest called Open Planet Ideas, in which anyone can propose solutions to global problems that employ Sony's state-of-the-art electronics, including wireless systems, presence-sensing systems, peer-to-peer software, and so on. *The Economist* magazine and Innocentive sponsor an ongoing open-source competition for "seekers" and "solvers": Any individual or corporation can propose a problem for solvers to work on, with a cash prize offered to the winning ideas.

The sum of all these social entrepreneurship efforts reflects a powerful trend away from large multinational corporations back toward human-sized enterprises where empathy, creativity, and personal passion—not profits—drive solutions. The monumental rise of grassroots social entrepreneurship proves that people are recognizing the value of using digital tools to create solutions that would never be executed in the traditional corporate world.

## EXERCISE INVESTOR LEVERAGE

Consumers also need to use their own wealth for socially responsible investing (SRI) at a level far greater than they have ever done in the past. Specialized SRI mutual funds have been available for more than a decade—climbing in number from 55 in 1995 to 260 today—but the total dollars invested in them is still small.[22] According to the Social Investment Forum, the estimated dollar value of social investing in 2010 is only about $3.07 trillion out of the $25.2 trillion in the U.S. investment marketplace, only about 12 percent of all investments.[23] Although these funds are valuable for launching new socially responsible companies working in sustainable industries, they are far from enough to compel traditional corporations to change.

Investing experts have suggested two reasons why SRI remains so low. First, the vast majority of individual investors have been wearing a profit-seeking hat for too long, failing to understand that their desire for profits is precisely what led to the chaos we face today. In other words, too many investors have seen themselves strictly as shareholders, rather than as *stakeholders* in a larger socioeconomic system—and it is time to change that misconception.

But the second reason should provide an even stronger reason to invest in socially responsible companies. If SRI comprises less than 12 percent of all U.S. investing, it means that those who own the other 88 percent of investments have virtually no motivation to move their investments into socially responsible companies. The system works for them, so there is no incentive to change it. The only way to alter this balance of investment power is for more consumers to invest in socially responsible funds, giving them a fighting chance to make a difference.

Certainly the amount of wealth controlled by average consumers may never be enough to match the investment dollars coming from the top 1 percent of the population. But if more people were to invest their wealth in SRI funds, it will, at the minimum, help launch new companies led by passionate and visionary CEOs who are eager to demonstrate that profit and purpose can be merged. These startups, such as those we see emerging today in the auto industry, can then begin to build a degree of leverage over large corporations, which will increasingly find themselves competing on a wider playing field.

> *Saving civilization is not a spectator sport. Each of us must push for rapid change. And we must be armed with a plan outlining the changes needed.*
>
> —Lester Brown, visionary and futurist

### CONSUMER ACTIONS FOR SOCIAL ACTIVISM

Imagine a world in which *all* consumers took independent action to become mindful, socially responsible shoppers, became involved directly or indirectly in social entrepreneurship and volunteering, and invested their assets exclusively in supporting responsible corporations and new socially oriented startups.

Not so hard to imagine, is it? Especially in light of the myriad opportunities listed above. So why hasn't it already happened—or, better yet, how can we make it happen?

At the root of the problem is the assumption that every consumer is willing to participate. The problem we face is that too many people are still too apathetic about change. To persuade corporations to become socially responsible, we need to encourage consumers by the millions to begin using their leverage to push for a better world.

The following actions exemplify the types of activities that consumers must engage in to become true agents working for social transformation. First, concerned consumers need to inspire others using all the tools of social media at their disposal. Second, they must create new ways to engage corporations in dialogue about how they might reengineer their strategies, business practices, and corporate values to contribute to the greater good.

### USE SOCIAL MEDIA TO INSPIRE ACTIVISM

Without a doubt, the use of social media is today overly devoted to trivial chatter. But such chatter is not useless; it provides and maintains the connective tissue of relationships that can be activated for social change. In other words, right now, social media is merely underemployed, not unemployable. As social-media adoption rises across the globe and its tools become more sophisticated, it will clearly emerge as an unprecedented change agent.

## OVERCOMING THE REALITY OF CONSUMER ANTIPATHY AND APATHY

In light of our dire economic situation and long history of corporate irresponsibility on social and environmental fronts, it is surprising that consumer surveys do not result in nearly unanimous support for change. The 3rd annual Edelman Goodpurpose survey in 2009 confirms that the majority of global consumers support corporate involvement in social-responsibility initiatives. But if you look at the inverse of the statistics, it has to make you wonder about the remaining portion of the population.

- 56 percent believe the interests of society and the interests of businesses should have equal weight in business decisions—*but 44 percent don't.*
- 66 percent believe it is no longer enough for corporations to simply give money away to a good cause; they need to integrate good works into their day-to-day business—*but 34 percent don't.*
- 59 percent have a better opinion of corporations that integrate charitable causes into their business—*but 41 percent don't.*
- 64 percent of consumers say they expect brands today to do something to support a good cause—*but 36 percent don't.*[24]

These results may reflect people who philosophically disagree that corporations owe any social responsibility to society. Another portion of respondents may not feel strongly one way or the other. But it also means that consumers in favor of We First capitalism need to focus harder on encouraging all these other voices, especially through social media, to reconsider their positions and join in their efforts at change.

The reason for this is that one of the most powerful characteristics of social media is that it opens the door for anyone and everyone to participate in social activism in many ways. Before the Internet, consumers could play only a limited number of roles in the brand-consumer relationship. They could be willing customers, private critics (talking to their friends about a product), or a public reporter (such as writing reviews in the traditional media). But today, through social media, consumers can participate to a far greater degree while reaching a potentially large audience of hundreds, if not thousands of other consumers. Consider all these roles consumers can now play:

- *Thought leaders and content creators.* Every consumer can originate ideas and present his or her content through emails, newsletters, websites, webinars, blogs, videos, tweets, and Facebook pages.

- *Distributors and syndicators.* Every consumer can spread ideas to other people in many ways: forwarding emails, equipping his or her blog with an RSS feed, retweeting links to content, posting a comment, or sharing content via Digg, FriendFeed, Google Buzz, or Paper.li—and asking others to do the same.
- *Curators.* Every consumer has the ability to use the same tools to collect, cull, and curate content to promote ideas and values important to his or her friends, followers, or fans.
- *Proponents and amplifiers.* Every consumer can demonstrate support within and across his or her social networks for an idea or a change initiative advanced by a company, a nonprofit, or a government relative to laudable brand CSR work, good work performed by nonprofit communities, or effective government initiatives that deserve recognition.
- *Disrupters.* Using the same tools and strategies, every consumer can challenge the motives, consequences, or simply the process and transparency of a company's actions, discrediting it if necessary.
- *Organizers of virtual and real-world activities.* Every consumer can help organize real-world or online activities using livecasting or streaming platforms, such as UStream, Justin.tv, or Skype; to host webinars or meetings, or to announce and organize boycotts or buycotts.

Consumers can choose any of these levels and modes of participation according to how they prefer engaging. Given that more than 90 percent of the American population and those of most Western nations are connected to the Internet, the door is open for potentially hundreds of millions of people to get involved in promulgating new ideas and taking part in social transformation. The availability of communication paths means that almost every individual can contribute to change efforts.

So what are the issues that people can get involved in over social media? What ideas can individuals contribute to as thought leaders, producers, distributors, or organizers? The next few sections provide suggestions for the types of public discussions the world needs to build a better future. These are the topics consumers must begin addressing themselves, as well as clamoring for answers from the corporations of the world.

*The role of Twitter is to allow people to share information that is meaningful to them in any way they want.*

—Evan Williams, cofounder, Twitter

## LOBBY FOR TRANSPARENT CAPITALISM

Consumers need to use social media to disseminate three critical economic issues into broad public awareness. Few people are interested in understanding the full complexity of economics, but through social media, those who can act as thought leaders on these issues can align themselves with those who enjoy acting as distributors, proponents, and organizers, and together, they can help educate the masses. The three issues detailed below relate to how we have allowed capitalism to dictate the lopsided ways in which economic progress and corporate profits are measured—and our need to change these methods.

### Ethonomics

Ethonomics is the field of study in which ethics is applied to economics. To date, ethonomics has been a topic of discussion only among legislators, politicians, and captains of industry, but it needs to become the subject of a much larger public discussion. Ethonomics asks us to examine the values expressed in specific types of economic decisions that corporations and consumers take. For example, if capitalism is based on creating value out of goods and services, we need to reflect on what are the economic values we want to live by. This is the focus of questions such as:

- What are fair tax rates that should be applied to people at different economic levels?
- Why does one country ask its citizens to pay one tax rate when another country asks its citizens to pay another?
- How much is a fair salary for a CEO compared to the average employee of that company?
- How do we justify short-term profits in the face of long-term damages?
- How can corporations balance the return investors or shareholders need to compensate for their risks with the social and environmental problems caused by excess and greed?
- What are the fair actions that corporations can take to minimize their taxes versus unjust loopholes to avoid paying their fair share?

In a capitalist society, questions like these need to be raised publicly and debated, much as we study history and civics to become better citizens. Business schools and MBA programs need to expose their students to ethonomics and infuse them with greater sensitivity to and knowledge of the value choices they will have to make in their future careers. Consumers and shareholders need to push back on corporate boards to drive ethonomic considerations into their judgments. For this to happen, consumers need to make it clear that such considerations are important to them. If we don't insist, the current divide between the ethical practice of economics and free market capitalism will continue. It's a choice that all consumers must make—whether they want to be engaged citizens invested in their well-being and the planet, or if they are satisfied to remain powerless.

> *It is not what a lawyer tells me I may do, but what humanity, reason and justice tell me I ought to do.*
>
> —Edmund Burke, statesman and philosopher

### The Economics of Negative Externalities

There is a growing awareness of negative externalities—the costs to society that businesses produce that they are not held accountable for, many of which taxpayers end up covering. For example, a chemical company that pollutes the air may pay for the direct costs of equipment to contain or clean up its pollution, but it is rarely held responsible for the higher health insurance premiums the area's residents often pay because they get sick more often than the general population. Similarly, companies in the fast-food, beverage, and candy sectors have not been asked to pay for the costs of higher rates of obesity that scientific research has shown are directly attributable to the foods they produce and sell. And companies that emit large amounts of carbon dioxide into the atmosphere are not asked to pay for the consequences of the increasing number of natural disasters such as hurricanes, tornadoes, and blizzards that scientists attribute to climate change.

The costs of negative externalities are not a trivial or imaginary problem in capitalism. Consumers need to begin talking about negative externalities to bring the issue to the surface of our economic debates. Either these costs must be built into the price of products and passed on to consumers, or society must force companies to deduct these costs from their profits. Ideally, companies should be asked to account for their true costs in a transparent way, which noted futurist Lester Brown called "externalities pricing mechanisms that tell the social and ecological truth."[25] This idea is not so far-fetched, and it could be included in a next generation of smartphone apps that consumers use in the shopping aisle.

### THE HAPPY PLANET INDEX: AN ALTERNATIVE TO GDP

The Happy Planet Index (HPI) is one of the newest efforts to create a more viable and meaningful measure of the human condition than gross domestic product (GDP). Developed by the New Economics Foundation (NEF), the index for each country is compiled from three sets of data—longevity, overall satisfaction, and each country's per-person ecological footprint. The calculations yield an indicator of how successful each country is at producing a good life for its citizens "that doesn't cost the Earth." As the HPI website says, "The Index doesn't reveal the 'happiest' country in the world. It shows the relative efficiency with which nations convert the planet's natural resources into long and happy lives for their citizens."

The first HPI came out in 2006, with an update (HPI 2.0) released in 2010, covering 143 countries and 99 percent of the world's population. The latest results indicate, of course, that people in richer countries enjoy the happiest and healthiest lives, but only because they consume at unsustainably high levels. Many less wealthy countries have high levels of life expectancy and life satisfaction with a low ecological footprint per head. The country that leads the HPI, in fact, is Costa Rica—where longevity and life satisfaction are almost as high as in many developed nations, but at less than half the ecological footprint.

Among Western nations, the Netherlands places highest when combining all three measures, while Germany, Italy, France, and the U.K. are in the middle of the rankings. But the United States is among the least efficient countries in producing longevity and life satisfaction, placing 114th out of 143 countries. Furthermore, HPI 2.0 discovered that most countries studied increased their HPI scores slightly between 1990 and 2005, while China, India, and the United States all saw their HPI scores drop in those years.[26]

NEF's aim in producing the HPI is to alert nations that the obsession with GDP is misplaced and unsustainable. Those nations that achieve longevity and life satisfaction at high levels of ecological consumption cannot continue to do so because the Earth simply cannot support such unsustainable policies. Luckily, HPI also provides instructive indicators that we can learn from, pointing the way to a different path—one that will allow us to do better in the future while respecting our environmental limits.

## Non-GDP Indices of Economic and Social Progress

The last economic measure consumers need to become aware of is the overreliance governments and the private sector put on gross domestic product (GDP) as the primary measure of growth and progress. Numerous experts point out that GDP is flawed because it blindly counts all of a country's economic outputs without regard to their utility, purpose, or consequences. When cars idle in traffic congestion, consuming gas and causing sales at the pump to rise, GDP rises. Rising sales of fast food and soft drinks that increase the need for obesity care and diabetes drugs also help GDP go up. Upswings in urban crime that cause home security systems to sell make GDP appear to rise. In short, using GDP as the main measure of a nation's economic growth yields a misleading and inaccurate picture of progress.

Many experts now agree that we need to fix this. Some suggest we update GDP with other inputs, such as by adding in the value of household work and child rearing. But many other experts believe we need to replace GDP completely, or at least complement it with alternative indices that take into account more meaningful indicators that measure improvements in the quality of life, not just the quantity of consumption.

One of the most significant efforts at spearheading a movement to eliminate GDP's dominance comes out of a commission established at the request of French president Nicolas Sarkozy. Chaired by Nobel-laureate economists Joseph Stiglitz and Amartya Sen, plus French economist Jean-Paul Fitoussi, the group agreed that GDP is a poor measure of economic progress. To replace it, they created a dashboard-style display showing readings in all the usual fields, including health, education, environment, and employment. But they also added a number of qualitative factors, such as interpersonal connectedness, political engagement, and quality-of-life indicators. The commission's guiding concept is that societies can get a more accurate picture of their true prosperity only when they take these social indicators into account.

AT THIS TIME, too few consumers are involved in the complexities of economics such as covered in the three issues discussed above. But if, as a society, we seek to discover and disseminate the truths about how capitalism creates and contributes to our economic, social, and environmental problems, we must initiate deeper public conversations that help advance more accurate and humanistic measures of economic growth. Consumers need to become better educated about these issues and take action to help others comprehend not only how capitalism fails us, but how we can make it work better.

*Access is the first tile in a domino effect of awareness, empathy, and action. The power of the social web lies in the sequence of its three capacities: To inform, to inspire, and to incite.*

—Maria Popova, blogger and editor, *Brain Pickings*

## PUSH BRANDS TO IMPLEMENT SOCIAL CONTRACTS

Traditional corporate law is based on the premise that businesses exist to make profits for shareholders and are not responsible to provide any benefits to society at large. By virtue of their legal status, corporations are protected from their mistakes by the grant of limited liability to their shareholders, except in cases of proven fraud or misconduct. Shareholders are functionally immune from whatever effects their corporations have on society.

In social contract theory, however, people seeking to participate in a society must agree to yield some of their natural rights in exchange for the benefits and protections that society provides them. All citizens living under the social contract of a democracy, for example, have a duty to act responsibly, to obey the laws, and to abandon certain self-interests that conflict with the general good in exchange for the security and protections that their government offers them.

It is now high time to apply social contract theory to corporations, especially given the 2010 Supreme Court decision, *Citizens United v. Federal Election Commission,* that grants corporations the same rights as individuals when it comes to political spending on election campaigns. Given this Supreme Court ruling, it only makes sense that if corporations want the same rights as individual citizens, they should be held just as accountable as citizens when it comes to their responsibilities as members of society. As such, consumers would do well to persuade companies to agree to some form of a social contract governing their operations. A brand's fans, for example, have every right to pressure a company to create a written document spelling out its efforts to contribute to society. And if a company refuses, consumers can use their leverage to create enough reputational damage that the company reassesses its decision. Consumers should never underestimate the persuasive power they have to promote greater social responsibility from companies in exchange for their loyalty and business. In many ways, Facebook has already made this easier by adding an "Unlike" button to complement the "Like" button on its profile pages. With a simple click, consumers can communicate that they don't like a brand's behavior—and if enough consumers begin doing this, the threat of "Unlikes" may be sufficient to effect change.

Here is an example for how such a social contract might read. This is a template, which can be modified to accommodate the specific circumstances of an industry or an individual company, the benefits to society it is trying to produce, and the latest in the emerging technologies it intends to use.

---

### WE FIRST SOCIAL CONTRACT BETWEEN BRANDS AND CONSUMERS

The goal of We First is a sustainable practice of capitalism. We First is based on the belief that selfish Me First thinking hurts our businesses and the lives of millions of people around the world. We First asserts that a brighter future depends on an integration of profit and purpose within the private sector. To achieve this, companies and customers must become partners in social change to build a better world. We First believes the following principles should guide our business practices:

1. We believe companies have a right to innovation, entrepreneurship, and profit-making, while consumers have a right to a healthy society and a healthy planet.

2. We recognize that an interdependent, global community requires an expanded definition of self-interest that acknowledges the needs of all inhabitants of the planet.

3. We define success through prosperity as that which ensures the well-being of many, not the wealth of a few.

4. We believe that the future of profit is purpose.

5. We believe that the interests of companies and consumers are best served through a sustainable practice of capitalism—economically, morally, ethically, environmentally, and socially.

6. We believe that corporations and consumers owe each other an equal duty of transparency, authenticity, and accountability.

7. We believe that social technology, business, and shopping have the potential to change our world through new modes of engagement, collaboration, and contribution.

8. We believe the values that inform our daily practice of capitalism include: sustainability, fairness of rewards, fiscal responsibility, accountability, purposefulness, engagement, and global citizenship.

9. We believe that corporations and consumers are duty-bound to serve as custodians of global well-being for this and future generations.

10. We believe that the private sector must cooperate, collaborate, and coordinate with governments and NGOs to create a unified force for social good.

## SEEK POSITIVE ENGAGEMENT WITH BRANDS

Not every incident requires a protest, nor does every corporate transgression deserve a boycott. There are many circumstances when consumers can be more effective in furthering change by engaging in positive dialogue with companies to emphasize forward-thinking goals, rather than focusing on past mistakes or missed opportunities.

Knowing when to protest versus when to try to negotiate in good faith with a company is not always a black-and-white decision. But as the power of the Wedia matures, consumers will gain experience and sophistication in learning how to use their consumer media to encourage corporations to adopt responsible business practices that eventually lead to deeper changes in their thinking and behavior. Both parties need to be good listeners and sensitive to the motives of the other and what they are trying to achieve together.

---

### WHEN BAD BRANDS DO GOOD THINGS

Almost every brand doing meaningful work can at some time be accused of providing a product or service that is harmful or causes a social problem. Meanwhile, many of the classic corporate villains also contribute significantly to important social programs. So what should consumers do with these brands? Should they be punished or not?

My view is that little is gained by taking an all-or-nothing approach to this issue. Of course, transparency, authenticity, and accountability from brands are paramount. But it's unrealistic to expect brands to exercise their duty to society and their shareholders without making some difficult compromises, which sometimes means companies that do good works still source, produce, and sell products and services in ways that are undeniably injurious to people and our planet.

This doesn't mean bad brands should get a free pass. However, a sustainable future won't be achieved by relentless demonization of these companies. Instead, it is better for consumers to work with them, celebrating what good they do and encouraging them to do more of it. If consumers can demonstrate to companies obsessed with only fulfilling their self-interest that doing public good is also good business, it is the start of teaching them how to expand their definition of self-interest. As consumers support the success of those initiatives, they can then encourage these brands to shift their offending products and services into alignment with their core values. In this way, consumers can help more companies learn how to successfully marry profit and purpose.

## VOLUNTEER YOUR EXPERIENCE TO NONPROFITS

There are an increasing number of online communities devoted to helping consumers find opportunities to donate their services to nonprofits and NGOs. Volunteerism empowers consumers to take action and circumvent the corporate track. Within just the past few years, dozens of online communities have arisen to connect consumers to responsible companies, causes, and volunteer opportunities. Here are a few resources to help you bring change to the world through your own volunteer efforts:

- *Volunteer Match:* A site for people and companies to find opportunities to volunteer to work with a nonprofit.
- *Idealist:* A clearinghouse where people interested in service can link up with nonprofits, and where nonprofits can exchange resources and locate opportunities and supporters.
- *Change.org:* A site that provides information on a wide variety of causes, from education to human rights to poverty, with opportunities for people to take action.
- *Causecast:* A site that partners with a wide array of nonprofits and provides users with opportunities to connect with people, thought leaders, charities, and brands that inspire them.

### THE EVOLUTION OF A RESPONSIBLE CONSUMER

The last chapter laid out a vision for how responsible brands might one day become magnets for large groups of global fans who support their products and plan for a better world. A similar evolution applies to consumers who, through their own shopping and investing actions and through their social activism, can grow to become fully participating members of a truly socially responsible society.

This consumer evolution encompasses seven stages. To some extent these stages overlap the diversity of roles we reviewed that consumers can play through social media, but the evolutionary hierarchy below encompasses a broader development of skills and expertise.

*Stage 1: Individual Commitment.* Consumers begin to change their own behaviors away from little or no consciousness of their responsibility. They examine how their consumption habits impact the world. They start doing more mindful and socially responsible shopping, using smartphone apps to gain product information, and transitioning their personal wealth into social investing.

*Stage 2: Community Engagement.* Consumers begin engaging in social media. They find a community and causes to get involved with. They identify brands that reflect their values and prefer purchasing them over all others. They read online magazines, blogs, and tweets to connect with like-minded individuals.

*Stage 3: Promotion of Values.* Consumers start to communicate with others about the values they believe in. They push back on corporations for breaches of integrity, and they celebrate those companies that demonstrate authentic commitments to their core values. They do this using social media to post product and company reviews on online sites, write favorable blogs, or tweet about their admiration for a brand.

*Stage 4: Driving Awareness.* In this phase, consumers decide to participate at a higher level, agreeing to help raise the awareness of issues among other people by producing, distributing, or curating content. They film and post videos or write articles for websites; they "Like" or "Recommend" articles they read, alerting their friends to them. They donate to crowd-funded media-buying platforms such as Loudsauce that promote television and outdoor advertising about ideas that matter. They are active proponents of a cause.

*Stage 5: Thought Leadership.* In this phase, consumers voluntarily assume the role of a thought leader who takes responsibility to analyze issues and produce the arguments that others need to persuade the public. The thought leader promulgates his or her ideas in many formats—books, articles, interviews, videos, webinars, blogs, and tweets. Thought leaders are driven not by ego, but by a conviction to ensure their ideas and values play a role in how society works.

*Stage 6: Building a Community.* In this phase, consumers (often thought leaders) seek to organize other people together into a community that shares their thinking and values. This work takes place either online or off-line, but wherever it occurs, it does not remain a virtual community, and it seeks to have an impact in the real world.

*Stage 7: Connecting Communities.* In this stage, a consumer tries to synchronize many communities into a bona fide movement with specific objectives and goals. At this point, there may be a need for greater organization and hierarchy to help maintain a unified message, as well as a strong strategic plan to ensure that social transformation occurs.

## WHERE DO YOU FIT IN?

Not every consumer will complete this evolutionary journey. Just as with green endeavors like recycling, it's up to each individual to decide how far he or she wants to go. We can expect the degree of participation to vary from person to person. Consumers need to work from their own comfort zone, in accordance with their specific skills and needs.

There is no doubt that achieving a major social transformation in capitalism will require millions of consumers with all sorts of skills. But if managed well, the crises we face represent an enormous opportunity for corporations, brands, and consumers to stake out a better future for the world.

## CHAPTER TAKEAWAYS

- Consumers are now in a position to co-create with corporations the world in which they want to live. They have the capability to drive a major shift in corporate thinking and behavior in a relatively short period of time.
- Social media offers the opportunity to raise the level of cognitive dissonance, forcing people to question whether Me First capitalism is the best system available.
- Critics of social media often say it creates only weak ties, promotes "slactivism," and lacks hierarchy, but these are premature assessments that fail to envision how social media can mature into a powerful consumer tool to change corporate behavior.
- Consumers need to begin by changing their own behaviors, practicing mindful and socially responsible consumption, becoming involved in social entrepreneurship, and leveraging their investments to force companies to change.
- Consumers should seek to inspire greater action against corporate irresponsibility by using social media to spread ideas, lobby for transparent models of economic progress, seek social contracts with brands, and volunteer for causes.

# 9 HOW CONTRIBUTORY CONSUMPTION CREATES SUSTAINABLE SOCIAL CHANGE

How much money would it take to build a better world? What size commitment would be required? To answer, let's start with a provocative idea—imagine that every commercial transaction included a contribution to build a better world.

Now let's isolate the retail sector as an example of the money that could be generated if only a small amount—say, just 1 percent or 2 percent—of every sale were used to fund solutions to our most severe global crises.

Take shoes, for example. More than 2 billion pairs of shoes are sold each year, which generates about $25 billion in annual revenues. Now throw in clothing and retail apparel sales, at $350 billion. Next, add in annual sales from supermarkets and grocery stores, at $465 billion, and furniture retailing, with $50 billion. Then there are florists, $5 billion; the car-wash industry, $6 billion; art dealers and galleries, $8 billion; cosmetics and beauty supplies, $10 billion; boat dealers, $11 billion; movie theaters, $12 billion; toys and hobbies, $15 billion; household appliance stores, $16 billion; computer hardware and software, $16 billion; bookstores, $17 billion; bakeries, $25 billion; jewelry stores, $30 billion; tire dealers, $30 billion; sporting goods, $35 billion; dollar stores and other general merchandisers, $50 billion; consumer electronics, $60 billion; department stores, $70 billion; discount department stores, $130 billion; drugstores, $220 billion; restaurants, $375 billion; and finally, automobile sales, $600 billion. So far that's total retail sales of $2.656 trillion. But why stop there?

Let's add in service industries, such as architecture businesses, which generate $38 billion; engineering, $260 billion; and residential real estate brokerage and management, $170 billion. We're now up to $3.124 trillion.[1] If just 1 percent of every dollar were repurposed for building a better planet—either by donating it to a philanthropy or charity or by redirecting it to a cause—that alone would amount to more than $30 billion. If retailers and brands agreed to 2 percent as a contribution, the total take would be $60 billion just among the aforementioned industries.

Now imagine that every single credit and debit card purchase donated 10 or 20 cents for a cause. Statistics show that there are more than roughly 30 billion credit and debit card transactions per year, so a cause contribution per transaction would amount to another $3 billion or $6 billion.[2] These amounts would bring the contributions up to between $35 billion at the low end (with a 1 percent donation and 10 cents) and $70 billion at the high end (with a 2 percent donation and 20 cents).

And this list includes only a small cross section of the full range of retail and service industries in the United States. If every single consumer-retail establishment and service sector were involved, the daily practice of capitalism could conceivably generate far more than the current corporate direct donations of about $14 billion. In fact, contributory consumption could generate as much as $100 billion at a 2 percent donation rate—*annual* funds that could be devoted to building a better world.

Furthermore, these estimates are for the United States alone. Imagine if all the major capitalist economies—Canada, Western Europe, Japan, Russia, and parts of Asia, Latin America, and Africa—all joined in. How much might contributions from their retail and service industries add? It would be hundreds of billions more.

Finally, let's extend the concept into uncharted waters by applying the same contributory model to the gaming and the virtual worlds. What if all the advertising and the purchases made within virtual worlds like Second Life, online games like World of Warcraft, and social games like FarmVille and Mafia Wars—all brimming with virtual goods—also generated contributions? And how much more might we expect to get as these industries explode in the coming years?

But to come back down to Earth, let's imagine only a small portion of enlightened companies, driven by their desire to build loyal off-line and online communities, participated. Even if only 5 percent of retail businesses, service industries, and gaming companies participated, contributing only 1 or 2 percent of sales, we would *still* exceed the current level of annual global corporate donations of roughly $14 billion.

This idea may seem fantastical, but it's not outside the realm of possibility. All manner of corporations, from multinationals like Starbucks to pioneering companies like TOMS Shoes, are already paving the way. The potential for modifying the entire engine of capitalism so that billions of daily transactions generate small but sustained contributions to eradicate poverty, malnutrition, disease, illiteracy, and homelessness is, to say the least, enormous.

## CONTRIBUTORY CONSUMPTION: SMALL CHANGE MAKES BIG SENSE

*We First* has so far argued that we need a new paradigm for free market capitalism, and that this begins with changes from within. For companies, it means understanding that civilization is hurtling toward a vastly different world— one in which complexity, interdependence, and global connectivity will have clear consequences on their business practices. In this new world, companies must learn how to meld profits with purpose. Societal values must guide capitalism toward becoming a benevolent economic system that operates with accountability, integrity, and transparency. Consumers, too, will need to make changes, reducing their consumption and redefining what a meaningful lifestyle looks like.

Companies and consumers alike must start implementing this new thinking in their behaviors and practices. On the corporate side, it begins with a new breed of leaders who can offer a vision of transforming their companies into socially responsible citizens. Meanwhile, consumers can tap into their collective purchasing power to encourage companies to invest in missions that serve both purpose and profit. Little by little, corporations and consumers need to start collaborating, using social media to engage in dialogue and partnerships that effect change. These actions alone would go a long way toward building a better world.

But the crises we face across the planet today are immense. The developed Western nations are losing ground in spreading prosperity to the nearly 4 billion people living elsewhere in relative poverty, with millions needlessly dying each year from malnutrition and controllable diseases. Governments are unequipped to handle this degree of assistance. Philanthropies are underfunded. The Great Recession has severely impacted charitable giving to the point that many nonprofits are disappearing.

*We First* therefore proposes yet another concept to help build a better world—*contributory consumption*. This is the idea that birthed this book, as explained in the prologue. It is the concept inspired by Bill Gates's challenge to the most successful corporations to find new creative models by which they could help the poorer nations of the world. It is perhaps the only way that capitalism can ever devise a response on the same scale as the severity of our crises.

What exactly is contributory consumption? It's a twist on free market capitalism that turns Me First into We First commerce. It takes two of the best elements of free market capitalism—corporate branding and conscious consumption—and merges them with corporate social responsibility and social media to create a new economic system that drives a perpetual motor of prosperity.

The opening pages of this chapter illustrate how contributory consumption could conceivably amass enormous financial resources by taking just a small fraction of every commercial transaction and devoting it to funding solutions for the crises we face. At first glance, the concept may seem radical—a plot to alter the foundations of capitalism. Many corporate executives might reject it as fanciful or just plain silly. But in fact, it is nothing less than the logical extension of current forms of corporate social responsibility, rooted in economic pragmatism and marketing logic. *Let's use day-to-day transactions to build renewal into every instance of consumption.*

### WHO PAYS FOR THE CONTRIBUTIONS, AND WHY?

The key question, of course, is: Who pays for the contributions? Should brands give up a portion of their profits? That's how some cause-related marketing (CRM) programs, including (PRODUCT)RED, work. Or should contributions be deducted from retail profits, as some stores now do on occasion? Or should consumers pay for the donation? They already do in some cause-related marketing campaigns when a brand inflates the price of its product to compensate for the extra costs of the contribution.

Ideally, brands themselves would agree to fund the majority of these contributions as compensation for the benefits they receive from society. Perhaps retailers would also agree to participate consistently rather than on a campaign basis, thereby doubling the contribution levels. Keep in mind that this recommendation comes directly from consumers, who in survey after survey confirm their wish for corporations to become more socially responsible. As a reminder of the strength of consumer conviction about this, let me repeat a few of the statistics already cited from the 2009 Edelman Goodpurpose survey: 71 percent of consumers think brands and companies spend too much on advertising and marketing and should put more into good causes; 64 percent say they expect brands today to do something to support a good cause; and 83 percent are willing to change their shopping habits if it makes the world a better place.[3]

These are all good reasons why corporations should shoulder the burden of contributory consumption. However, given that many corporations already donate to specific charities, conduct CRM campaigns, or fund eponymous foundations, it is understandable if they prefer to participate less heavily in these transactional contributions. Many brands have already built a reputation on and expertise around specific causes related to their business, so it would be natural for them to want to remain focused on those programs.

Nevertheless, some level of participation in contributory consumption would be appropriate from all corporations, because the fact is, the world could double, triple, or quadruple the resources dedicated to renewal each year, and it would still be not enough. Furthermore, if a brand truly wants to earn the goodwill of consumers, it should be seen as transparently bearing the costs of bettering the lives of others and the planet, because only authenticity creates genuine admiration and loyalty. When a company passes contributory costs onto consumers, it risks being interpreted as just another example of a brand trying to get away with cause-washing.

Finally, the burden of adding another 1 to 5 percent to cause contributions may turn out to be trivial, given the two potential benefits that brands can gain. First, the brand would likely see an increase in sales and a boost to its reputation among consumers. Second, the actual dollar costs of the donations will likely be balanced out by the reduced need for traditional marketing and advertising budgets in a world of free social media.

But let's assume some corporations will find it impossible to bear the burden alone. They could pass a portion, perhaps half, of the transactional contribution costs back onto consumers via price increases. Consumers already know this is how many CRM campaigns operate, but more significantly, research shows that in some cases people are willing to absorb a small premium for products linked to causes or produced via sustainable means. A 2009 SCA and Harris Interactive survey, for instance, showed that 47 percent of American adults agreed they would be willing to pay more for environmentally friendly products; 63 percent would spend more for organic, fair-trade, or locally sourced food; and 62 percent would pay more for environmentally friendly cleaning supplies. On average, these respondents were willing to pay 17 to 19 percent more in each of these cases.[4]

Meanwhile, an insightful study from 2009 confirms that not only are consumers willing to pay more for a product from a socially responsible company, but they are also quite happy to punish unethical companies by refusing to buy their products at full price. June Cotte, a professor of marketing at the University of Western Ontario's Ivey School of Business, and doctoral candidate Remi Trudel conducted a series of experiments, one of which was to ask coffee drinkers to help a local grocery store select a new brand of coffee to sell. The coffee brand was made-up, but the presentation was realistic enough that the subjects did not suspect this. One group was shown a coffee brand described as practicing fair-trade policies, with a lengthy description of all the benefits for the farmers who grow the coffee. Another group was introduced to the same coffee brand, but it was described as having been criticized for unsustainable farming that might be harmful to the environment and for using child labor. A control group was shown the same coffee brand with no description whatsoever.

The results were astonishing: Consumers in the test groups were willing to pay an extra $1.40 per pound over standard coffee prices for fair-trade coffee, but their threshold for buying the unsustainable coffee brand required a discount of $2.40 per pound. As the authors concluded, "Negative information concerning trade practices had almost twice the impact of positive information on the coffee consumer's willingness to pay."[5] The researchers repeated the experiment with t-shirts made with different percentages of organic cotton and found that consumers were again willing to pay a premium for t-shirts with any amount of organic cotton, but required a discount for t-shirts made with zero organically grown fiber.

These results suggest that it is feasible for companies to raise their prices to pass the cost of contributory consumption back to consumers. Ultimately, most companies would probably implement a range of practices to fund their contributions—sometimes absorbing the complete donation themselves, sometimes sharing it with consumers, or a hybrid across their product lines.

## PRECURSORS FOR CONTRIBUTORY CONSUMPTION

Contributory consumption is not such a radical idea in the rapidly evolving world of commerce. Numerous inspiring precursors already exist.

The first is the entire industry of cause-related marketing itself—the hundreds of campaigns in which a brand affiliates itself with a cause and challenges consumers to show their support by purchasing the brand's products in exchange for a donation. Contributory consumption differs from CRM in several ways, but its method—contributions generated through purchases—is the same. Where it differs, however, is significant: Cause-related marketing efforts are largely independent or one-off campaigns designed by a single brand in the name of a single cause. Such campaigns ask too little of corporations in a world that demands bigger actions on a more consistent and coordinated basis.

A second precursor to contributory consumption is 1% for the Planet, started in 2002 by Yvon Chouinard, founder of Patagonia, and Craig Mathews, owner of Blue Ribbon Flies. As sportsmen and passionate environmentalists, the two men devised the concept as a way to involve the larger business community in helping to preserve the planet. They launched it in San Francisco, with 22 retailers signing up to donate 1 percent of their gross sales to environmental groups around the world. By 2005, there were more than 200 members, largely retail stores and outdoor-oriented companies whose business depends on a clean, healthy environment. As of this writing, 1% for the Planet has more than 1,200 member companies in 38 countries. In its eight years of existence, it has generated more than $50 million in donations to environmental organizations.

A third precursor to contributory consumption is (PRODUCT)RED, the program launched by Bono and Bobby Shriver in 2006 that licenses its name to leading brands, which then produce special co-branded products. When these products are sold, the licensed brand donates 50 percent of its profit to the Global Fund, which uses the donations to fund HIV and AIDS care and prevention programs in Africa. So far, this unique program has licensed its name to some of the world's most iconic brands, including American Express, Apple, Bugaboo, Converse, Dell, Emporio Armani, Gap, Hallmark, Nike, Penguin, and Starbucks, generating more than $150 million to help 5 million people.

Finally, a fourth precursor for contributory consumption is SocialVest, founded in 2010 by social entrepreneur Adam Ross. SocialVest is a combined on- and off-line shopping platform that links consumers to a list of more than 600 top retailers, online vendors, services, and brands—including Kohl's, Macy's, Saks Fifth Avenue, Lancôme, Sears, Staples, and many others—that have agreed to rebate a percentage of each member's purchases back to causes. Some vendors donate 1 percent, some 3, 5, or 7 percent, and some as high as 10 percent.

Consumers begin by joining the website and can then either shop at the online stores directly or register a credit card that they will later use at participating bricks-and-mortar stores. Each consumer has his or her own "Giving

Account," into which the participating retailers or vendors deposit the donations earned through the member's purchases. There is no cost to consumers, since the donations come from the participating stores.

With the money in their Giving Account, consumers can choose from any of 1.5 million 501(c)(3) charitable not-for-profit organizations registered in the United States. The balance is transferred once a month to the consumer's selected charities in minimum increments of $10 using Network for Good, a PayPal-style electronic funds-transfer tool. SocialVest is also starting to tap into social media, using Facebook's Causes feature to expand awareness of its programs and make donating easier.

In many ways, the We First vision of contributory consumption is the next evolution of these four precursors. It extends the value proposition of transaction-based donations into the entire universe of real-world and online shopping, using actual and virtual goods, and inviting all brands, retailers, and consumers to use capitalism as a driver of change. We First also envisions contributory consumption being applied to transactions that are increasingly made through smartphones equipped with social shopping apps, augmented-reality apps, and emerging product-scanning technologies. And finally, it also looks to the additional revenues that gaming and "g-commerce" (gaming commerce) can make through the purchase of real or virtual goods in social games.

Let me synthesize clearly how We First contributory consumption departs from these precursors, especially cause-related marketing, to offer brands and consumers a more comprehensive opportunity to generate donations in the name of social transformation.

### Capitalism's Purpose

Whereas corporate charity and CRM initiatives accept capitalism and corporate profits as givens—and in fact, corporations often conduct a cause-related marketing campaign to enhance their profits—contributory consumption seeks to retool the engine of capitalism by turning every single purchase into a generator of funds to be used for long-term social change. This represents a systemic shift deep in capitalism's purpose by integrating contribution into consumption.

### Remedial versus Proactive

CSR and CRM are effectively remedial treatments on behalf of companies to fix social problems ex post facto. In contrast, contributory consumption seeks to enable all commerce to become a form of *preventative* medicine to change society. Selling, buying, and contributing become fundamentally intertwined into one process, transforming the fundamental nature of commerce into a motor for global progress.

### Ad Hoc versus Systematic

Corporate philanthropy campaigns are often ad hoc, disconnected, or one-off efforts conducted by individual corporations. Systematic campaigns like (PRODUCT)RED and 1% for the Planet solve this problem by offering a comprehensive program, but each focuses on a specific cause. SocialVest offers an expanded program, but the scale of current crises necessitates that we go even further with contributory consumption to transform all capitalism—on- and off-line, in the real and digital worlds, selling actual and virtual goods—into a constant source of funding.

### Small-Scale versus Large-Scale

Capitalism exists nearly everywhere on the planet, but corporate contributions do not. Many corporate programs are finite and small relative to how many transactions occur on a daily basis. Contributory consumption, on the other hand, seeks to raise social change to a level of consciousness never seen before by engaging brands and consumers in a daily collaboration via transactions directed to social change.

## IMPLEMENTING CONTRIBUTORY CONSUMPTION

To bring contributory consumption to fruition, brands, retail stores, and consumers need to accept its value proposition—and that will take a certain amount of dedicated persuasion and conviction. But before it's dismissed as admirable but unrealistic, let's see how it could work in the four worlds of shopping—the real world of bricks-and-mortar stores, the virtual world of click-to-buy, the new mobile world, and the gaming world—that collectively offer tremendous sources of transactional funding.

### CONTRIBUTORY FUNDING FROM REAL-WORLD SHOPPING

In a We First world of shopping malls, warehouses, grocery stores, and streets lined with Mom-and-Pop retail shops, consumers go about their business just as they do now. They select branded or generic products according to their usual preferences. Nothing about their existing habits changes, but behind the

scenes, for every purchase made, many or most of the manufacturers and retail stores agree to contribute a percentage of each sale as a donation to pressing social causes.

On top of this more common real-world shopping scenario, however, contributory consumption allows for many unique levels of personalization and
customization. Brands, retailers, and consumers can tailor their cause programs
and contributions in all kinds of ways. They can use mobile apps, online platforms, and social media to create different paths for contributory consumption at various consumer "touch points" to transform the real-world shopping
landscape. Let me enumerate some ideas.

### Retail-Driven Contributions

The retail shopping world is getting smarter and more interactive. For example, there's a new "smart" cash register from Intel and Frog Design that could
serve the contributory cause world very well. Looking like a sleek desk with a
TV screen, it flashes products and marketing messages to passersby. When customers are ready to check out, they flash their radio-frequency identification
(RFID) store loyalty card on the screen inset into the desktop, and up comes
their shopping history, personal interests, and wish lists. This ability was originally designed to enable salesclerks to engage customers in friendly conversation about their purchasing habits, but it could also be used very well for
contributory consumption.

Imagine, for example, how flashing the store loyalty card over the register
might immediately give customers information on the social responsibility of
the store and the brands being purchased, and then provide them with the opportunity to select a cause to support through a portion of their total purchase.
(Alternatively, the customer's store loyalty card could be personalized with a
QR code that, when scanned at checkout, automatically credits the customer's
preferred causes.) In addition, the store clerk could then invite customers to
register their praise or criticism about brands in their shopping profile, which
creates a database of customer sentiment that management can use to formulate its future buying strategy.[6]

In such a We First shopping world, contributing and being able to direct
one's contributions becomes a meaningful form of personal expression. Retail becomes Wetail, as consumers begin to see themselves not just as shoppers but as agents of change. In turn, brands and retailers can learn how to
use contributions to drive business and customer loyalty. Over time, the social currency of shopping rises to the point that stores and brands are able

to entice consumers on the basis of contributions to causes instead of discounts. They begin engaging consumers through a variety of creative offers to make donations in exchange for active expressions of loyalty, such as "Liking" a brand on Facebook or text-messaging friends about the store or the brand.

### Social-Media-Driven Contributions

As more and more stores get involved, we may also see more campaigns that use social media to drive donations. Some might imitate Procter & Gamble, which launched a "Give Health" widget that bloggers could embed into their websites for a specific period of time. Anyone reading that blog has only to click on the widget and P & G will donate a day's worth of clean drinking water—about two liters—to someone in need—and send the clicker a coupon for P & G products. The company calls the campaign its "Clean Water Blogivation." The same idea can be applied by any retail store, offering a widget to bloggers on behalf of a variety of causes.

Or consider the Starbucks Facebook application, which lets people buy a coffee remotely for a friend. Imagine how in a We First world, every coffee purchase might also generate a contribution. This same concept could launch a whole new generation of remote gift-giving for causes that expands to include hundreds of products. Rather than going to stores to shop for a gift, we could begin to see millions of people log onto Facebook to send their friends a birthday present or a thinking-of-you gift, while simultaneously making a donation to a cause in that person's name.

## CONTRIBUTIONS THROUGH ONLINE SHOPPING

All these CRM strategies can be replicated in the online shopping world, too. Given that 92 million Americans already shop online, contributory consumption could also be applied to the websites of the major retailers and web-only vendors like Amazon and Zappos, which would agree to donate a portion of all their sales to causes.

All the online price comparison and product information sites could participate, too. For example, sites like PriceGrabber, Pricewatch, DealTime, and MySimon that currently allow consumers to compare prices, get product information, and decide which store to buy from are all candidates to become involved in contributory consumption. They can help consumers learn about a brand's social responsibility profile and start automatically matching them with the online shopping sites that donate to their preferred causes.

### Coupon-Driven Contributions

Contributory consumption is also a great match for the fast-growing coupon industry that includes category leaders Groupon and LivingSocial, as well as a growing legion of emerging competitors. What if, when consumers went to such coupon sites, they discovered that they could increase the value of their coupon by donating directly to a cause? For example, take the 25 million consumers who use Groupon—why not arrange it so that when the daily deal "tips" (meaning it becomes valid when there are enough buyers), either Groupon or the retailer makes a celebratory contribution to a cause? Then there is the new Walmart-sponsored version, CrowdSaver, which posts ads on Facebook with special deals. With its market dominance, it would be profitable for Walmart to donate a percentage of consumers' savings to a cause, pegging the amount to how many consumers agree to the deal. For example, if 5,000 people purchase a TV at $x$ price, Walmart will contribute $y$ dollars to a cause; but if 10,000 people buy the TV, the product's price goes down while the company's contribution goes up—further motivating consumers to buy.

### Integrated Shopping Opportunities

Many commentators are predicting that we will soon begin to see a total merger of the on- and off-line worlds for shopping. For example, writing on the blog TechCrunch.com, David Zong, founder and CEO of the mobile-payment company Zong, described a future scenario that starts with an application on a smartphone.

> A user would launch the app, see what special deals are in her area (location + group buying), which of her friends already bought the coupon/item (social graph), local reviews from friends (social graph + reviews), and then she could buy the desired coupon in one click on her handset. She could walk into the local business with a discount code, bar code, or maybe at some point in the future, an enabled RFID tag, and redeem what she just bought.[7]

This futuristic-sounding scenario is speeding toward us, and it, too, can be considered a potential driver of purchase-driven cause donations.

### Contributions via Social Network Shopping Websites

Beyond these usual shopping outlets that can be adapted to contributory consumption, there is also a new category that we might refer to as "online social network shopping" that can be tapped into. For instance, ShopSocially.com allows groups of friends to recommend products to each other and learn about what others have purchased. In contributory consumption, members could use the site to notify their friends about how the purchases they made that day contributed to specific causes, and then invite them to make matching contributions. Groups of friends could also challenge each other to see who can generate the largest donations in the same way that teams of people compete in Yoplait's Lids to Save Lives breast-cancer campaign.

### Contributions from Cause-Oriented Brands

In this vision of a contributory world, another recent phenomenon could also become a model for contributions—that of the many on- and off-line brands whose mission is deeply linked to causes. Take TOMS Shoes, for instance, which pioneered the "one-for-one" concept. For each pair a consumer buys, TOMS gives away a pair to a child in need. The company also promotes the idea of turning charity into a fun social event, such as its "Style-a-Shoe parties" whereby a host invites friends to decorate their very own pair of white canvas shoes purchased from TOMS in bulk orders of at least 25 pairs (generating, of course, an equal donation). TOMS's buy-one-give-one concept could be a model for many other shopping experiences in a contributory world. Indeed, it has already caught on among at least a dozen other brands, including BoGo Light and One Million Lights (solar-powered and LED flashlights, respectively), One World Futbal (soccer balls for refugee camps or poor communities), Baby America (blankets and pillows), Warby Parker (prescription glasses), and Whitten Grey (dresses for little girls).

### Contributions from Other New Ideas

In a We First world, there is also ample room for many new kinds of websites to serve charities. Causes.com is a model of one such idea. Founded in 2007 by Napster founder and former Facebook president Sean Parker and social activist Joe Green, the site serves as a home base for any charity or cause that signs up to send its potential supporters and donors rather than investing in making its own website. The charities use the site to collect their donations, while Causes.com, which operates as a for-profit company, collects consulting fees for helping to design fund-raising campaigns and by asking donors for a voluntary 10 percent "tip" to defray its costs. So far, Causes.com has attracted 119 million donors and generates about $1 million per month in contributions.

To boost contributions, Causes is also launching a new off-line method of donation that uses "cause gift cards," available in amounts of $25 or $50 at Safeway and Vons supermarkets. Recipients of the cards log onto Causes.com and distribute the amount among their preferred charities. Parker notes that a successful retail gift-card program can do $500 million of business per year, which he hopes to convert to charitable causes.

An equally powerful concept is Jumo.com, created by Facebook cofounder Chris Hughes to match consumers with nonprofits based on needed skills and interests. Hughes's focus is on creating a space for real human interaction be-

---

### A NEW RETAIL FUTURE

The world of technology is changing faster than most shoppers can imagine. The number of creative ideas in development exceeds our ability to conceive of how they might transform our lives. But here's a preview of a few new ideas.

We already have digital billboards in cities like Los Angeles, but Japanese designers are expecting to soon release billboards that actually *watch* consumers shop and adjust the advertising to match their demographics in real time. There are plans for entire city streets to be geo-tagged to create an increasingly sophisticated ongoing dialogue between customers, stores, and products. Customers simply hold their camera-enabled smartphone up to view the street and can immediately see filterable tags synthesizing information from the stores in front of them. Inside a store, they can point the phone at a display wall and immediately see product recommendations. If they have checked in using an app like Foursquare, they might receive an automatic message left there by a friend with a recommendation for what to buy.

Imagine cities in which QR codes appear on digital walls, notifying shoppers about sales, discounts, and cause promotions in the nearby shops. Imagine holding your phone up to a building and seeing all the tweets emanating from shoppers inside those stores. Or picture a scene where customers instinctively check in throughout their day to earn points that can be traded for real-world products, coupons, or cause donations specific to their current location.

Overall, we can expect that as these digital languages develop, marketers will need to extensively reformulate how they attract customers to their brand and keep them loyal. Technology aside, the fact is that consumers are looking for interactions that add meaning to their lives, and cause-related marketing will remain a crucial factor for brands to achieve connection.

fore any requests for money or time are made. Describing his site, he told *Fast Company,* "This is not just a click on a banner ad and give $10 to a needy child. I believe people really want to engage."[8] After being matched, people can follow their nonprofits' news and interact with other members.

As web experiences become increasingly personalized, so too will opportunities for donations. According to Facebook's chief operating officer, Sheryl Sandberg, in the next three to five years, every website will be tailored to a specific user's interests. "People don't want something targeted to the whole world—they want something that reflects what they want to see and know," she says.[9] Given HTML's capacity for user tagging and targeting, visitors to any website who have already chosen to share the causes they care about may start to see those sites providing donation opportunities specific to their interests. In this way, the web will become an even more persuasive platform for social change because it can deliver custom-tailored content unique to each visitor's vision of social change.

## CONTRIBUTORY FUNDING FROM MOBILE SHOPPING

The mobile world is perhaps the most dynamic frontier for contributory consumption, as text messaging is already linked to cause contributions and smartphones will soon effectively replace credit cards. The power of mobile devices to drive charity support was resoundingly proven after the Red Cross raised $32 million in its text-to-give campaign following the 2010 Haiti earthquake. This equaled about 13 percent of all U.S. donations to Haiti that came in via mobile texting. Overall, text or SMS message donations to other charities more than doubled after the quake, according to a study by Blackbaud.[10]

In a follow-up study conducted by Cone, 27 percent of Americans said they were more likely to donate via text message if there is a credible endorser (person, company, or nonprofit); 27 percent said they would be more likely to text in a donation if a company or organization matched their gift; and 19 percent said they would rather text than donate through other means, such as writing a check or going online.[11]

The significance of this has not been lost on the 1.5 million nonprofits in the United States as they increasingly move to soliciting donations via text. Causecast, along with mobile-payment provider Obopay and software company Benevity Social Ventures, has raced to fill the need, giving philanthropies easy access to text-to-pay technology. Their platforms enable nonprofits to instantly take advantage of mobile philanthropy using the memes "text2give," "text2pledge," and "text2broadcast," along with a short code that identifies the specific charity recipient.[12] The philanthropy then publicizes the number on its website and in its marketing materials, but it also broadcasts the number through the retailers and brands that support the philanthropy, thus facilitating a growing direct partnership among brands, retailers, and NGOs.

In a We First world, direct donating to causes is not the only way consumers can use their smartphones to contribute. There is also a new wave of creative ideas to link real-time shopping with donations using mobile apps. Consider, for example, the existing bar code readers GoodGuide and Barcoo, which help consumers learn about the social responsibility footprint of a company before they purchase a product. In a world of contributory consumption, this information could be enriched to include how the brand contributes to causes, what NGOs it works with, and how it supports the U.N. Millennium Development Goals—information which then helps consumers make a more informed decision to purchase and donate.

There are even more interesting possibilities for the new generation of quick-response bar code readers like Stickybits for iPhone and Android phones. A QR code already allows for multimedia links so that anyone scanning it can view related photos or video. In a We First world, QR codes become rich communication tools to inform consumers about a brand's causes. We might start seeing QR codes that contain videos to inspire consumers to support causes, ideas for what they can do to participate to help nonprofits and NGOs, or how they can work with the brand as a partner in change.

Location-based applications, too, hold great opportunities for contributory consumption as they grow in appeal as a way to build engagement and loyalty. Stores that today reward consumers for "checking in" via Facebook Places or Foursquare when they arrive at their location might subscribe to services that allow for charitable donations linked to check-ins. For example, Facebook has launched Facebook Deals, in which a store or brand rewards people with special deals when three of the user's friends check in at a location—and the same principle could be applied to cause donations. Another example is CauseWorld, which offers a check-in reward by which consumers earn "karma points that, when a certain level is reached, result in a donation to a cause of the user's choice." Imagine many apps like these giving out cause donations as the primary or extra incentive for people to check in and help publicize a store or a special offer.

Location-based applications accelerate the social shopping experience, and again offer tremendous potential for contributory consumption. Apps like GetGlue publicize users' comings, goings, and doings, linking their check-ins to their Twitter and Facebook accounts—and therefore, to their broader social networks. Apps such as these and the currencies they use for check-ins—points or badges—could be effectively used to generate donations and brand contributions. Meanwhile, retail stores have already begun using location-based apps to broadcast deals and incentives to subscribers within a certain range of the property. In the future, these could include cause appeals to consumers to make a purchase to benefit a charity they care about.

Augmented-reality (AR) applications are changing how people move through their environment, adding layer upon layer of opportunities for communication between brands and consumers. For example, the N Building, near the Tachikawa subway station in Tokyo, has a façade entirely covered by a digitized QR code. Passersby simply hold up their phones to scan the constantly changing codes, which reveal what is going on inside the building. Consumers can browse for information, make reservations, and download coupons from the digital billboard. This is the beginning of a wave of smartphone-enabled dialogues between shoppers and their environment.

Now imagine these same AR apps being used to inspire cause donations. For example, in a We First world one might imagine retail stores employing technology to allow consumers to hold up an AR-enabled smartphone and see all the various causes associated with an aisle or on a display of products. Or imagine that as consumers walk through the streets of a city, they can scan a QR code and see a video or read a brief, geo-tagged synopsis about their location's history in exchange for a small donation to a cause. Brands could sponsor QR codes in or on trains and buses, and in airports that generate increasingly larger contributions to a cause based on each scanner's engagement level, starting with visiting the brand's website and posting a status update on Facebook all the way to purchasing a product.

Each of these activities can be executed by individuals alone or in groups. As Christopher Penn, vice president of strategy and innovation at Blue Sky Factory, suggests, nonprofits could use things like donor rankings on their websites and start using "game mechanics" to inspire groups of people to race to the top. "Create reasons for teams, guilds, groups, or other gatherings . . . who might gain something from each other, and have them compete for progressions, badges, and leaderboards," he writes.[13]

When we put all these enhancements together—smart cash registers and personalized RFID cards, websites, remote gifting, competitions for causes, donate-by-text technologies, smartphone bar code readers, QR code readers, and location-based apps—we get a potentally transformative picture of the future of shopping in a We First world.

## CONTRIBUTIONS AND THE VIRTUAL WORLD OF GAMES

There is an enormous arena where the notion of charitable contributions has yet to catch more than a toehold—the world of virtual games. These include individual games, small group games, massively multiplayer online role-playing games (MMORPGs), and games played from mobile phones. It is estimated that 67 percent of American households play computer or video games[14] and one in five adults over age 18 plays every day.[15] This translates into roughly 60 million active players in the United States. Add in other gamers around the globe, and the total number of active players goes up to 500 million people who spend at least one hour per day playing games. And in the next decade there will be *1 billion more gamers,* thanks to low-energy wireless and mobile consoles that the gaming industry is creating.[16]

The leading social-game maker Zynga, whose titles include FarmVille, FrontierVille, and Mafia Wars, reports that its games attract more than 360 million people around the world each month, with a daily average of 47 million players.[17] Such large numbers explain how the worldwide market for gaming is estimated to reach $70 billion by 2015.[18]

As these virtual worlds have evolved over the past five years, an astonishing phenomenon has taken place—they have become effectively limitless marketplaces for the sale of "virtual goods" that players use while playing online games. In FarmVille, for example, players purchase (with actual cash) virtual money and coins to use in the game to buy such items as farm equipment, crop seeds, animals, and tractors. In World of Warcraft, players purchase weapons, armor, and so on.

The concept of selling virtual gaming goods originated in South Korea more than a dozen years ago, and today racks up $4 billion in sales in that nation. In 2009, the U.S. market for virtual goods was estimated to be about $1 billion; it is projected to rise to $1.6 or perhaps $2 billion in 2010, and to continue rising up to $6 billion by 2013.[19] Also noteworthy is that the sale of virtual goods has started to exceed advertising sales on mobile phones. The analytics firm Flurry reports that apps that require users to purchase virtual goods are now generating four times more revenue each month than advertising revenues from free apps, except in December when holiday advertising is strongest.[20]

From a We First point of view, the virtual world represents an enormous untapped market to mine for charitable donations in four ways. The first and most encouraging is the most obvious—leveraging the cash revenues generated by the sale of virtual goods, whether through direct payments to causes or via Facebook Credits (which are now the exclusive currency for virtual goods in many games, including those from Zynga and Electronic Arts). Just as We First proposes that real-world shopping can evolve toward contributory consumption, it is only logical that the game makers and consumers who relate in the virtual world might become equal partners in building a better *real* world. And since the overhead for virtual goods is nil, requiring no manufacturing costs, this is a market where consumers and gaming companies might consider even higher levels of contribution—perhaps 5 to 10 percent—than brands' real-world donations of perhaps 1 to 5 percent. In fact, Zynga has already used sales of virtual goods to support Haitian earthquake relief (generating over $3 million in two campaigns) and to build the UCSF Benioff Children's Hospital in San Francisco.

The second way to put gaming revenues to use is for brands that advertise in virtual-game worlds to make contributions. As in the real world, the virtual world of games is replete with advertising. The popularity of virtual games has been driving enormous advertising campaigns on virtual-game sites, especially on Zynga's Facebook pages, where its games are played, and the company estimates that it serves up more than 1 billion ad impressions per day. These amounts need not be oppressive, as they can be bundled into the costs of advertising, which is absorbed by companies' marketing budgets.

And these budgets are vast. *Advertising Age* reports that Zynga's partnership with SocialVibe has placed more than 100 campaigns in its games from such brands as Apple, Discover, Kia, Macy's, Microsoft, MillerCoors, and Visa. Zynga has also done marketing campaigns with McDonald's, 7-Eleven, and Cascadian Farms. These ads engage gamers by offering them a chance to earn currency or points for watching a movie trailer or doing another activity, like taking a quiz, on behalf of a brand—and then sharing their experience on Facebook. SocialVibe charges advertisers by how specifically the ad is pitched to users (e.g., Moms 35 to 44 years old, Millennial males, etcetera).[21] That this kind of targeting and automatic in-network sharing are already in place bodes well for cause activism in this realm.

An emerging technology called gestural advertising could further enhance donations from in-game advertising. New software like Move and Microsoft's Kinect, which use cameras and motion trackers to capture a user's appearance and moves, will enable gamers to personalize brand advertising to feature video and images of themselves. We know that such messages are far more appealing when they come from a friend rather than the brand alone, so Kinect allows the gamer to upload the content to his or her Facebook page in exchange for a further incentive—which could be a coupon or, following the contributory consumption model, a donation.

In a We First world, virtual world advertising would turn into a significant driver of contributions. Ideally, game companies like Zynga would partner with brands—and perhaps with nonprofits as well—to donate a portion of the ad revenues to causes or, better yet, to incorporate donations to a player's favorite charities as an incentive to view the ads. SocialVibe's idea of sharing one's ad experience on Facebook could turn ads into viral contributory opportunities, as one player views an ad and gets game points while also making a contribution, then shares it with the members of his or her network on Facebook, who then all have a chance to do the same. Think of the reach, in terms of donated funds, that a highly viral ad could bring.

A third way that brands and consumers can use virtual worlds for contributory transactions is to create opportunities for free-flowing exchanges between the virtual and real worlds. In the We First vision, consumers, for example, might earn points in the games they play in the virtual world, and could then exchange those points for branded products that elicit real-world donations. It can work in reverse as well: allowing consumers' real-world purchases to accrue points for virtual games, which then trigger a donation. This concept is entirely possible, given that Zynga and American Express formed a partnership in November 2010 that allows gamers to use rewards earned through their American Express credit card to buy virtual goods on Zynga games. Furthermore, Facebook now sells its Facebook Credits in the form of gift cards—which are used as virtual money in more than 150 games and applications—at bricks-and-mortar stores like Walmart and Best Buy. It's only a small step to convert these dynamics into vehicles for social contribution. Ultimately, the creative options for channeling donations between the real and virtual worlds are endless.

And finally, there is a fourth level available to transform virtual worlds into agents of social change. This notion grows out of explorations into ways to use the attraction of virtual worlds to connect people for the purpose of doing good. It involves merged on- and off-line competition that organizes the players of a virtual game into teams with an assignment they must accomplish in the real world. Games might seek out brand sponsors, which would subsidize prizes for the top teams, including a donation to charity in the winners' names.

This type of scenario is, once again, not so far-fetched. Visitors to CommonDeeds.com may register a cause, become a participant on a team working for a cause, or sponsor a team in their brand's name. In essence, the site is an online clearinghouse to facilitate the assembly of all the necessary ingredients for social transformation: purpose, people, and sponsors.

Clearly the virtual world represents a huge field of opportunity for causes, as the popularity of games will only increase. Clay Shirky and others have called this development "gamification." As James Currier of Ooga Labs, a San Francisco–based developer of consumer Internet businesses, writes,

> gamification is coming to everything in the next few years. The next portal is a game. The next email is a game. The next social network is a game. Your next trip to the supermarket could be a game. Your next job could be a game. That means a lot of things, but for one, people with an understanding of those mechanics and how to create contexts will be highly valued. Second, gamification is just the beginning, and will continue for decades.[22]

If gaming is to become the world's obsession, however, society must admit to a sad irony about the virtual world—that consumers will spend billions of dollars on incidental virtual goods while billions of people alive on this planet suffer needlessly from a lack of food, shelter, and basic human services. Just as we cannot allow social media to become a tool for the trivialization of our lives, we must not allow gaming to become a rudderless pastime for those with disposable income and little interest in contributing to our world.

This conundrum is precisely the sentiment expressed in an interview with Premal Shah, president of Kiva.org, one of the most innovative microlenders. Reflecting on his company's future, Shah commented, "I think our biggest competitor is actually probably Zynga. It's not other nonprofits. It's actually competing for people's attention. That fantasy football player in Canton, Ohio, who might play two hours of FarmVille at night—how do we get them to think about Uganda? ... If building a real farm on Kiva can be as compelling as building a virtual farm on Facebook, then I think we've done our jobs really well."[23]

The fact is, social games can help transform our world by leveraging the global reach and addictive nature of gaming to help generate donations far

---

### ZYNGA, FARMVILLE, AND HAITI: HARNESSING THE VIRTUAL WORLD FOR DONATIONS

The notion of tapping into sales of virtual goods for contributions is not without precedent. Following the 2010 earthquake in Haiti, Zynga created limited-edition virtual goods for sale in its games FarmVille, FishVille, Mafia Wars, and Zynga Poker, which they sold to players in 47 countries with the proceeds going to earthquake victims. All the items had a distinctly Creole theme, such as Haitian white corn in FarmVille, a Haitian drum in Mafia Wars, a Haitian fish in FishVille, and a Haitian chip package in Zynga Poker. Links for further donation were promoted on Zynga's other games, including Café World, PetVille, and YoVille, and on Zynga.org.

In the end, Zynga generated $1.5 million in donations, with more than $1 million of that total coming from FarmVille players. This was the first time that Zynga gave 100 percent of its revenues from the sale of virtual goods to a charity—in this case, the World Food Program—and it serves as a model for how virtual gaming can become an agent for social change.

One of the advantages of generating funds from gaming is that it is painless for consumers. The world has seen too many relief efforts frustrated by donor fatigue, limited resources, or even public fear. All three of these factors affected the amount of relief funding raised for the 20 million victims of the tragic floods in Pakistan in 2010. Social games can help ease the extra pressure on real-world NGOs by monetizing fun.

The use of social technology to help others is the next stage in the necessary integration of living and giving that capitalism needs to embrace. As Dan Pallotta explains in his insightful book, *Uncharitable,* the separation between the lives we live and the comparatively small donations we give means that we cannot escape the multiple global crises we face. Social gaming has the potential to make such giving sustainable and fun, while offering perhaps an even greater reward—the knowledge of having helped others.

beyond those of real-world fundraising efforts. Add to that the mass adoption of gaming among children and teens, ensuring future generations will grow up playing social games, and you can see how the virtual world can become a mainstay of collective giving in the future. But only once the concept of contributory consumption is applied to the exchange of real and virtual goods through g-commerce can unprecedented resources can be raised to enable massive social change.

*In a [social] game, you need to give people chances to express themselves in front of their friends.*

—Brian Reynolds, chief game designer, Zynga

## CONTRIBUTIONS AND THE WORLD OF GAMES FOR GOOD

"Games for good" represent an entirely new category of online interaction. Such pursuits implement game mechanics in new ways to challenge people to accomplish positive change in their own lives and in the world. They differ from virtual games in that they are not meant as entertainment and do not feature imaginary contests or worlds. Instead, their ultimate goal is to teach players something meaningful that can be applied in the real world, and they encourage group problem solving. For this reason, they are sometimes called "serious games," because they are collaborative, rather than competitive, and aim to teach things like leadership, negotiation, and teamwork.

One of the pioneers in this field is Dr. Jane McGonigal, director of research and development at the Institute for the Future in Palo Alto, California. She is responsible for designing several massive multiplayer online games focused on social issues. In her article "Why I Love Bees: A Case Study in Collective Intelligence Gaming," McGonigal notes that French philosopher Pierre Lévy argued as early as 1994 that the Internet would facilitate the rapid, open, and global exchange of data and ideas. Coining the term "collective intelligence," Lévy believed that over time the network could "mobilize and coordinate the intelligence, experience, skills, wisdom, and imagination of humanity" in new and unexpected ways. As Lévy put it, "We are passing from the Cartesian *cogito*"—I think, therefore I am—"to *cogitamus*"—*we* think, therefore we are.[24]

Speaking at a TED conference in 2010, McGonigal explained how games might help us mend our world. She pointed out that people currently spend 3 billion hours per week playing games. That may seem like a lot of wasted time, but McGonigal wishes it were 21 billion hours, because she believes gamers would then be better able to solve problems like hunger, poverty, global climate change, and conflict. Her rationale is that games teach people four critical skills that we need to solve the world's crises.

- *Urgent optimism.* Gamers develop a sense of urgency that they must accomplish their goal as soon as possible, yet they remain optimistic they can achieve it.
- *Sensitivity to social fabric.* Gamers learn how to cooperate with each other and perform problem solving collaboratively.
- *Blissful productivity.* Gamers are happiest when they are engaged in problem solving and hard work.
- *Pursuit of epic meaning.* Gamers want to feel they are involved in addressing global threats of gigantic proportion.

Having these four skills enables gamers to achieve what McGonigal calls an "epic win," an outcome that is so extraordinarily positive they had no idea it was even possible. "It is almost beyond the threshold of imagination, so that when you get there, you are shocked that you were truly capable of it," she says. For McGonigal, being able to capture epic wins in the virtual world teaches people how to achieve epic wins in the real world. She even suggests that our formal educational systems need to include both instruction and practice in how to construct and contribute to the type of collective intelligence we need to solve our crises. She points out that the average young person growing up in a country with a strong gamer culture spends 10,000 hours playing online games by the time he or she is 21 years old—the same amount of time that experts of cognitive science say it takes to become a virtuoso in any profession.[25]

Let me give you a few examples of socially oriented serious games of the type that McGonigal refers to.

### 3rd World Farmer

This is an online simulation that depicts the standard plight of poor farmers in unstable and impoverished countries. Originally developed by students at IT University in Copenhagen, Denmark, the game has gone through several upgrades to incorporate feedback from relief agencies and game designers. In the game, the player manages an African farm, complete with all the difficult choices that poverty and conflict bring. One mistake can cause people to die from starvation; players might encounter a corrupt official, be raided by guerrillas, or get caught in a civil war.

### Darfur Is Dying

This game, created in partnership with the Reebok Human Rights Foundation and the International Crisis Group, is an online simulation in which players act out being a displaced Darfurian in a refugee camp who must survive in the face of attacks by the Janjaweed militias. In the process of the game, players learn about the 2.5 million refugees and more than 400,000 dead in the Darfur region of Sudan. They come to understand the ways they can help stop human rights abuses and provide humanitarian assistance.

### World Without Oil

Developed by Jane McGonigal, this one-off simulation took place over 33 days in 2007, and simulated the first 32 weeks of a global oil crisis. People could play the game by agreeing to create a personal story about what their life would be like if all the world's oil were shut off. They then had to email, blog, film, photograph, podcast, tweet, or phone in their story. The game encouraged excellence from its 1,900 participants with daily awards and recognition for authentic and intriguing stories.

### SuperStruct

The premise of this online game, also by McGonigal and the Institute for the Future, is that the world will end in 23 years. Anyone could play the game by providing ideas as to how the world could be saved by reinventing agriculture, energy, health, security, and the social safety net. It's no longer live, but participants generated 500 new solutions.

IN A WE FIRST CONTRIBUTORY WORLD, serious games could play a double role—not only teaching people how to solve the problems of the world, but also helping to generate donations through game playing. Funds can be derived in many ways, such as brand sponsors (possibly solicited by consumers) or through the purchase of virtual goods that trigger a donation. Now is the time for online game companies to explore socially oriented serious games whose goal is to generate funds for charities.

In what is perhaps the first blend of large-scale gaming with social responsibility, Tim Kring created Conspiracy for Good, an "augmented-reality drama" that began as a scavenger hunt for clues in the real-world streets of London in the summer of 2010. Sponsored in part by Nokia, game players traveled around London using their Nokia phones to find and decipher codes hidden throughout the city. As a key part of the game, players also helped the Pearson Foundation donate books to libraries in Zambia. The game was repeated over several weekends, with Polaroid also supporting the event by donating phones and taking photos of contestants that they could turn in for a £5 donation to a charity.[26]

In a We First future, large-scale public games will find their way into the social consciousness. Like Conspiracy for Good, some of these games may have major brands as sponsors, while others might be funded through players' donations. Support for this concept already exists. Geoff Livingston, the cofounder of social-media communications agency Zoetica, which works primarily with nonprofits, organized a crowdsourcing event called CitizenGulf to help children whose families were affected by the BP oil spill. Events in 20 cities raised $11,000. Livingston noted how the collaborative aspect energized participants, who had paid to be part of it. He wrote, "I think when people are empowered to become a part of something—not told what to do, but literally, make it their own, make it part of their life, make it feel like their $10 and two hours of time means something—wow, that's powerful."[27]

The future of serious gaming will move increasingly toward alternate-reality games (ARGs), which combine online episodic storylines with pairs or teams of players who interact in the real world to solve a problem. Their answer then determines the course of the next episode presented to them online, making the game unpredictable, always fresh, and constantly challenging. These AR games will become ever more complex as they come to employ online videos, mobile phones, facilitators, and global teams who communicate using Twitter and other social-media networks.

> *We are witnessing no less than a mass exodus to virtual worlds and online game environments.*
>
> —Edward Castronova, economist

## THE EVOLUTION OF REVOLUTION IS CONTRIBUTION

What I have attempted to portray in this chapter can be encapsulated into a single phrase: *We can no longer draw a line between living and giving if we hope to build a better world.* We cannot continue to live with a form of capitalism that creates profits while ignoring purpose, then makes an inadequate charitable contribution that attempts to rectify the wrong.

We need an economy that functions in the name of sustainable development, that puts purpose on the same plane as profit, that operates in alignment with human values, and that legitimates mutual interest. We need a version of capitalism that delivers a wider and fairer degree of prosperity around the world. We need businesses and corporations to begin acting in the interests of the greater good.

In this modern era, *the evolution of revolution is contribution.* The word *contribution* has multiple connotations here. First, it refers to the very essence of We First—that along with creating profits, the corollary goal of capitalism should be to contribute to the world. All businesses must have at their core some redeeming element which embeds contribution to society into their core principles.

The second meaning of contribution refers to the specific idea of contributory consumption in which every transaction includes a donation to a cause. Given that the U.N. itself seeks to raise $195 billion per year from the world's 22 richest countries, only 5 of which have managed to live up to their pledge, the resources for global social transformation are sorely lacking. We will never solve our nation's—or the world's—crises with the current levels of contribution. We need to transform capitalism into a perpetual motor of renewal.

This proposition will become even more relevant as more nations begin participating in free market capitalism, which if left unchecked will only cause more hardship and chaos. It is already reported, for example, that the growing disparity in China between a small, wealthy elite and the rest of its population already threatens to tear apart the fabric of their society. With roughly 300 million people who can now afford Western-style consumption, and 1 billion people who cannot, China is heading for the same problems that have plagued most developed nations.

If you accept that the world is in trouble—if you accept that the existing pillars of change are insufficient, if you accept that governments are burdened by historic debt, that philanthropies lack sufficient resources, and that corporations mostly practice only self-interested and potentially destructive behavior—then it is only logical to accept that we need to look for a new solution. And the major reservoir of resource creation as yet untapped is the private sector.

*Capitalism hasn't finished evolving yet. It's the most powerful engine of opportunity creation and innovation that's ever been devised, but that doesn't mean that it's finished evolving; it can get better.*

—Jay Coen Gilbert

## CHAPTER TAKEAWAYS

- The crises our planet faces are immense, and governments and charitable donations have never been enough. We First proposes a new system of funding—contributory consumption—in which every transaction generates a charitable contribution.
- Ideally, brands themselves would agree to fund the majority of these contributions from their profits as compensation for the benefits they receive from society.
- Numerous surveys confirm that consumers are willing to absorb a small premium for products linked to causes or produced via sustainable means.
- There are many precursors to the idea of comprehensive contributory consumption: cause-related marketing and programs like (PRODUCT)RED, 1% for the Planet, and SocialVest.
- Contributory consumption can be applied to the real and virtual marketplaces, as well as to brands existing both on- and off-line, coupon deals, social entrepreneurial websites, mobile-phone transactions, online games and virtual goods, and the growing field of serious games.
- We can no longer separate living and giving if we hope to build a better world. The evolution of revolution is contribution.

# 10 THE GLOBAL BRAND INITIATIVE

## THE FUTURE OF THE PRIVATE SECTOR

Humans are organizational creatures. We've evolved to live in increasingly complex systems—from families and tribes to villages and towns to cities and nations. We instinctively congregate around one another, and we rely on the members of our communities to help us in our moments of need.

Whenever humans have a good idea, we tend to build it out using organizations, because they make sense. This has held true for religions, fraternal organizations, labor unions, and even for charitable causes. In the early 1900s, many cities in the United States had "community chests," social organizations that collected money from businesses and workers to use for civic projects. In 1948 more than 1,000 of these organizations were merged into the United Foundation. In 1963 it became United Way; in 1971, United Way of America; and today it is United Way Worldwide.

Charitable organizations are now evolving even further. Network for Good (NFG), founded in 2001, is a prime example. When AOL, Cisco, and Yahoo saw in the emergence of the online world a totally new opportunity for charitable fundraising, the companies teamed up to form a one-stop shop where brands, nonprofits, and consumers could all work together for causes. NFG is effectively a clearinghouse that leverages the online world and social media to facilitate charitable donations in a variety of ways. It assists in developing corporate-sponsored good-works campaigns of all types: from grant-matching to crowdsourced voting that rewards popular charities with corporate monies, to campaigns that ask people to pledge volunteer time, acts of kindness, or dollars to achieve a common goal.

Along with its partner Zoetica, a communications company specializing in serving nonprofits and socially conscious companies, NFG has helped pioneer a variety of creative concepts for online fundraising. It produces "charity badges"—fundraising widgets that any company, charity, or individual can add to a website to enable visitors to donate. It built a web application where volunteers can search a database of opportunities for their work (it is now the provider of choice for the official statewide volunteer offices and programs in California, Illinois, and Louisiana). And whenever natural disaster strikes, NFG can set up online donation centers for corporations and nonprofits that sponsor emergency fundraising efforts.

Computerworld, *Forbes,* the ePhilanthropy Foundation, *Wired,* and MarketingSherpa have hailed NFG for "revolutionizing philanthropy." In its decade of existence, it has processed over $400 million in donations for more than 50,000 nonprofits, including household names like Malaria No More and SocialVest.[1]

## INTRODUCING THE GLOBAL BRAND INITIATIVE

Network for Good is just one of many precursors to have laid the groundwork for one more idea I am proposing for how brands and consumers can build a better world. Called the Global Brand Initiative (GBI), this will be an association of corporate brands and their advertising partners that willingly agree to work together to advance corporate social responsibility and charitable donations. The GBI would have three primary tasks.

- To act as a clearinghouse of corporate social responsibility information and action among all brands participating in We First capitalism.
- To administer, manage, and direct the flow of monies derived from brands and retailers that make donations through contributory consumption transactions.
- To organize new collaborations and partnerships among participating brands that can positively impact the speed and efficiency of social transformation.

The goal of the GBI is not to reinvent the wheel of corporate philanthropy or cause-related marketing, but to engage the untapped cross-pollination of brands to enhance the private sector's response to the world's problems. Operating as the hub in a hub-and-spoke structure, the GBI would follow a decentralized but federated organizational model of administration and decision making. Every brand that participates in the GBI would remain in charge of its own cause-related marketing efforts, the funds it collects under contributory consumption, and any donations it brings in otherwise. But each brand could also choose to pool its funds in a common cash reserve used to support NGOs that need larger sources of monies that usually cannot be generated through traditional fundraising.

The GBI would adhere to a charter developed among its originating member companies laying out its foundational principles, mission, and rules. It would host a centralized office staffed with representatives from all participating brands and advertising partners. Management and employees, working with government and NGO representatives, would help the GBI establish and monitor clear one-, three-, and five-year goals on which the member corporations would vote and approve. The GBI would then allocate roles and responsibilities among its members to ensure that the goals are met with the best efficiencies of the private sector.

This concept raises many questions, of course. Why would companies, especially competitors, join the GBI? What do they get out of it? Why do we need it? Why can't companies just continue doing their own CRM? Let's explore my answers.

## PRECURSORS OF THE GBI

There is a good reason that the time is right for brands to form an association like the Global Brand Initiative—*they are already evolving in the direction of collaboration, which experience shows is what solving the world's problems needs.* While this state is not fully realized yet, there are fewer and fewer impediments to global collaboration among corporations, while much evidence exists proving that the dynamics needed for the GBI are already taking shape. Let's examine four broad categories in which we can see the precursors of palpable change: (1) corporations becoming increasingly involved in socially transformative thinking or actions; (2) corporations partnering together for change; (3) corporations directly participating with NGOs; and (4) corporations working to assist governments. All these are signs that contributory consumption and the GBI offer realistic, practical, and actionable solutions to the crises we face around the world.

## CORPORATIONS INVOLVED IN SOCIALLY TRANSFORMATIVE ACTIONS

The number of individual corporations involved in socially oriented projects is skyrocketing. I have already mentioned a few of the exceptional efforts that are indicative of the emerging new thinking and action in the corporate world, such as Patagonia's Common Threads recycling program and its Footprint Chronicles, which measures the company's sustainability profile for every one of its products. We also looked at Unilever's goal to implement 100 percent sustainable packaging by 2020, and Sony's Open Planet Ideas in conjunction with World Wildlife Fund, which is a crowdsourcing effort inviting the public to create new ideas to solve problems using Sony technologies. I pointed out how many major multinational companies are reaching out in truly novel and creative ways to alleviate some of the most difficult global problems, such as P & G's Children's Safe Drinking Water program, which provides $20 million to purify 2 billion liters of water, and its Pampers program to vaccinate expectant mothers in 12 African countries.

These are good news and solid precursors of how individual companies are undertaking actions that were unheard of a decade or two ago. Many corporate programs are now regularly making headlines in business magazines and websites like Fast Company, TechCrunch, Mashable, Springwise, and others that in turn drive the movement forward.

And there are hundreds more worthy of being called out. Consider, for instance, Google's Project $10^{100}$, which began in October 2008 as a crowdsourcing call for ideas to change the world. In this competition, Google asked members of the public to submit their biggest ideas that could help the most number of people possible, out of which the company would donate $10 million toward the five best ideas. The results were astonishing: Google received more than 150,000 entries, which took more than two years to sort through and select the five top ideas which were finally announced in September 2010.

There are also many other types of laudable activities being conducted by individual companies to demonstrate their social responsibility, ranging from creating new ways to invest to the development of new indices to help measure economic progress. For example, one of the most significant accomplishments in raising awareness about the need to move corporations toward greater social responsibility is an effort from B Labs under a grant from the Rockefeller Foundation in association with the Global Impact Investing Network. The goal of this effort is to start moving substantial amounts of institutional capital from the usual private investment portfolios into "impact investments." Impact investing differs slightly from socially responsible investing in that it seeks to fund companies whose missions are literally to solve social and environmental problems, whereas SRI is solely about investing in companies that avoid irresponsible practices.

To encourage the growth of impact investing, B Labs is launching in 2011 the Global Impact Investing Rating System (GIIRS), which will function somewhat similar to the Morningstar rating system for mutual funds or the S & P credit risk ratings. For companies, the system will produce ratings of individual companies in the form of an overall rating, plus ratings in about 15 subcategories and key performance indicators (KPIs). For funds, the system will produce a rating based on an aggregated and weighted scale of the underlying portfolio companies. Both ratings will also help investors decide what companies and funds are truly involved in socially transformative businesses.

The GIIRS rating system is just one of many new tools being created to help consumers, investors, and corporations better understand the impact of capitalism on our society. Indeed, there is a vast wave of thought leaders who are proposing many types of indices that will provide more accurate feedback on social responsibility and environmental concerns. We explored earlier the Walmart Sustainability Index and the Happy Planet Index, but there is also the Prosperity Index, the Social Competitiveness Index (SCI), and the Commission on the Measurement of Economic Performance and Social Progress, chaired by economist Joseph Stiglitz. While all these new indices differ slightly in how they measure progress, they all agree we can no longer rely solely on measures of production and output such as GDP that reflect the profit-for-profit's-sake thinking of free market capitalism.

There are also companies creating their own accountability metrics, such as Timberland, and companies voluntarily joining networks such as the Global Reporting Initiative (GRI) and Social Accountability International that ensure that their corporate social responsibility practices are not only authentic but measurable in order to justify them to corporate boards and shareholders.

The trend toward socially responsible behavior is also being captured among business schools. For example, Thunderbird Business School is the first MBA program that asks all its students to agree to a pledge, The Thunderbird Oath, which commits them to create sustainable economic and social value. In 2008, about 500 MBA programs around the world adopted a similar voluntary pledge that originated at Harvard, the MBA Oath, which students can take to swear their commitment to responsible business practices. Such oaths may be literally predictive about the future of capitalism since MBA students will shortly comprise the leadership of thousands of corporations.

## CORPORATIONS PARTNERING TOGETHER FOR CHANGE

Also unimaginable a decade ago is the number of corporations working with other firms to collaborate on significant change efforts. This is occurring with increasing frequency both within industry groups and across sectors.

Examples include Timberland's membership in the Outdoor Association, in which 200 companies have agreed to a new industry Eco-index regarding the environmentally sound production of outdoor sport gear and equipment. Unilever is a founding member of the Roundtable on Sustainable Palm Oil, set up in cooperation with the World Wildlife Fund (WWF) in 2004, and the Round Table on Responsible Soy, both industry-wide associations of companies that seek to adhere to higher socially responsible standards. Unilever also worked with Nestlé and Danone to establish the Sustainable Agriculture Initiative Platform (SAI Platform) in 2002, which now involves more than 20 companies from the food and beverage industry that agree to advance sustainable agriculture in four areas: dairy, arable and vegetable crops, coffee, and fruit.

Numerous C-suite executives also team up with Whole Foods CEO John Mackey in his Conscious Capitalism Alliance (CCA), an association of executives that endorses transforming business into a more responsible and interdependent global marketplace. Other examples of new business associations focused on social responsibility include B Labs "Declaration of Interdependence" for B Corporations and Bono's (PRODUCT)RED license, which connects participating companies together to support collective fundraising for HIV/AIDS in Africa.

There are also many organizations now existing that serve as networking groups for corporations, executives, and entrepreneurs who want to work collectively to push corporate practices further toward social responsibility. For example, both the World Business Academy and Social Venture Network sponsor meetings and conferences that highlight new ideas and best practices.

When we consider the growth in the number and range of such collaborative efforts, it is clear that many corporations are no longer reluctant to join forces with other companies to share ideas on how they can improve their business practices in regard to sustainability, environmental issues, and social responsibility.

## CORPORATIONS WORKING FOR CHANGE WITH NONPROFITS

For decades, corporations simply donated money to nonprofits. Then in the 1990s, more companies began offering in-kind donations such as products, expertise, and the volunteer time of their employees. Today, the level of corporate cooperation with NGOs is impressive, confirming the potential role that the GBI could serve in encouraging greater corporate-NGO partnership activities.

Consider, for example, the extraordinary story of how the World Wildlife Fund has succeeded in working directly with many companies to help them understand the critical importance of sustainability in their business practices. In a fascinating TED talk entitled "How Big Brands Can Help Save Biodiversity," WWF Vice President Jason Clay explained that all businesses must acknowledge that sustainability is no longer a choice. As Clay put it, consumers should no longer be able to choose between an unsustainable product and a sustainable one. "Sustainability has to be a pre-competitive issue. It has to be something we all care about. And we need collusion. We need groups to work together that never have. We need Cargill to work with Bungee. We need Coke to work with Pepsi. We need Oxford to work with Cambridge. We need Greenpeace to work with WWF. Everyone has to work together. China has to work with the U.S. We need to begin to manage this planet as if our life depended on it, because it does."[2]

To achieve this goal, WWF began studying how it could partner with companies to directly impact their business practices. At first WWF was daunted, realizing that as many as 60,000 companies were involved in depleting the Earth's natural resources. But upon further investigation, WWF saw that only about 100 companies controlled 25 percent of the market across these sectors. If WWF could persuade just those 100 firms, their competitors would naturally follow.

This became its strategy. WWF invited the top eight companies involved in salmon aquaculture to attend a roundtable. Despite the fact that three of the eight companies were suing each other in court, they all came to the meeting, where Clay persuaded them to agree to new standards for sustainable salmon aquaculture. WWF is now conducting roundtables for the market leaders in other industries such as palm oil, forestry, and coffee and cocoa farming, demonstrating that even competing companies can find common ground to work on behalf of sustainability, particularly where the very future of their business is at stake.

Another example of nonprofit-corporate cooperation is Ceres (pronounced "Series"), a network of investors, environmental organizations, and other public interest groups that works with companies to establish new policies and practices regarding sustainability and global climate change. Originally launched following the *Exxon Valdez* oil spill in 1989, Ceres has had surprising success creating new standards and pushing for corporate compliance in many key areas. In 1989, it proposed its 10-point Ceres Principles for corporate environmental behavior, which are now followed by 50 major corporations. The organization's current push is the "Ceres 20–20 Plan," which proposes four pillars of substantive change in business: accounting that takes carbon emissions into account; higher standards of business leadership; accelerated green innovation; and new policies that reward performance for sustainability.

The Nike Foundation's Girl Effect program is another example of a nonprofit-corporate cooperation. Proposed by Maria Eitel, president of the Nike Foundation, the concept focuses on finding ways to educate the estimated 600 million adolescent girls throughout the developing world who live in poverty, are at risk for HIV, and are often abused by their families. By funding schools and programs to ensure these girls stay in school where they can learn the skills to become employable, the program helps them escape a life of early marriage and motherhood, often as young as 12 or 14 years old. The "girl effect" thus offers these adolescents—and their future daughters—a chance to break the cycle of poverty. Educating women in the developing world has also been shown to improve the economic growth and health of their communities and their nations. As Eitel explained in a *Fast Company* interview, "A girl is the mother of every child who is born into poverty, and a girl will determine the future of the next generation. The Girl Effect: you don't just transform her life, but the family's, the community's, the nation's."[3]

Another example is Hewlett Packard's (HP) collaboration with the Clinton Health Access Initiative (CHAI), aimed at bringing urgent treatment to tens of thousands of infants infected with HIV in Kenya. By building five data centers, HP and CHAI have set themselves a goal of reducing diagnosis response times from several months to just days. HP seeks to reach 70,000 of the infected infants in the first year of the program. As President Bill Clinton stated, this partnership serves to "demonstrate how the private sector can and should operate in the developing world."[4]

The WWF effort, the Nike Girl Effect, and the HP/CHAI partnerships illustrate significant advances in how the nonprofit world can work directly with

## LESSONS FOR NGOS FROM COCA-COLA

At a special Bill and Melinda Gates Foundation TEDxChange in September 2010, Melinda Gates delivered an insightful presentation on what nonprofits can learn from the business world. Her focus was on Coca-Cola, which is ubiquitous throughout the world, delivering 1.5 billion servings of its beverages each and every day, even in the most remote and poverty-stricken areas. Her advice for NGOs: "If we can learn from Coke, we can learn to fix the world."

Gates then proceeded to analyze three lessons that Coke can teach NGOs. First, the company seeks to maintain real-time market data on every one of its products, which helps it create a powerful feedback loop. Coke knows where every can and bottle of its products is sold. If sales begin to drop, it can adjust or boost its marketing. In contrast, NGOs usually don't collect data until the end of their projects, which Gates described as "bowling in the dark."

Second, Coke taps into the natural human impulse for entrepreneurialism. The company noticed how in places like some parts of Africa, where there are no roads (and hence, no delivery trucks), local people in every village would manage to buy products in bulk and resell them to neighbors. So Coke offered them loans and trained them to become "micro-distribution centers." Coke now has 3,000 such centers in Africa, which collectively employ 15,000 people who sell Coke products from bicycles, pushcarts, and wheelbarrows. In contrast, NGOs often struggle to deliver their services to remote areas. One NGO in Ethiopia found success by following Coke's model, training 35,000 health extension workers to deliver basic healthcare services throughout the country.

Third, Coke is an expert at marketing, making its products aspirational purchases. People desire Coke because in their mind, it makes their life better. Where Coke shines is in localizing its aspirational message—Coke delivers happiness, but since what that entails varies around the world, the company has learned to adapt its messages to each country. By contrast, NGOs often erroneously believe that people want exactly the improvements they plan to deliver. Gates pointed out, for example, that putting toilets in villages where children die from diseases caused by open defecation is not enough to make people change their sanitary habits. Instead, NGOs must find ways to imbue their services with meaning, such as the state of Haryana, in India, where toilets were linked to courtship: women would not marry men who did not have a toilet.

corporations to build support and agreement on substantial social and environmental change issues. The distance between nonprofits and corporations is shrinking every day.

## CORPORATIONS WORKING WITH GOVERNMENT

As a last category of precursors to the GBI, we are also witnessing more and more instances of companies working closely with government on social change activities. One of these, Change the Equation, involves a network of 100 CEOs who are committing their companies to help rebuild science and math literacy in America's school systems. Companies such as Intel, Kodak, Sally Ride Science, Time Warner Cable, Xerox, and ExxonMobil have agreed to start aligning all the separate programs they each conduct in schools to help boost science, technology, engineering, and math (STEM) skills. Change the Equation will begin by taking a baseline of all the corporate programs, then it will create a scorecard and assessment criteria so that companies can measure their effectiveness. From that input, the program will establish a core curriculum for STEM skills that can be taught in 100 sites across the country.

Another intriguing example of government availing itself of new ideas from the private sector is the April 2010 State Department–sponsored TED talks. Over 700 State Department officials attended the event, which also served as the launch of Secretary of State Hillary Clinton's Global Partnership Initiative, opening up the State Department to more partnerships with foundations, businesses, non-governmental organizations, universities, and faith communities. With the theme for the day being "New ideas for a better world," Secretary Clinton invited the State Department attendees to be open to new ideas from all those sectors to meet the challenges that the world faces. Clinton also made the same point again in October 2010, when she spoke to an audience of Bay Area technology leaders at a meeting in San Francisco, inviting them to assist the State Department in conquering the problems of poverty and disease in the Third World. As she told this audience,

> part of our approach is to embrace new tools like using cell phones for mobile banking or to monitor elections. But we're also reaching [out] to the people behind these tools, the innovators and the entrepreneurs themselves. . . .
> We know that many business leaders want to devote some of their companies' expertise to solving problems around the world, but they often don't know how to do that. What's the point of entry? Which idea is going to have the

## THE ASCENDANCY OF OPEN-SOURCE THINKING

According to law professor Yochai Benkler, author of *The Wealth of Networks,* there is a radical shift occurring in the way information production and exchange are being capitalized. In the past, the costs of producing information had to be centralized and market based. Today, the costs of information and knowledge are now distributed throughout the world, as the Internet links a billion people together who each absorb part of the cost in the purchase of the computers or smartphones. This effectively puts the elements of knowledge creation in the hands of every connected person around the planet. And as we move increasingly toward information economies—where wealth is created through information and knowledge—we're experiencing a revolution that Benkler calls open-source economics. A prime example is how Wikipedia is slowly replacing the market-based information source *Encyclopaedia Britannica.*

The evolution of open-source economics is affecting nearly every domain via social media. The creation of content and knowledge is being outsourced in nearly every field. Benkler calls it the creation of a fourth system, one of social sharing and exchange that occurs outside the prior systems of market-based companies, nonprofits, and government.

Equally important, though, is the fact that social media also introduces into the equation our human tendency to do things to help others *because it gives us meaning or a set of social relations.* People are increasingly using social media to participate in information sharing—and hence problem solving—just because they like it. They are willing to spend five minutes here, an hour there, to work on a problem for which they have expertise to contribute.

This is why we are now seeing a huge rise in the number of open-source problem-solving websites such as Sony's Open Planet Ideas, Innocentive, One Billion Minds, and OpenIDEO.

Many of these sites are based on the type of platform used in OpenIDEO, which posts a challenge and then employs three development phases to solve problems—inspiration, concepting, and evaluation. During inspiration, anyone can upload ideas in any form—photos, text, videos, sketches, snippets of code. In concepting, anyone can build off any of the inspirations provided to create a full-blown concept for solving the problem. Participants can provide feedback to each other at any time. Between phases, the staff at IDEO provides input to shape the process. At the end, a top concept is chosen which people can then offer the world to solve the challenge. The whole enterprise is open sourced, shared, and public.

There is no doubt that more and more of the world's problems will be cast into open-source thinking—nor should there be doubt that the collective of humanity is well equipped to solve its own problems.

most impact? . . .To bridge that gap, we are embracing new public-private partnerships that link the on-the-ground experience of our diplomats and development experts with the energy and resources of the business community.[5]

## THE MERITS OF THE GLOBAL BRAND INITIATIVE

We already have tens of thousands of corporations participating in some form of social transformation through their foundations, charitable donations, cause marketing efforts, and employee volunteer programs. They are increasingly collaborating with other companies, NGOs, and governments. These efforts represent a massive collection of individual attempts that are slowly advancing us in the right direction. In fact, CSRWire's 2009 summary of corporate social responsibility characterized the progress we have recently seen as follows:

> Perhaps the biggest CSR development of the year was not readily visible, as it was an idea: that CSR represents not just a trend or professional discipline, but a social movement. In other words, CSR is not a random collection of ad hoc, discrete actions to revise corporate behavior, but rather a coherent aggregation of sustained, widespread efforts to reform (or even revolutionize) the role of corporations, shifting from negative to positive impacts on society, environment, and economy.[6]

But all these efforts could be tremendously enhanced if the corporations of the world would come together to pool their resources, expertise, knowledge, and talent into one focused global initiative to change the world together. The Global Brand Initiative is designed to play precisely this role.

## THE STRUCTURE AND OPERATION OF THE GBI

How might such a large alliance of corporations work? First, as stated earlier, it would be voluntary, operating as a federation of brands, each one still maintaining its independence and sovereignty over its own internal efforts for social transformation but agreeing to work with other member companies on joint projects, as it deems appropriate. Here are some specifics as to the GBI's membership, governance, tasks, costs, and decision-making process.

## MEMBERSHIP

Companies could choose to become permanent members or just sign on for a finite period. To accommodate various levels of participation, there could even be different levels of membership, just as with the G20 or G7 and the U.N., such that those who assume greater responsibility and contribution would become permanent members.

Each participating brand would have a representative to present its interests and views, though preferably not the CEO so as to avoid conflicts of interest. This person represents his or her organization, but is also bound to act in concert with other members to honor the overarching goals of the GBI. All participating members sign a charter or an agreed-upon code of conduct, with breaches resulting in that particular organization being expelled or losing its voting rights. Ideally, there should be members from all major industries so the body of the GBI reflects the full gamut of the private sector. From a collaborative point of view, this also boosts the opportunities for cross-pollination of ideas from different sectors.

## GOVERNANCE STRUCTURE

The GBI would employ a governing structure similar to the United Nations. There would be a governing board, composed of representatives half from the permanent companies, half from the larger set of companies, whose tenures would rotate, limited to a specified term. To avoid a monopoly of power among larger corporations versus smaller ones, a maximum three-year term among all governing board members would be enforced.

Participating member corporations would select an acting Director who would serve a term of two or three years. The GBI would maintain an office for the Director and some support staff, with space for live meetings and all the necessary technology for virtual meetings among member companies, NGOs, and government officials when they are working on projects together. The Director could appoint standing committees whose focus might parallel the eight U.N. Millennium Development Goals, plus ad hoc committees that are tasked with analysis and decisions on specific social projects.

## TASKS AND RESPONSIBILITIES

The activities of the GBI would be geared entirely around finding ways to maximize the private sector's capabilities to assist governments and NGOs in the work of alleviating global poverty, malnutrition, joblessness, lack of sanitation and healthcare, illiteracy, gender discrimination, and all the other crises that plague the planet.

As such, the GBI's tasks might include analyzing and assessing the current efforts among members so as to create a scorecard and database of existing social transformation projects; recommending opportunities for partnerships and joint projects among corporations or between corporations, NGOs, and government for new projects or ways to enhance existing ones; evaluating current levels of research and development for products and services that could boost social transformation; examining current levels of funding to see where there may be areas where reallocating resources to the most promising solutions could help fast-track them to implementation; maintaining a database of corporate expertise and technical knowledge that NGOs and government could have access to as needed; and coordinating suppliers and distribution channels for solutions that reflect the most effective and efficient methods of responding to chronic and acute crises.

## OPERATING COSTS

The GBI will have operating costs, and these would be covered through membership dues paid by participating brands and advertising agencies (which could be rated on a sliding scale according to size of company). The dues could also be adjusted by putting a dollar value on the in-kind contributions—such as R & D, expertise, management training, or advertising, marketing, and media contributions—that a member company might contribute. In return, member companies will benefit from the PR, CSR, and HR advantages they receive by virtue of their membership in the GBI.

## DECISION MAKING

Working with NGOs and governments, various committees within the GBI working on specific causes would prepare an annual budget to project where money is needed and where it could be most effectively utilized to bring about the most benefit. These committees would form competing agendas whose decisions would be placed in front of the Governing Board for debate and approval, then sent directly to the GBI's Director for final sign-off. The Governing Board might base its priorities each year on the status of the research under way or on the potential for a certain project to accomplish a major change that could impact millions of lives.

## TECHNOLOGY

The GBI would endeavor to use the latest technologies in all solutions to maximize their effectiveness, and will aim to equip NGOs with the newest tools that can help them relay information between their operational headquarters and sites on the ground. The GBI will also seek to emphasize technology-based solutions that can substantially improve a program's coverage or capabilities while maintaining or reducing its costs.

## AWARDS

In order to aid the recognition of participating members, the GBI would create a variety of awards linked to causes and effective actions. An awards ceremony would recognize the leading companies each year for their contributions at different levels for various causes. This ceremony would also serve as a global public awareness ceremony that increases visibility for the GBI, all its member brands, and most importantly, the progress made toward easing crises and the causes that remain to be solved.

## THE GBI AND DONATIONS FROM CONTRIBUTORY CONSUMPTION

There is another vital role for the GBI—to act as the clearinghouse for the funds that come from the contributory consumption programs of its member companies. So how would the GBI manage these funds?

Companies could decide, if they prefer, to continue funding the causes their brands have become known to assist. Or they could publicize to consumers that a percentage of each sale would go to the Global Brand Initiative to be pooled with other corporate donations that will all help another cause. Alternatively, brands could let consumers choose if they would like the brand's donation to go to its usual cause or to one of the GBI causes that is more in line with their personal concerns.

However, if the brand decides to allocate its donations from contributory consumption to the GBI, those funds would be deposited into a common escrow account that collects the donations of all brand members. These monies could then be used to help fund the U.N. Millennial Development Goals, or unexpected and costly emergency relief efforts, or to fund special programs that NGOs cannot manage on their own.

Some of the funds collected from consumer purchases would also go to critical Research & Development activities to create new technologies and tools, such as vaccines, water purification equipment, or renewable energy technologies. A portion of funds would also be used for the personnel staffing needed in relief programs, such as teachers, doctors, and administrators. Finally, a small portion of the brand contributions would help cover the cost of running the GBI itself in the event of deficits from dues. Based on a distributed model, these costs would be small compared to the large operating costs of institutions like the U.N., the World Bank, or the International Monetary Fund, as the GBI organization itself would effectively reside in the corporate headquarters of multiple companies throughout the world.

As it moves forward, the GBI might create its own list of goals and milestones that it will seek to fund using brand contributions. Such new goals might include some of the ideas that Olav Kjorven, assistant secretary general of the United Nations for development policy, proposed in 2010, including cutting greenhouse gas emissions by 50 percent; converting at least 40 percent of agricultural lands to ecologically sustainable production; transitioning 13 million of the 22 million fishing boats into alternate activity in order to save and replenish depleted global fish and seafood stocks; and reduce average animal protein intake among the top billion people by 20 percent.[7] These are all goals that will require funding for research, development of solutions, as well as marketing and advertising communications to convey them to the public.

Given that the GBI would be in charge of potentially billions of dollars, the issue of transparency is of paramount importance to its success. The GBI Director and Governing Board would establish rules and procedures that guarantee complete transparency with regard to funds. All of the participating corporations, nonprofits, government partners, and consumers would have access to monthly reporting to see how money is spent. The GBI would adopt effective indices that can clearly report on the number of projects undertaken and their impact.

## THE BENEFITS OF THE GBI

What are the benefits of membership that would motivate companies to participate?

One is that the GBI can take advantage of the collective intelligence of thousands of companies in every sphere of human activity. If just 100 or 500 or 1,000 of the 50,000 or 60,000 corporations in the world participated in the

GBI, it would amass a brain trust unmatched in intellectual prowess combined with pragmatic thinking and focus.

As a related perk of the GBI, research increasingly demonstrates that a distributed model of intelligence yields greater results than a top-down, authoritarian model. In his book *The Wisdom of Crowds*, James Surowiecki notes that the success of problem solving increases with the number of participants as long as four elements are in place: diversity of opinion, independence, decentralization, and the aggregation of decisions into one choice. Similarly, in a notable TED talk, "Institutions vs. Collaboration," Clay Shirky argues that in today's technological world, collaboration is how we ensure that we don't miss the contributions of the least expected but often the best or most useful solutions. Shirky points out that while 80 percent of the work invariably comes from the top 20 percent of the people, we cannot afford to risk losing the brilliant idea from someone in the 80 percent tail which might offer the solution that bests all others.[8]

The message of Surowiecki and Shirky suggests that we need to embrace collaboration as the new model of human interaction that can help us solve our problems and achieve our goals with greater efficiency and efficacy. In conjoining hundreds or thousands of corporations, the GBI will effectively act as a collaborative network that inspires companies to contribute to the collective intelligence far more than they could accomplish on their own.

Another benefit of the GBI is that it can generate a reliable stream of financial resources enabling nonprofits to plan further in advance. The private sector is accustomed to planning for goals years in advance, and this is a critical skill and capacity it can offer nonprofits. This is true for large, complex, and long-term crises as well as humanitarian emergencies that necessitate thorough preparation to ensure the most effective responses.

A third benefit of the GBI is that it can fulfill a dire need for greater coordination among NGOs. Many of the challenges facing philanthropies and NGOs stem from the extreme chaos and circumstances under which they operate. In Haiti there are over 10,000 NGOs seeking to help the country, with insufficient coordination between them. India has over 1 million NGOs working on scores of causes and projects. NGOs also report that they often lack the power and clout to persuade local governments to allow them to work in certain territories or to implement the solutions the NGO believes are most effective.

These are barriers that a coalition of multinational corporations could more easily overcome. For example, consider the 2010 floods in Pakistan that put 6 million people at risk. In that situation, P & G Children's Safe Drinking Water (CSDW) Program partnered with World Vision, Save the Children, Read Foundation, HOPE, and other NGOs to provide more than 5 million PUR packets to purify contaminated water. But imagine if they could have also called on five other corporations to assist with the relief effort, helping to coordinate donations and delivery.

## THE FUTURE OF TECHNOLOGY AND THE GBI

Another valuable lesson that companies participating in the GBI can learn is how the same technologies and innovations that help solve the problems of the developing world can be used to improve their own operations or serve their customers. As advances in technology make the job of building a better world increasingly more efficient and effective, even the future of First World innovation will derive and benefit in part from the answers created to meet the needs of the developing world.

This point was driven home in a *New York Times* column by Thomas Friedman, who noted that some of the most creative and disruptive innovations are being developed to assist poor countries where there is little or no infrastructure for transportation or communications. Friedman points out that the cheap connectivity of mobile phones and their ability to close the "last mile"—the gap where government services end and the consumer's need begins—encourage enterprising technology gurus throughout countries like India and Bangladesh to innovate low-cost solutions that get around the problems so many developing nations have. As a result, many new applications are being developed for smartphones that, for example, help people in remote or poor villages do banking, transfer money, take out loans, take classes, train for jobs, sell their crops, or check commodity prices—all tasks that previously could not be done and thus kept millions of people locked in underdevelopment with no access to prosperity. As Friedman concluded, "If you thought the rate of change was fast thanks to the garage innovators of Silicon Valley, wait until the garages of Delhi, Mumbai, and Bangalore get fully up to speed."[9]

## THE PROMISE OF THE GBI

The GBI is designed to maximize the impact that the corporate world can bring to social transformation. Its organizational and administrative efficiencies can replace the patchwork of corporate social responsibility (CSR) activities that, while essential and generous, have yet to achieve large-scale global transformation. The role of the GBI is to bring the best of private-sector thinking, skills, and resources to bear on our greatest social challenges while also preventing capitalism's worst excesses.

Taken as a whole, contributory consumption and the GBI have the potential to create a powerful virtuous lifecycle of constructive benefits for all. Consumer power motivates brands to participate and agree to contribute in order to maintain their loyal customers; consumer purchases drive the brand contributions to the GBI; these contributions fund the various actions necessary to effect social change on a global level; and, finally, those same social changes slowly improve the world for consumers and the business environment for brands. Consumers, brands, and the world prosper as one.

In this way, *We First* establishes a comprehensive system to build a better world. Each element is designed to build on the last in an ever-larger framework for change. It instills into our economic system a new vision of mutual self-interest, purpose, sustainability, and values. It aligns brands and consumers together as partners for change. It radically boosts the opportunity to generate the funds that global social transformation desperately needs. And, through the GBI, it unites much of the corporate world into a single body that can bring its expertise and resources to bear on fulfilling the vision of a more prosperous and peaceful world.

## CHAPTER TAKEAWAYS

- We First proposes the Global Brand Initiative (GBI), an association of corporate brands and their advertising partners that willingly work together to advance corporate social responsibility and charitable donations.
- The efforts of corporations to assist with social change could be tremendously enhanced by coming together to pool their resources, expertise, knowledge, and talent into one focused global initiative to change the world together.
- The GBI would be voluntary, operating as a federation of brands, with specific operational regulations, membership rules, budgets, and responsibilities to boost the capabilities of government and

NGOs and to manage the flow of money from contributory consumption.

- The GBI unites much of the corporate world into a single body that can bring its expertise and resources to bear on fulfilling the vision of a more prosperous and peaceful world.

# EPILOGUE

I opened this book by asking the question: Is this the world you want? For the many reasons outlined in its pages, my answer is no. Still, the future has never looked brighter. The challenges we face are enormous, but the opportunity to shape our future has never been greater. *There is no time to waste.*

Whether we are corporate executives, entrepreneurs, consumers, concerned citizens, or activists, we must begin working on behalf of our planet and those without power. If we continue to neglect these two issues, their combined impact will permanently harm the Earth and destroy the fabric of our societies. Characterizing the plight of the African American community decades ago in his "I have a dream" speech, Martin Luther King Jr. spoke of "a lonely island of poverty in the midst of a vast ocean of material prosperity." Tragically, in today's global community, that metaphor still holds true, but it has reversed: Our world is now an ever shrinking island of extraordinary wealth fortifying itself against a widening ocean of abject poverty and broken dreams.

Yet the shift we seek has begun. Citizen-controlled social media now competes with the multinational monopolies to write and tell the story of our future. As more people chime in, the more their needs and hopes are being reflected. And the stories they create are being framed around values that unite rather than divide us. Business is rising to the challenge. Top-down, hierarchical organizing principles rooted in fear are being superseded by organic, distributed, and free-flowing structures. Leading-edge companies are integrating values into their business strategies and embracing their role as enduring custodians of community and planetary well-being. Billionaires and corporate leaders are willingly following the example of Bill Gates, Warren Buffett, Sergey Brin, and Mark Zuckerberg, whose personal successes feed their public generosity. Slowly, the false separation between economic and moral values is dissolving. As it does, the unit of measure for success is shifting from the gross domestic production of a single country to global well-being for all humankind.

*The great hope for business is the business of hope.*

Technological change is accelerating this shift on two levels—speed and scale. Both must be enlisted if we are to accomplish our goals before it is too late. The merger of mobile, social, and gaming technology portends even greater transformative opportunities that leverage both the real and virtual worlds. Still, the world we want will not be built by fiber optics, cell-phone towers, or social-media platforms. It will be created choice by choice, in our hearts and minds, and with our hands. That innate desire for a better world is easily awakened. As Jonathan Haidt explains in *The Happiness Hypothesis:* "The emotions that promote the meaningful life are powerfully contagious, which increases their chance for propagation, and their encoding into our nervous systems and their ritualization into cultural practice."[1] New studies by behavioral economists draw the same conclusions; as one of the field's leaders, Herbert Gintis, states: "It is increasingly obvious that people are motivated by morality; people are motivated by ethics. We may be seeing a possible renaissance of economic theory."[2]

Given this, the most critical role that social technology can play is to compound this contagious quality and hasten the half-life of change. It will enable this generation to serve as an example for others in the future, effectively creating a self-perpetuating (re)generational cycle of responsibility. *The gift we give our children is the world we leave behind.*

Whether or not we realize it, this outcome depends on our choices as individuals. It is our personal responsibility to manage our thinking, behavior, and lives so that we bring our best selves to the challenges ahead. Every daily choice, task, and commitment represents a chance to shape our future and add meaning to our lives.

We are the only ones who will build the world we want. I invite you to join the We First movement. Let's put each other first.

# RESOURCES

**AUTHOR'S BLOG**

Enjoy three or more posts each week for free on the latest in social change and emerging technology by subscribing to Simon's blog.

www.simonmainwaring.com

**WEBSITE FOR *WE FIRST***

This site features in-depth information about the book as well as consulting case studies, training materials, seminar details, and Simon's weekly blog.

www.wefirstbook.com

**VIDEO FOR *WE FIRST***

Watch as Simon takes you through why he wrote the book and the benefits it can offer brands, non-profits, and consumers.

www.wefirstbook.com

***WE FIRST* BRAND CONSULTING WEBSITE**

If you're interested in working directly with Simon to define and build your brand, simply go to the *We First* website for contact details.

www.wefirstbranding.com

***WE FIRST* TRAINING (DVD/AUDIO SETS)**

Learn how leading brands use social media to build their customer communities, profits, and positive impact on the world.

www.wefirstbranding.com

***WE FIRST* SEMINAR**

For in-depth and personalized training on how to build your brand community and profits, attend Simon's next We First "Brand Leadership" seminar.

www.wefirstbranding.com

# REFERENCE GUIDE

The following is a list of some of the leading companies using social media to build their brand communities and make a positive impact on the world.

Aflac: Aflac Cancer Center and Blood Disorders Service
    http://www.facebook.com/aflaccancercenter
Allstate: Good Hands Community
    http://www.goodhandscommunity.org/
American Express: Small Business Saturday
    http://www.facebook.com/SmallBusinessSaturday
Avon: Avon Breast Cancer Crusade
    http://www.avonfoundation.org/breast-cancer-crusade/
Best Buy: @15
    http://www.at15.com/
Campbell Soup: Let's Can Hunger
    http://www.letscanhunger.com/
    *Labels for Education*
    http://www.labelsforeducation.com
Canon: Canon Envirothon
    http://www.envirothon.org
Chase Bank: Community Giving
    http://www.facebook.com/ChaseCommunityGiving
Chevron: Will You Join Us
    www.willyoujoinus.com
Coca-Cola: Open Happiness
    http://www.facebook.com/cocacola
Deloitte: Women's Initiative
    http://blogs.deloitte.com/winblog/
Disney: Project Green
    http://disney.go.com/projectgreen/
Dove: Campaign for Real Beauty
    http://www.campaignforrealbeauty.com/
Ebay: Giving Works
    http://www.facebook.com/EbayGivingWorks
Fannie Mae: Help the Homeless Walkathon
    http://www.facebook.com/helpthehomelessdc
Ford: Invisible People
    http://www.thefordstory.com
GAP: Recycle Your Blues
    http://www.facebook.com/event.php?eid=154626797903926
General Electric: Ecomagination
    http://www.ecomagination.com
General Mills: Box Tops for Education
    http://www.facebook.com/BoxTopsForEducation
General Motors: Teach Green
    http://teachgreen.gmblogs.com
Google: Google Powermeter
    http://www.google.com/powermeter
Hyundai: Hope On Wheels
    http://www.hyundaihopeonwheels.org/
Intel: CSR@Intel
    http://blogs.intel.com/csr/
Kellogg: Kellogg Cares
    http://www.facebook.com/Kelloggcares

Kodak: A Thousand Words Blog
    http://1000words.kodak.com/
L'Oreal: Women of Worth
    http://www.facebook.com/womenofworth
    *Color of Hope*
    http://www.facebook.com/lorealcolorofhope
Levi Strauss: Care for Our Planet Pledge
    http://www.us.levi.com/care/pledge.aspx
    *Care to Air*
    http://www.us.levi.com/care/contest.aspx
Mastercard: The Mastercard Foundation
    http://www.themastercardfoundation.org
McDonald's: Values in Practice Blog
    http://www.aboutmcdonalds.com/mcd/csr/blog.category.3043609.html
MTV: think
    http://think.mtv.com/
Nestlé: Dear Nestlé
    http://www.nestle.com.my/dearnestle/index.htm
Nike: Girl Effect
    http://www.youtube.com/user/girleffect
Pepsi: Pepsi Refresh
    http://www.refresheverything.com
Petsmart: Petsmart Charities
    http://www.facebook.com/savehomelesspets
Procter & Gamble: Give Health
    http://givehealth.changents.com/
Starbucks Corp.: Being a Responsible Company
    http://www.starbucks.com/responsibility
Stonyfield: Have-A-Cow
    http://www.stonyfield.com/healthy_planet/importance_of_organic_farming/have_a_cow/
        index.jsp
Target: Bullseye Gives
    http://www.target.com/community
    http://www.facebook.com/target
Toyota: Your Ideas For Good
    https://www.yourideasforgood.com/
Tyson: Hunger Relief
    http://hungerrelief.tyson.com
Virgin: Virgin Unite
    http://www.virginunite.com
Volkswagen: TDI Truth & Dare
    http://tdi.vw.com/
Whirlpool: Building Blocks
    http://www.facebook.com/whirlpoolbuildingblocks
Yoplait: Save Lids Save Lives
    http://www.facebook.com/YoplaitPledge
Zappos: Health & Fitness Zappos Family Blog
    http://blogs.zappos.com

# NOTES

PROLOGUE
1. Bill Gates, "A New Approach to Capitalism in the 21st Century," speech delivered at World Economic Forum, Davos, Switzerland, January 24, 2008, http://www.microsoft.com/press-pass/exec/billg/speeches/2008/01-24wefdavos.mspx.

CHAPTER 1
1. John Kenneth Galbraith, *A Short History of Financial Euphoria* (New York: Viking Penguin, 1993), 62.
2. Carmen M. Reinhart and Kenneth Rogoff, *This Time Is Different* (Princeton, NJ: Princeton University Press, 2009), 208.
3. Michael J. Moore, "Wall Street Sees Record Revenue in '09–10 Recovery from Bailout," *Bloomberg BusinessWeek,* December 28, 2010, http://www.businessweek.com/news/2010-12-12/wall-street-sees-record-revenue-in-09-10-recovery-from-bailout.html.
4. Catherine Rampell, "Corporate Profits Were the Highest on Record Last Quarter," *New York Times,* November 23, 2010, http://www.nytimes.com/2010/11/24/business/economy/24econ.html.
5. "U.S. Companies Hoarding Almost $1 Trillion Cash: Moody's," October 26, 2010, http://www.reuters.com/article/idUSTRE69Q00T20101027.
6. Robert Reich, "The Great Decoupling of Corporate Profits from Jobs," The Huffington Post, July 26, 2010, http://www.huffingtonpost.com/robert-reich/the-great-decoupling-of-c_b_660048.html.
7. Arianna Huffington, *Third World America* (New York: Crown Publishing Group, 2010), 4.
8. *The Rachel Maddow Show,* MSNBC, July 27, 2010, http://today.msnbc.msn.com/id/38446591/ns/msnbc_tv-rachel-maddow-show/.
9. G. William Domhoff, "Wealth, Income, and Power," *Who Rules America* blog, August 2010, http://sociology.ucsc.edu/whorulesamerica/power/wealth.html.
10. Jason DeParle and Robert M. Gebeloff, "Living on Nothing But Food Stamps," *New York Times,* January 2, 2010, http://www.nytimes.com/2010/01/03/us/03foodstamps.html?hp.
11. The World Bank, *2008 World Development Indicators, Poverty Data,* The World Bank, 2008, http://siteresources.worldbank.org/DATASTATISTICS/Resources/WDI08supplement1216.pdf.
12. Anup Shah, "Poverty Facts and Statistics," Global Issues website, September 20, 2010, http://www.globalissues.org/articles/26/poverty-facts-and-stats.
13. Anup Shah, "Today over 22,000 Children Died around the World," Global Issues website, September 20, 2010, http://www.globalissues.org/article/715/today-over-22000-children-died-around-the-world.
14. Food and Agriculture Organization of the United Nations, http://www.fao.org/publications/sofi/en/.
15. UNESCO Institute for Statistics, http://www.uis.unesco.org/ev_en.php?ID=6401_201&ID2=DO_TOPIC.
16. Committee Encouraging Corporate Philanthropy, *Shaping the Future: Solving Social Problems through Business Strategy, 2010,* http://www.corporatephilanthropy.org/pdfs/resources/Shaping-the-Future.pdf.
17. Winston Churchill, http://www.quotationspage.com/quotes/Sir_Winston_Churchill/11.

CHAPTER 2
1. Norimitsu Onishi, "Trying to Stop Cattle Burps from Heating Up Planet," *New York Times,* July 13, 2010, http://www.nytimes.com/2010/07/14/science/earth/14australia.html?ref=globalwarming.
2. Creditcards.com, "Credit Card Statistics, Industry Facts, Debt Statistics," http://www.creditcards.com/credit-card-news/credit-card-industry-facts-personal-debt-statistics-1276.php#Credit-cards.

3. Nayan Chanda, "A Review of Globalinc: An Atlas of the Multinational Corporation," Yale Global Online, http://yaleglobal.yale.edu/about/globalinc.jsp.

4. Trading Economics, "India GDP Growth Rate," http://www.tradingeconomics.com/Economics/GDP-Growth.aspx?Symbol=INR.

5. BBC News, "India Billionaires Double in 2009," http://news.bbc.co.uk/2/hi/8562957.stm.

6. eBizMBA, "Top 15 Most Popular Social Networking Websites," http://www.ebizmba.com/articles/social-networking-websites.

7. Associated Press, "Followers Good, Dollars Better for Social Media," Media Biz on MSNBC.com, http://www.msnbc.msn.com/id/35110370/ns/business-media_biz/.

8. "What Americans Do Online," Nielsen Wire, August 2, 2010, http://blog.nielsen.com/nielsenwire/online_mobile/what-americans-do-online-social-media-and-games-dominate-activity.

9. Ben Parr, "Facebook Is the Web's Ultimate Time-sink," Mashable.com, February 16, 2010, http://mashable.com/2010/02/16/facebook-nielsen-stats.

10. Nicholas Christakis, "The Hidden Influence of Social Networks," speech delivered at TED Conference, February 2010, http://www.ted.com/talks/nicholas_christakis_the_hidden_influence_of_social_networks.html.

11. Stuart L. Hart, Capitalism at the Crossroads, 2nd ed. (Philadelphia: Wharton School Press, 2007), 34.

12. United States Energy Information Administration International Energy Outlook 2009, http://www.eia.doe.gov/oiaf/ieo/world.html.

13. Hart, 35.

14. Jared Diamond, "What's Your Consumption Factor?," New York Times, January 2, 2008, http://www.nytimes.com/2008/01/02/opinion/02diamond.html?scp=4&sq=jared+diamond&st=ny.

15. Thomas Friedman, Hot, Flat, and Crowded (New York: Farrar, Straus & Giroux, 2008), 27.

16. Larry Weber, Sticks and Stones: How Digital Business Reputations Are Created Over Time and Lost in a Click (Hoboken, NJ: Wiley, 2009).

17. Kevin Kelly, "The New Socialism: Global Collectivist Society Is Coming Online," Wired, May 22, 2009, http://www.wired.com/culture/culturereviews/magazine/17-06/nep_new socialism?currentPage=all.

18. Rainforest Facts website, http://www.rain-tree.com/facts.htm.

19. Food and Agricultural Organization of the United Nations, March 7, 2005, http://www.fao.org/newsroom/en/news/2005/100095/index.html.

20. FAO, July 16, 2008, http://www.fao.org/newsroom/en/news/2008/1000884/index.html.

21. FAO, July 2, 2008, http://www.fao.org/newsroom/en/news/2008/1000874/index.html.

22. Paul Hawkins, commencement speech given at the University of Portland on May 3, 2009. Text available at: http://globalmindshift.wordpress.com/2009/05/21/the-unforgettable-commencement-address-by-paul-hawken-to-the-class-of-2009-university-of-portland-may-3-2009.

## CHAPTER 3

1. Michael J. Hiscox and Nicholas F. B. Smyth, "Is There Consumer Demand for Improved Labor Standards? Evidence from Field Experiments in Social Product Labeling," Working Paper 2008–0058, Weatherhead Center for International Affairs, Harvard University, November 2005, http://www.people.fas.harvard.edu/~hiscox/SocialLabeling.pdf.

2. 2009 Edelman 3rd Annual Goodpurpose Report, "Put Meaning into Marketing & Profit Through Purpose,"™ Study, November 1, 2010, http://edelmaneditions.com/wp-content/uploads/2010/11/edelman-goodpurpose-study-2009.pdf.

3. Cone Cause 2010 Evolution Study was conducted using a sample of 1,057 adults in July 2010, with a margin of error of ±3 percent, http://www.coneinc.com/files/2010-Cone-Cause-Evolution-Study.pdf. The Cone Cause Survey, 2008, is available at: http://www.coneinc.com/stuff/contentmgr/files/0/8ac1ce2f758c08eb226580a3b67d5617/files/cone25thcause.pdf.

4. Carlye Adler, "Cleaning Up," Newsweek, May 3, 2010, http://www.newsweek.com/2010/05/03/cleaning-up.html.

5. Danielle Sacks, "Jeffrey Hollender: Seventh Generation, Triple Bottom Line Entrepreneur," Fast Company, February 2, 2010, http://www.fastcompany.com/article/jefferey-hollender-seventh-generation-triple-bottom-line-entrepreneur?partner=rss.

6. The Foundation Center, "Foundation Yearbook," July 2009, http://foundationcenter.org/gainknowledge/research/pdf/fy2009_highlights.pdf.

7. Statue of Liberty Facts, http://www.statueliberty.net/Statue-of-Liberty-Facts.html.

8. "Cause Marketing," *Wikipedia,* last modified October 29, 2010, http://en.wikipedia.org/wiki/Cause_marketing.

9. The Center on Philanthropy at Indiana University, "Giving USA 2010: The Annual Report on Philanthropy for the year 2009," published by GivingUSA Foundation, 2010, 13, http://www.givingusareports.org/products/GivingUSA_2010_ExecSummary_Print.pdf.

10. "Giving in Numbers, 2010 Edition," Committee Encouraging Corporate Philanthropy, http://www.corporatephilanthropy.org/pdfs/giving_in_numbers/GivingNumbers2010.pdf; Victor Brudney and Allen Ferrell, "Corporate Charitable Giving," *The University of Chicago Law Review* 69 (2002): 7.

11. Skoll Foundation, "Investment Strategy: Our Capital Model," http://www.skollfoundation.org/approach/investment-strategy/.

CHAPTER 4

1. For more on the population decline on Easter Island, see Jared Diamond, *Collapse: How Societies Choose to Fail or Succeed* (New York: Viking, 2004).

2. UN Documents: Gathering a Body of Global Agreements, "Report of the World Commission on Environment and Development: Our Common Future," 27, http://www.un-documents.net/ocf-ov.htm#I.

3. Andrew W. Savitz with Karl Weber, *The Triple Bottom Line* (San Francisco, CA: Jossey-Bass, 2006).

4. "A New Era of Sustainability," United Nations Global Compact/Accenture CEO Study 2010, http://www.unglobalcompact.org/docs/news_events/8.1/UNGC_Accenture_CEO_Study_2010.pdf?utm_medium=email&utm_source=MonthlyBulletin&utm_content=413458303&utm_campaign=UNGlobalCompactBulletinJuly2010subscribers&utm_term=Download.

5. Carmen M. Reinhart and Kenneth Rogoff, *This Time Is Different* (Princeton, NJ: Princeton University Press, 2009), 292.

6. Dambisa Moyo, *Dead Aid: Why Aid Is Not Working and How There Is a Better Way for Africa* (New York: Farrar, Straus & Giroux, 2009).

7. Global Footprint Network, http://www.footprintnetwork.org/en/index.php/GFN/page/footprint_basics_overview/.

8. New Economics Foundation, "9 October: The Day Humanity Starts Eating the Planet," http://www.neweconomics.org/press-releases/9-october-day-humanity-starts-eating-planet; "Tuesday 23 September: The Day Humanity Starts Eating the Planet," http://www.neweconomics.org/press-releases/9-october-day-humanity-starts-eating-planet; and "We've Gone into the Ecological Red," http://www.neweconomics.org/blog/2010/08/23/weve-gone-into-the-ecological-red.

9. John Roach, "Arctic Summers Ice Free by 2040, Study Predicts," National Geographic News, December 12, 2006, http://news.nationalgeographic.com/news/2006/12/061212-arctic-ice.html.

10. Carnegie Institution for Science, "Carbon Emissions 'Outsourced' to Developing Countries," March 8, 2010, http://carnegiescience.edu/news/carbon_emissions_outsourced_developing_countries.

11. Rainforest Facts, "The Disappearing Rainforests," http://www.rain-tree.com/facts.htm.

12. Juliet Eilperin, "Global Extinction Crisis Looms, New Study Says," *Washington Post,* October 26, 2010, http://www.washingtonpost.com/wp-dyn/content/article/2010/10/26/AR2010102607146.html?wpisrc=nl_pmheadline.

13. Nick Klopsis, "World's Oceans Could Be Completely Depleted of Fish in 40 Years: UN Report," *New York Daily News,* May 18, 2010, http://www.nydailynews.com/news/world/2010/05/18/2010-05-18_un_warns_that_global_fish_stock_could_be_depleted_by_2050.html.

14. Ryan J. Donmoyer, "83 Percent of Companies Had Tax-Haven Units, GAO Says (Update1)," January 16, 2009, Bloomberg News, http://www.bloomberg.com/apps/news?pid=newsarchive&sid=aK0aqjwsiSCA.

15. Gretchen Morgenson, "Death of a Loophole, and Swiss Banks Will Mourn," *New York Times,* March 28, 2010, http://www.nytimes.com/2010/03/28/business/28gret.html.

CHAPTER 5

1. Information and background for this report was drawn from the following sources: Greenpeace, "Sweet Success for Kit Kat Campaign: You Asked, Nestlé Has Answered," May 17, 2010, http://www.greenpeace.org/international/en/news/features/Sweet-success-for-Kit-Kat

-campaign/; Greenpeace, "Public Pressure for Indonesia's Forests Works, Ask Unilever," January 14, 2009, http://www.greenpeace.org/international/campaigns/forests/asia-pacific/dove-palmoil-action/; Greenpeace, "Palm Oil," http://www.greenpeace.org.uk/forests/palm-oil; Paul Armstrong, "Greenpeace, Nestle in Battle Over Kit Kat Viral," CNNWorld, March 19, 2010, http://articles.cnn.com/2010-03-19/world/indonesia.rainforests.orangutan.nestle_1_sustainable-palm-oil-greenpeace-video-sharing-web-site?_s=PM:WORLD.

2. World Growth, http://www.worldgrowth.org/who/.

3. Michael Prager, interview with Janine Benyus, November 20, 2008, http://www.michael prager.com/green_hero_janine_benyus.

4. Eliot Spitzer, "We Own You: How Technology Can Help Stockholders Take Control of the Corporations They Own," *Slate*, January 12, 2010, http://www.slate.com/id/2241191.

5. Richard Edelman, "Edelman Trust Barometer 2010—A New Mandate for Business," *6 A.M.* (blog), January 25, 2010, http://www.edelman.com/speak_up/blog/archives/2010/01/edelman_trust_b_1.html.

6. Naresh Kumar, "Nike Launches Open-Source App to Encourage Sustainable Design," PSFK, http://www.pskf.com/2010/12/nike-launches-open-source-app-to-encourage-sustainable-design.html.

7. Advertolog, "Livestrong Apparel (movie) Chalkbot," http://www.advertolog.com/nike/adverts/movie-chalkbot-13732655/.

8. Gordon Brown, "Wiring a Web for Global Good," speech delivered at TEDGlobal 2009, July 20, 2009, http://www.ted.com/talks/gordon_brown.html.

9. As reported by Yasmin Anwar, "Social Scientists Build Case for 'Survival of the Kindest,'" *ScienceDaily*, December 9, 2009, http://www.sciencedaily.com/releases/2009/12/091208155309.htm.

10. Umair Haque, *The New Capitalist Manifesto: Building a Disruptively Better Business* (Cambridge, MA: Harvard Business Review Press, 2010).

CHAPTER 6

1. David Brooks, "The Underlying Tragedy," *New York Times*, January 15, 2010, http://www.nytimes.com/2010/01/15/opinion/15brooks.html.

2. Republic of Haiti, *Document de Stratégie nationale pour la Croissance et de la Réduction de la Pauvreté*, November 2007, http://siteresources.worldbank.org/INTPRS1/Resources/Haiti-PRSP%28march–2008%29.pdf.

3. The World Bank, "Haiti: The Challenges of Poverty Reduction," August 1998, http://web.worldbank.org/WBSITE/EXTERNAL/TOPICS/EXTPOVERTY/EXTPA/0,content MDK:20207590~isCURL:Y~menuPK:443285~pagePK:148956~piPK:216618~the SitePK:430367,00.html.

4. Douglas MacMillan, "Philanthropy: Causes, the Socially Conscious Network," *Bloomberg Business Week*, October 21, 2010, http://www.businessweek.com/magazine/content/10_44/b4201045340465.htm?campaign_id=rss_null.

5. "How Companies Manage Sustainability," *McKinsey Quarterly*, March 2010, https://www.mckinseyquarterly.com/Energy_Resources_Materials/Strategy_Analysis/How_companies_manage_sustainability_McKinsey_Global_Survey_results_2558.

6. Clive Cook, "The Good Company," *The Economist*, January 20, 2005, https://netfiles.uiuc.edu/julio/www/CSR_1.pdf.

7. Committee Encouraging Corporate Philanthropy, "Shaping the Future: Solving Social Problems Through Business Strategy," based on research by McKinsey & Company (New York: CECP, 2010), http://www.corporatephilanthropy.org/pdfs/resources/Shaping-the-Future.pdf.

8. Scott Henderson, "In a Connected Society, Corporations Must Focus on the Social Good," *Chronicle of Philanthropy*, August 26, 2010, http://philanthropy.com/blogPost/Corporate-Responsibility/26469.

9. Andrew Savitz, *The Triple Bottom Line* (San Francisco, CA: Jossey Bass/John Wiley & Sons, 2006), 21.

10. "Business's Social Contract: Capturing the Corporate Philanthropy Opportunity," Committee for Encouraging Corporate Philanthropy, 2009, http://www.corporatephilanthropy.org/pdfs/research_reports/SocialContract.pdf.

11. Steve Lohr, "How Crisis Shapes the Corporate Model," *New York Times*, March 28, 2009, http://www.nytimes.com/2009/03/29/business/29unbox.html?_r=1&scp=9&sq=Rakesh%20Khurana&st=cse.

CHAPTER 7

1. Potato Pro, "Biodegradable Snack Food Packaging for Sunchips Introduced," April 16, 2009, http://www.potatopro.com/Lists/News/DispForm.aspx?List=813b91f5-f5b5-46ec -95e2-463829ed0100&id=2536.

2. Richard Gray, "Potatoes Could Boost Water Supplies," *Telegraph UK,* October 31, 2010, http://www.telegraph.co.uk/earth/earthnews/8082956/Potatoes-could-boost-water -supplies.html.

3. "Pepsi's Dream Machine Aims to Make Recycling a Slam Dunk," Greenbiz.com, May 4, 2010, http://www.greenbiz.com/news/2010/05/04/pepsi-dream-machine-recycling-slam-dunk.

4. Ariel Schwartz, "Pepsi: Agricultural Hero?," *Fast Company,* October 20, 2010, http:// www.fastcompany.com/1696618/pepsicos-i-crop-farming-system-manages-water-co2 -emissions?partner=rss.

5. Brenna Ehrlich, "Pepsi: Refresh Project Racks Up More Votes than Last Presidential Election," Mashable, September 21, 2010, http://mashable.com/2010/09/21/pepsi-refresh -project-racks-up-more-votes-than-last-presidential-election.

6. Natalie Zmuda, "Pepsi Expands Refresh Project," *Advertising Age,* September 7, 2010, http://adage.com/article?article_id=145773.

7. J. Scott Trubey, "Capitalism Must Change, Says Coca-Cola's Isdell," *Atlanta Business Chronicle,* September 28, 2009, http://atlanta.bizjournals.com/atlanta/stories/2009/09/ 28/story1.html?page=1.

8. "64 Percent of the World's Largest Company CEOs Are Not Social Online, According to New Weber Shandwick Study," October 12, 2010, http://www.webershandwick.com/ Default.aspx/AboutUs/PressReleases/2010/64PercentoftheWorld%E2%80%99sLargest CompanyCEOsareNotSocialOnlineAccordingtoNewWeberShandwickStudy.

9. Adam Ostrow, "CEOs at the World's Biggest Companies Still Social Media Averse," Mashable.com, http://mashable.com/2010/10/13/social-media-ceos/?utm_source=feedburner &utm_medium=feed&utm_campaign=Feed%3A+Mashable+%28Mashable%29.

10. Erik Qualman, "3 Reasons CEOs Hate Social Media," blog post, August 9, 2010, http:// socialnomics.net/2010/08/09/3-reasons-why-ceos-hate-social-media/.

11. Beth Kanter, "Tweeting for Social Good in Davos," *Harvard Business Review* blog, Monday, February 1, 2010, http://blogs.hbr.org/kanter/2010/02/twittering-for-social-good -in.html?utm_source=feedburner&utm_medium=feed&utm_campaign=Feed:+harvard business+%28HBR.org%29&utm_content=Google+Reader.

12. Kate Andersen Brower, "Kraft, PepsiCo Pledge to Aid First Lady's Campaign," *Bloomberg BusinessWeek,* May 17, 2010, http://www.businessweek.com/news/2010-05-17/kraft -pepsico-pledge-to-aid-first-lady-s-campaign-update1-.html.

13. "Timberland Expands Its Green Product Rating, Embraces 'Eco Index,'" Greenbiz.com, August 16, 2010, http://www.greenbiz.com/news/2010/08/16/timberland-expands-its-green -product-rating-embraces-eco-index#ixzz11hRfcaFN.

14. John Hagel III, John Seely Brown, and Lang Davison, *The Power of Pull: How Small Moves, Smartly Made, Can Set Big Things in Motion* (New York: Basic Books, 2010).

15. "Consumers Bullish on Cause Marketing," *Philanthropy Journal,* September 29, 2010, http://www.philanthropyjournal.org/news/consumers-bullish-cause-marketing.

16. Stowe Boyd, "Social Strategy and Social Architecture," blog entry, April 11, 2010, http:// www.stoweboyd.com/post/857666678/social-strategy-and-social-architecture.

17. Piers Fawkes, "Coca Cola: The Original Social Construction Brand," PSFK, May 25, 2010, http://www.psfk.com/2010/05/coca-cola-the-original-social-construction-brand.html.

18. Brian Solis, "Are Your Ears Burning? In Social Networks, One-Third of Consumers Talk Brands Every Week," blog post, July 6, 2010, http://www.briansolis.com/2010/07/are-your -ears-burning-in-social-networks-one-third-of-consumers-talk-brands-every-week.

19. Arathi Menon, "8095 Report: For Millennials, Taking Action Is a Core Value," PSFK.com, October 19, 2010, http://www.psfk.com/2010/10/8095-report-for-millennials-taking -action-is-a-core-value.html.

20. Cited in Scott Henderson, "In a Connected Society, Corporations Must Focus on the Social Good," *The Chronicle of Philanthropy,* August 26, 2010, http://philanthropy.com/blogPost/ Corporate-Responsibility/26469/.

21. Jeffrey Hollender, "Another False Witness Against Corporate Responsibility," CSRNewswire, August 30, 2010, http://csrwiretalkback.tumblr.com/post/1038150951/ another-false-witness-against-corporate-responsibility.

22. "ENGAGEMENTdb: Ranking the Top 100 Global Brands," WetPaint/Altimeter Group, July 2009, http://www.engagementdb.com/downloads/ENGAGEMENTdb_Report_2009.pdf.

23. Sarah Perez, "Bar Code Scanning Up 700% This Year," ReadWriteWeb.com, October 13, 2010, http://www.readwriteweb.com/mobile/2010/10/mobile-barcode-scanning-up-700 -percent-in-2010.php?utm_source=feedburner&utm_medium=feed&utm_campaign =Feed%3A+readwriteweb+%28ReadWriteWeb%29&utm_content=Google+Reader.

24. Ryan Flinn, "Wanted: Social Media Sifters," *Bloomberg BusinessWeek,* October 21, 2010, http://www.businessweek.com/magazine/content/10_44/b4201020317862.htm.

25. "Compass Labs Launches at TechCrunch Disrupt Startup Battlefield," CompassLabs.com, May 25, 2010, http://www.compasslabs.com/news/20100525.html.

26. Paloma Vazquez, "Moore's Law, Sensors, and an Impending Data Explosion," PSFK.com, June 1, 2010, http://www.psfk.com/2010/06/moores-law-sensors-and-an-impending-data -explosion.html.

27. Information for this story was compiled from several news accounts and articles, primarily Kenji Hall's "How the Homeless Are Fighting Nike in Shibuya's Miyashita Park," *CNNGo,* May 12, 2010, http://www.cnngo.com/tokyo/play/brawl-over-miyashita-park-shibuya -snares-nike-565070.

28. Cone 2010 Cause Evolution Study 19.

29. Carol Holding, "CSR's Impact on Brands Grows," PolicyInnovations.org, August 23, 2007, http://www.policyinnovations.org/ideas/commentary/data/csr_brand_impact.

30. Katherine Mangu-Ward, "Clay Shirky Is Kind of Annoying. He Is Also Right," *Reason,* November 1, 2010, http://reason.com/blog/2010/11/01/clay-shirky-is-kind-of-annoyin.

31. "2010 World's Most Ethical Companies," Ethisphere Institute, http://ethisphere.com/wme 2010.

32. Brian Solis, *Engage!: The Complete Guide for Brands and Businesses to Build, Cultivate, and Measure Success in the New Web* (New York: Wiley, 2010).

33. Altimeter Group, "Engagementdb Report: Ranking the Top 100 Brands," July 2009, http:// www.engagementdb.com/downloads/ENGAGEMENTdb_Report_2009.pdf.

34. McKinsey Global Institute, "Lions on the Move: The Progress and Potential of African Economies," June 2010, http://www.mckinsey.com/mgi/publications/progress_and _potential_of_african_economies/pdfs/MGI_african_economies_full_report.pdf.

35. Susan Whiting, "The Global Consumers: Diverse, Demanding, Connected," *Point Magazine,* Vol. 3, Spring 2010, http://www.zinio.com/reader.jsp?issue=416126295&RF=point _spring10&o=ext&p=9.

36. World Telecommunication/ICT Development Report 2010, "Monitoring the WSIS Targets: A Mid-Term Review" (Geneva: International Telecommunication Union, 2010), http://www .itu.int/ITU-D/ict/publications/wtdr_10/material/WTDR2010_ExecSum-en.pdf.

37. Mark Landler, "Google Searches for a Foreign Policy," *New York Times,* March 27, 2010, http://www.nytimes.com/2010/03/28/weekinreview/28landler.html.

38. Stuart Elliott, "Marketers Trade Tales About Getting to Know Facebook and Twitter," *New York Times,* October 14, 2010, http://www.nytimes.com/2010/10/15/business/media/15adco .html.

## CHAPTER 8

1. As described in a speech Johnson delivered at the 2010 ConnectNow Conference in Sydney, Australia.

2. Malcolm Gladwell, "Small Change: Why the Revolution Will Not Be Tweeted," *New Yorker,* October 4, 2010, http://www.newyorker.com/reporting/2010/10/04/101004fa_fact _gladwell?currentPage=5#ixzz12OyBRW1S.

3. Ibid.

4. Henry Jenkins, "Perhaps a Revolution Is Not What We Need," *Aca-Fan: The Official Weblog of Henry Jenkins,* October 6, 2010, http://henryjenkins.org/2010/10/perhaps_a _revolution_is_not_wh.html.

5. Chuck Salter, "Meet Livestrong CEO Doug Ulman, the Most Savvy Health Care Leader in Social Media," *Fast Company,* November 2010, http://www.fastcompany.com/1695101/ livestrong-ceo-doug-social-media.

6. Liz Gannes, "Twitter Founders: Gladwell Got It Wrong," GigaOm, October 11, 2010, http://gigaom.com/2010/10/11/twitter-founders-gladwell-got-it-wrong/.

7. Biz Stone, "Biz Stone on Twitter and Activism," *The Atlantic,* October 19, 2010, http:// www.theatlantic.com/technology/archive/2010/10/exclusive-biz-stone-on-twitter-and -activism/64772.

8. Maria Popova, "Malcolm Gladwell Is #Wrong," *Brain Pickings,* October 6, 2010, http:// changeobserver.designobserver.com/entry.html?entry=19008.

9. "A World of Tweets," Twitter blog, October 22, 2010, http://blog.twitter.com/2010/10/world-of-tweets.html.
10. Stone, *The Atlantic.*
11. Malcolm Gladwell, "Does Egypt Need Twitter?" *The New Yorker,* February 2, 2011, http://www.newyorker.com/online/blogs/newsdesk/2011/02/does-egypt-need-twitter.html.
12. Jennifer Preston, "Movement Began with Outrage and a Facebook Page That Gave It an Outlet," *New York Times,* February 5, 2011, http://www.nytimes.com/2011/02/06/world/middleeast/06face.html.
13. Brian Solis, "Malcolm Gladwell: Your Slip Is Showing," Brian Solis Blog post, February 5, 2011, http://www.briansolis.com/2011/02/malcom-gladwell-your-slip-is-showing/.
14. Stowe Boyd, "Revolution = Messiness at Scale, Again," blog post, February 4, 2011, http://www.stoweboyd.com/post/3105227293/revolution-messiness-at-scale-again.
15. Zeynep Tufekci, "What Gladwell Gets Wrong: The Real Problem Is Scale Mismatch (Plus, Weak and Strong Ties Are Complementary and Supportive)," *Technosociology,* September 27, 2010, http://technosociology.org/?p=178.
16. Karen Egolf, "BBMG Launches The Collective," *Advertising Age,* April 6, 2010, http://adage.com/goodworks/post?article_id=143144.
17. David D. Burstein, "A Changed Generation: Scott Harrison | charity:water," *Fast Company,* May 18, 2010, http://www.fastcompany.com/1638747/scott-harrison-charity-water?partner=rss&utm_source= feedburner&utm_medium=feed&utm_campaign=Feed%3A+fastcompany%2Fheadlines+%28Fast+Company+Headlines%29&utm_content=Google+Reader.
18. Ashoka, "Facts: Philosophy," http://www.ashoka.org/facts.
19. Victor Ma, "ATM Machines Offer Embedded Charity with Every Purchase," Springwise.com, May 4, 2010, http://springwise.com/non-profit_social_cause/choosechange/?utm_source=feedburner&utm_medium=feed&utm_campaign=Feed:+springwise+%28Springwise%29&utm_content=Google+Reader.
20. Springwise.com, "Grocer Lets Customers Direct Its Community Giving," August 28, 2008, http://springwise.com/nonprofit_social_cause/grocer_lets_customers_direct_i/.
21. David Zax, "How Could Facebook Empower Individual Entrepreneurs?," *Fast Company,* October 19, 2010, http://www.fastcompany.com/1696264/could-facebook-empower-individual-entrepreneurs.
22. Social Investment Forum, "Social Investment Facts," http://www.socialinvest.org/resources/sriguide/srifacts.cfm.
23. Ibid.
24. 2009 Edelman Goodpurpose Report, "Put Meaning into Marketing & Profit Through Purpose," http://edelmaneditions.com/wp-content/uploads/2010/11/edelman-goodpurpose-study-2009.pdf.
25. Cited in John Elkington and Pamela Hartigan, *The Power of Unreasonable People: How Social Entrepreneurs Create Markets That Change the World* (Cambridge, MA: Harvard Business Press, 2008), 181.
26. See Happy Planet Index report at http://www.happyplanetindex.org/public-data/files/happy-planet-index-2-0.pdf.

## CHAPTER 9

1. All statistics taken from First Research and generally reflect data from 2010, http://www.firstresearch.com/industry-profiles.aspx?source=VRb.
2. The 2010 Federal Reserve Payments Study, December 8, 2010, http://www.frbservices.org/files/communications/pdf/press/2010_payments_study.pdf
3. 2009 Edelman 3rd Annual Goodpurpose Report, "Put Meaning into Marketing & Profit Through Purpose,"™ Study, November 1, 2010, http://edelmaneditions.com/wp-content/uploads/2010/11/edelman-goodpurpose-study-2009.pdf.
4. "Cause Branding and Corporate Responsibility Endure Despite the Recession," *Cone LLC Landscape Review,* March 2009, http://www.coneinc.com/stuff/contentmgr/files/0/deb4642e2d1bd5c2318798b306b1ca50/files/cause_and_cr_endure_despite_recession_march_2009.pdf.
5. June Cotte and Remi Trudel, "Does It Pay to Be Good?," *MIT Sloan Management Review,* Winter 2009, Vol. 50, Number 2, http://sloanreview.mit.edu/the-magazine/articles/2009/winter/50213/does-it-pay-to-be-good/.
6. Andrew Blum, "Intel Cash Register Knows Who You Are, What You Want," Wired.com, January 9, 2009, http://www.wired.com/epicenter/2009/01/intel-cash-regi.
7. David Marcus, "The Future of Local Commerce = Facebook + Foursquare + Yelp + Groupon," TechCrunch.com, October 30, 2010, http://techcrunch.com/2010/10/30/the

-future-of-local-commerce-facebook-foursquare-yelp-groupon/?utm_source=feedburner &utm_medium=feed&utm_campaign=Feed%3A+Techcrunch+%28TechCrunch%29&utm _content=Google+Reader.

8. Ellen McGirt, "Facebook Chris Hughes, Jumo.com," *Fast Company,* March 18, 2010, http://www.fastcompany.com/1587959/facebook-chris-hughes-jumocom.

9. Marshall Kirkpatrick, "Facebook Exec: All Media Will Be Personalized in 3 to 5 Years," ReadWriteWeb.com, September 29, 2010, http://www.readwriteweb.com/archives/facebook _exec_all_media_will_be_personalized_in_3.php.

10. Zachary Sniderman, "Social Good Is as Easy as Texting," Mashable.com, October 19, 2010, http://mashable.com/2010/10/19/text-to-donate.

11. Cone Trend Tracker, "Disaster Relief: Cone 2010 Text-to-Give Trend Tracker," 2010, http://www.coneinc.com/stuff/contentmgr/files/0/f4e6f613f1d49d917abc33813dc6c629/ files/2010_cone_text_to_give_trend_tracker.pdf.

12. Causecast Mobile Fundraising, "How Does Text2Give Work?," http://www.causecastmobile fundraising.org/how-does-text-to-give-work.

13. Christopher S. Penn, "Game Mechanics for Nonprofits," Awaken Your Superhero, September 13, 2010, http://www.christopherspenn.com/2010/09/game-mechanics-for-nonprofits.

14. Essential Facts about the Computer and Game Industry, 2010, Entertainment Software Association, http://www.theesa.com/facts/pdfs/ESA_Essential_Facts_2010.PDF.

15. Amanda Lenhart et al., "Video Games: Adults Are Players Too," Pew Research Center Publications, December 7, 2008, http://pewresearch.org/pubs/1048/.

16. Statistics cited in TED presentation by Jane McGonigal, "Gaming Can Make a Better World," speech delivered at TED Conference, February 2010, http://www.ted.com/talks/ jane_mcgonigal_gaming_can_make_a_better_world.html.

17. Michael Learmonth, "Zynga Grows One Thing Advertisers Want: Mass Reach," Crains-Detroit Business, October 25, 2010, http://www.crainsdetroit.com/article/20101025/ BESTOFCRAINS/101029926/zynga-grows-one-thing-advertisers-want-mass-reach#.

18. David Jenkins, "Games Market to Reach $70 Billion by 2015," Gamesindustry.biz, May 27, 2010, http://www.gamesindustry.biz/articles/games-market-to-reach-usd70-billion-by -2015.

19. Dean Takahaski, "U.S. Virtual Goods Revenue Expected to Hit $1.6 Billion This Year," VentureBeat.com, January 26, 2010, http://venturebeat.com/2010/01/26/as-farmville -players-buy-little-pink-tractors-u-s-virtual-goods-revenue-is-expected-to-hit-1-6b.

20. Dean Takahashi, "Virtual Goods Sales Are Overtaking Ad Revenues on the iPhone," VentureBeat.com, October 14, 2010, http://venturebeat.com/2010/10/14/virtual-goods-sales -are-overtaking-ad-revenues-on-the-iphone.

21. Michael Learmonth, "Zynga Grows One Thing Advertisers Want: Mass Reach," *Advertising Age,* October 25, 2010, http://adage.com/digital/article?article_id=146670.

22. James Currier, "Gamification: Game Mechanics Is the New Marketing," OogaLabs.com, November 5, 2008, http://blog.oogalabs.com/2008/11/05/gamification-game-mechanics-is -the-new-marketing.

23. Evelyn Rusli, "Kiva President on the Next Five Years," TechCrunch.com, October 13, 2010, http://techcrunch.com/2010/10/13/kiva-ceo-on-the-next-5-years-and-why-zynga-is-their -biggest-rival-tctv.

24. Jane McGonigal, "Why I Love Bees: A Case Study in Collective Intelligence Gaming," February 2007, http://www.avantgame.com/McGonigal_WhyILoveBees_Feb2007.pdf.

25. Jane McGonigal, "Gaming Can Make a Better World," speech delivered at TED Conference, February 2010, http://www.ted.com/talks/jane_mcgonigal_gaming_can_make_a_better _world.html.

26. Nick Mendoza, "Gaming + Mobile + Social = 'Conspiracy for Good' from Tim Kring," Mediashift, July 28, 2010, http://www.pbs.org/mediashift/2010/07/gaming-mobile-social -conspiracy-for-good-from-tim-kring209.html.

27. Sarah Kessler, "5 Trends Facing the Future," September 2010, Mashable, mashable.com/ 2010/09/15/5-trends-social-good/.

## CHAPTER 10

1. Network for Good, "About Us," http://www1.networkforgood.org/about-us.

2. Jason Clay, "How Big Brands Can Help Save Biodiversity," speech delivered at TEDGlobal, July 2010, http://www.ted.com/talks/jason_clay_how_big_brands_can_save_biodiversity .html.

3. Alice Korngold, "Nike at CGI: Helping Girls and Women Achieve Their Potential and Change the World," *Fast Company,* September 24, 2009, http://www.fastcompany.com/

blog/alice-korngold/leading-companies-good/nike-cgi-envisioning-and-achieving-greater
   -potential.
4.   David Zax, "HP, Bill Clinton to Help Infants with HIV in Kenya," *Fast Company*, No-
     vember 30, 2010, http://www.fastcompany.com/1706487/hp-bill-clinton-to-help-infants
     -with-hiv-in-kenya?partner=rss.
5.   E. B. Boyd, "Clinton to Tech Innovators and Entrepreneurs: 'We Want You,'" *Fast Com-
     pany*, October 16, 2010, http://www.fastcompany.com/1695514/hillary-clinton-silicon
     -valley-commonwealth-club?partner=rss.
6.   Bill Baue, "Opinion: When CSR Became a Movement," *Business Ethics*, January 22, 2010,
     http://www.business-ethics.com/2010/01/22/1034-corporate-social-responsibility
     -movement/.
7.   Andrew Revkin, "A 10-Year Checkup on Global Goals," NYTimes.com, September 20,
     2010, http://dotearth.blogs.nytimes.com/2010/09/20/a-10-year-checkup-on-global-goals/
     ?partner=rss&emc=rss.
8.   Clay Shirky, "Institutions Versus Collaboration," speech delivered at TEDGlobal, July 2005,
     http://www.ted.com/index.php/talks/clay_shirky_on_institutions_versus_collaboration.html.
9.   Thomas Friedman, "Do Believe the Hype," *New York Times*, November 2, 2010,
     http://www.nytimes.com/2010/11/03/opinion/03friedman.html?hp.

EPILOGUE
1.   Jonathan Haidt, *The Happiness Hypothesis: Finding Modern Truth in Ancient Wisdom*
     (New York: Basic Books, 2005).
2.   Jeremy Mercer, "The Altruism in Economics," *Ode*, June 24, 2010, http://www.ode
     magazine.com/blogs/behavioral-economics/16828/the_altruism_in_economics.

# INDEX